STALINIST CITY PLANNII

MW01154493

Professionals, Performance, and Power

Based on research in previously closed Soviet archives, this book sheds light on the formative years of Soviet city planning and on state efforts to consolidate power through cityscape design. Stepping away from Moscow's central corridors of power, Heather D. DeHaan focuses her study on 1930s Nizhnii Novgorod, where planners struggled to accommodate the expectations of a Stalinizing state without sacrificing professional authority and power.

Bridging institutional and cultural history, the book brings together a variety of elements of socialism as enacted by planners on a competitive urban stage, such as scientific debate, the crafting of symbolic landscapes, and state campaigns for the development of cultured cities and people. By examining how planners and other urban inhabitants experienced, lived, and struggled with socialism and Stalinism, DeHaan offers readers a much broader, more complex picture of planning and planners than has been revealed to date.

HEATHER D. DEHAAN is an associate professor in the Department of History at Binghamton University.

Stalinist City Planning

Professionals, Performance, and Power

HEATHER D. DEHAAN

UNIVERSITY OF TORONTO PRESS
Toronto Buffalo London

© University of Toronto Press 2013
Toronto Buffalo London
www.utppublishing.com
Printed in the U.S.A.

Reprinted in paperback 2016

ISBN 978-1-4426-4534-9 (cloth)   ISBN 978-1-4875-2166-0 (paper)

∞ Printed on acid-free, 100% post-consumer recycled paper.

Library and Archives Canada Cataloguing in Publication

DeHaan, Heather D., 1974–
Stalinist city planning : professionals, performance, and power /
Heather D. DeHaan.

Includes bibliographical references and index.
ISBN 978-1-4426-4534-9 (casebound) ISBN 978-1-4875-2166-0 (paperback)

1. City planning – Soviet Union – History – 20th century.   2. City
planning – Political aspects – Soviet Union – History – 20th century.
3. City planners – Soviet Union – History – 20th century.   4. Architecture –
Political aspects – Soviet Union – History – 20th century.   5. Stalin, Joseph,
1879–1953 – Influence.   I. Title.

HT169.S64D44 2013   307.1′2160947   C2012-907938-3

This book has been published with the help of a grant from the Canadian
Federation for the Humanities and Social Sciences, through the Awards to
Scholarly Publications Program, using funds provided by the Social Sciences
and Humanities Research Council of Canada.

University of Toronto Press acknowledges the financial assistance to its
publishing program of the Canada Council for the Arts and the Ontario Arts
Council, an agency of the Government of Ontario.

**Canada Council
for the Arts**

**Conseil des Arts
du Canada**

ONTARIO ARTS COUNCIL
CONSEIL DES ARTS DE L'ONTARIO

an Ontario government agency
un organisme du gouvernement de l'Ontario

Funded by the
Government
of Canada

Financé par le
gouvernement
du Canada

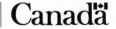

Contents

Figures

Acknowledgments

Although I did not realize it, I launched this project already in 1996, when I first travelled to Nizhnii Novgorod under the auspices of an undergraduate study abroad program. I arrived knowing next to nothing about Russia, not even the language, and I lacked experience in overseas travel. Greeted hospitably, I found what others might have viewed as a dull provincial city to be large and interesting – not only because it was Russian, but also because I grew up in a rural community. Even my undergraduate institution was surrounded by farmers' fields. Any city anywhere would have offered adventure; being a Russian city, Nizhnii Novgorod added the delightful challenge of navigating a foreign language and culture, both of which I soon came to love.

I owe my ability to conduct serious research on Nizhnii Novgorod to a host of individuals whom I met on that very first trip. Staff at the International Office of Nizhnii Novgorod State University offered both friendship and assistance, helping me obtain travel visas, access to the archives, and strong scholarly connections. Olga Artamonova offered friendship, a place to stay, and expert language consultation, as well as access to books at the Pedagogical University. The Zhuravin and Elsukov families likewise offered literature and advice, together with all the comforts of home – kindness, superb food, and a warm and clean bed.

The specialists upon whom I relied in the course of my research offered a highly welcome mix of warmth and professionalism. The archivists at GOPANO and TsANO – the former party and state archives of Nizhnii Novgorod, respectively – taught me how to navigate the Russian archives, and in 2001 they offered generous assistance as I gathered my materials. Staff at the provincial library dug old newspapers out of the basement of the church in which the library was then located, a dusty and unpleasant site where they served faithfully, despite inadequate recompense. Local scholars and writers also offered a great deal of advice and expertise. Of these, I need to give special mention to Olga Orel'skaia, Mikhail Zelenov, Mikhail Maslovskii, and Marina Ignatushko.

I also owe many thanks to scholars, colleagues, friends, advisers, and family members here in North America. To family members, I owe thanks for their patience, encouragement, and confidence. My husband James, who read multiple drafts of this manuscript, deserves whatever award may exist for "Stakhanovite" reviewing. To Lynne Viola, Robert Johnson, Thomas Lahusen, Susan Solomon, Elizabeth Wood, Veronica Aplenc, Ben Eklof, Kimberly Elman Zarecor, and Karl Qualls, I owe sincere gratitude for their generous advice, encouragement, intellectual exchange, and invaluable commentary. My colleagues at Binghamton University have been wonderfully supportive. I must also extend a heartfelt thank you to the anonymous reviewers whose critique of an earlier draft resulted in a number of critical alterations to this book.

Finally, I need to give credit to the institutions that financed this research. The Canadian Federation for the Humanities and Social Sciences subsidized the publication of this book through its Aid to Scholarly Publications Program, using funds provided by the Social Sciences and Humanities Research Council of Canada. This latter institution also provided funding for several years of research and writing between 2001 and 2005. The Centre for Russian and East European Studies (now the Centre for European, Russian, and Eurasian Studies) at the University of Toronto supported my research travel, as did Binghamton University. The Kennan Institute of the Woodrow Wilson Center granted this project a Title VIII fellowship, enabling me to further research and revise several chapters. Research funds awarded with the Tucker-Cohen Prize also helped bring this manuscript to completion.

A Note on Transcription, Translation, and Toponyms

Although most transcriptions in this manuscript follow the Library of Congress system, in the main text I render certain Russian terms in more familiar form. The name Maksim Gor'kii is therefore transliterated as Maxim Gorky, just as the names Aleksandr, Ol'ga, and Aleksei are presented as Alexander, Olga, and Alexei, respectively.

To make this manuscript more accessible to English-language readers, I also translate several terms that most scholars simply transliterate. So, I refer to the gorodskoi soviet or gorsoviet as the "city council" or "municipal government," never as the "city soviet." Similarly, I use the word "province" to refer to Nizhnii Novgorod gubernia, krai, and oblast'.

As readers will notice, the name of the city of Nizhnii Novgorod changed to Gorky in 1932, returning back to the original Nizhnii Novgorod only in 1991. When referring to the early years of Soviet rule, this manuscript therefore refers to Nizhnii Novgorod, while using the term Gorky to refer to the city after 1932.

гГОРЬКИЙ

БОР

Sormovo

Old Nizhnii
Novgorod

Former
Kanavino

Avtozavod

АВТОЗАВОД

РАЙОНЫ
I СОРМОВСКИЙ
II СТАЛИНСКИЙ
III ЛЕНИНСКИЙ
IV АВТОЗАВОДСКИЙ
V КУЙБЫШЕВСКИЙ
VI СВЕРДЛОВСКИЙ
VII МЫЗИНСКИЙ

Key to districts:

I.   Sormovo
II. Stalin District (region of former trade
     fair, once part of Kanavino)
III. Lenin District (also former Kanavino)

IV. Avtozavod (site of the Ford factory)
V.   Kuibyshev District
VI. Sverdlovsk District (historic Nizhnii
     Novgorod)
VII. Myza

District map of the City of Gorky, 1935. *Gor'kovskii rabochii* 43 (21 Feb. 1935), 2.

General city plan (1935–1936), completed by the Lengiprogor planning team. The Volga River runs across the top of this map from west to east, while the Oka River flows northward into it. At its founding, historic Nizhnii Novgorod occupied only the right bank of the Oka River. In the early nineteenth century, with the founding of the trade fair on the left bank, the city began to occupy both banks of the Oka River.

Olga Orel'skaia, *Arkhitektura epokhi sovetskogo avangarda v Nizhnem Novgorode* (Nizhnii Novgorod: Promgrafika, 2005), 143.

STALINIST CITY PLANNING

Professionals, Performance, and Power

Introduction: Planners, Performance, and Power

Man loves to create roads – that is beyond dispute. But ... may it not be ... that he is instinctively afraid of attaining his goal and completing the edifice he is constructing? How do you know, perhaps he only likes that edifice from a distance and not at all at a close range, *perhaps he only likes to build it, and does not want to live in it.*

Dostoevsky, The Underground Man

In 1928, authorities in Nizhnii Novgorod made arrangements to transform their merchant town into a socialist entity. Seeking more than just industrial growth, they envisioned street lights, pavement, broad thoroughfares, and tall residential buildings with all modern conveniences, as well as rational order and logic in the flow of people, waste, energy, and everything else needed to fulfil their vision for the modern city. For this purpose, they hired a planning team, which would soon be led by renowned city planner Alexander Platonovich Ivanitskii. A man already at the vanguard of his profession, Ivanitskii not only helped to redesign the city, but also to refashion the very discipline of city planning, which he worked to distinguish from the related disciplines of architecture and engineering.

Engaged to lay the infrastructure of a new Soviet society, Ivanitskii's task would be central to the Soviet state project of building socialism. As Ivanitskii fashioned the material world after a contested socialist ideal, he served as the architect of urban life, providing the transportation, education, public health, and energy systems that would foster the emergence of a healthy, engaged Soviet citizenry. To this end, he worked to harmonize the activities of a number of Soviet agencies, each of which endeavoured to make its own particular contribution to the project at hand. Because his allocation or refusal of space to these agencies could potentially affect their operational capacity, Ivanitskii found himself at the centre of battles over land, power, and the definition of socialist living. Facing the hostility of industry, citizens, municipal leaders, and even fellow planning professionals, Ivanitskii strove for the sort of scientific objectivity that might, in theory, transcend such disputes.

Stalinist City Planning: Professionals, Performance, and Power explores how Soviet urban planners addressed the political, aesthetic, and ideological disputes inherent to this work. Focused on the problem of power, this book discusses how Soviet city planners acted on the city, not only in the sense that they strove to manage and shape urban growth, but more importantly in that the city became a stage for the enactment and defence of their authority as Soviet professionals. Whether laying claim to scientific command or accepting the imperatives of Stalinist planning, whereby their legitimacy was grounded in their adherence to Party-imposed practices, Soviet city planners strove for the power to control the messy, volatile, and emotive passion of social, economic, and professional politics, not to mention the construction of the city itself. Neither victims nor collaborators, but rather actors on a complex and competitive urban stage, Soviet city planners concerned themselves as much with the cityscape as with their place, as Soviet professionals, within it.

Planning the Future of Self, City, and Profession

In 1928, Alexander Platonovich Ivanitskii arrived in the Russian provincial city of Nizhnii Novgorod to assist the local planning team – the Industrial Commission. Composed of an energetic group of local professors, scientists, and amateur enthusiasts who were committed to modernization, the Industrial Commission set out to solve a complex problem – namely, to coordinate growth at the site where the Oka River flows into the Volga River. Here, adjacent to the historic city of Nizhnii Novgorod, stood two smaller cities as well as a smattering of workers' settlements, which were largely clustered around major factories. Existing transportation, sanitary infrastructure, and cultural facilities were strewn somewhat haphazardly across the region, with no such services whatsoever in the area's smallest villages and outlying settlements. Parks, cultural institutions, running water, and schools were vastly insufficient, as were facilities for water treatment and waste disposal.

When Ivanitskii arrived in 1928, he confronted a city on the verge of rapid-fire growth. In the next four years, as part of the Soviet First Five-Year Plan, twenty new enterprises would be built, while others would be upgraded and expanded. The urban population would soar from 259,000 to 452,000 people.[1] As provincial authorities sought to coordinate an ever-expanding area of industrial production, they annexed new industrial lands to the city, whose spatial expanse grew from 67 to 326 square kilometres.[2] In Nizhnii Novgorod, as elsewhere, the very scope of such hasty development overwhelmed the city's sanitary and administrative resources. Recent migrants to the city had to find shelter wherever they could – in ramshackle homes, a rented room corner, in overcrowded barracks, and in dark and damp basements.[3]

A similar story could be told of all Soviet cities in these years. Although purportedly a program designed to build socialism – or, at least, the industrial foundations of modern living, the First Five-Year Plan wreaked social, economic, and even professional havoc on Soviet citizens. Seeking to extract from agriculture the wealth necessary for industrial development, Soviet authorities attacked the village, whose private trade, low-productivity farms, and religion-infused culture were deemed barriers to socialism. The resultant violence, which in turn contributed to the outbreak of famine, drove peasants to the city, where factory managers desperate for labour quickly recruited them, although few places of employment could offer housing, sanitary infrastructure, or access to transportation and other services.[4] Local governments lacked the money required for their provision, and industry had other priorities.

Despite such mounting challenges, Ivanitskii appears to have greeted the Soviet era with gusto – not necessarily because he embraced Marxism or the Bolsheviks, but simply because he relished the idea of wielding the state apparatus for the sake of building a healthier, more productive, and vibrant society.[5] Such ambition generally led planners such as Ivanitskii to accept, if not welcome, the Soviet assault on private property and capital, which many viewed as an undue limit on their prerogative as masters of urban space.[6] Whatever his personal views, Ivanitskii worked diligently to establish state standards and regulations for urban planning, while developing and standardizing programs to train the next generation of planners.[7] Unlike many experts, who rejected the long arm of state oversight, Ivanitskii actually worked to expand it.[8]

Members of the Industrial Commission apparently shared Ivanitskii's enthusiasm, doing their utmost to "build socialism," which was the mission of the day.[9] Committing themselves to human betterment, in the midst of the 1917 Revolution and ensuing civil war, many helped found a People's University dedicated to educating the masses.[10] Although the documents do not specify their attitude to Soviet power, these experts clearly embraced the Soviet state's modernizing ambition.[11] Indeed, upon Ivanitskii's arrival, they mobilized two hundred students, who voluntarily helped tabulate wind and traffic patterns, as well as the quantity and quality of housing. In braving the heat of summer and the bitter cold of Russian winter in order to complete their work, these students resembled the 25,000ers and the shock brigades of the Communist Youth League, for they applied the utmost of their talent and enthusiasm to the challenge of building a society founded on science, industrial production, and rational administration.[12] Although they did not walk the streets with these volunteers, Ivanitskii and the Industrial Commission apparently felt the same pull.

Such sentiments extended to the art and architectural community, including a small cohort of visionary thinkers developing a city plan for a new factory town to be located just a few kilometres up the Oka River from Nizhnii Novgorod. There, next to what would become, in all but name, a Ford automotive facility, these representatives of the Soviet Union's avant-garde continued their decade-long debate over the proper foundations of socialist architecture and the socialist city. Earlier, some had garnered world renown for such creative concepts as non-cities, garden cities, and flying cities, not to mention for their architecture of unique forms, shapes, materials, and colours. Taking their work with utmost seriousness, perhaps out of a Nietzschean sense that the artist bore the burden of creatively rethinking society, they engaged in visceral, often vindictive debates, breaking into "rationalists," whose designs reflected their concern for the way in which colour and form impact the human psyche, and "constructivists," who felt that buildings should give expression to their functional purpose and to the materials out of which they are formed. There were still other schools of thought, but in general, avant-garde proposals for the factory town near Nizhnii Novgorod would testify to their eager desire to create society anew.[13]

Despite its need for scientific and artistic expertise, in the midst of the First Five-Year Plan the Party encouraged a new, Soviet generation of professionals to attack such "bourgeois" professionals. The reasons for such violence can be traced to the October Revolution, in the wake of which many Bolsheviks expressed hostility to the managerial and professional classes, many of whom had opposed the Bolsheviks' seizure of power in 1917.[14] Besides, Party leaders refused to view science as ideologically neutral, insisting instead on the inherently biased, class-based nature of all scientific research.[15] Newer Party members, the *praktiki* who lacked the pre-revolutionary Party's education and theoretical bent, reinforced such hostile sentiments, for they generally despised the abstract theorizing for which artists and scientists were known.[16] Besides, the younger generation was eager to win power and prestige by forming a new, more proletarian elite. Exploiting the opening provided by the Cultural Revolution (1928–1931), a period that ironically witnessed the blossoming of avant-garde design and production, this group sought to oust its supposedly bourgeois predecessors.[17]

Because Ivanitskii and the Industrial Commission neither worked on the shop floor nor engaged in high-profile aesthetic disputes, they were largely sheltered from the volatile politics of the Cultural Revolution. Indirectly, however, they could not escape the violence that enveloped their contemporaries. Ivanitskii could not help but know that many of his students had joined the newly formed All-Union Association of Proletarian Architects (VOPRA) in 1929. Promoting themselves as representatives of a new working-class generation, VOPRA members accused Ivanitskii's peers and less proletarian students of alien class origins, isolation from the people, and bourgeois taste in design. Many of the accused thereafter lost their positions as students or teachers in educational institutions. The violence, which died with the Cultural Revolution, brought the avant-garde's iconoclastic experimentation in the arts to a close, while paving the way for the Party's decision to force all architectural movements and groups into a single Union of Soviet Architects in 1932.[18]

Although driven by the social frustrations of a rising generation of professionals, this violence was also forged out of clashing visions of the *how* of Soviet governance. For the sake of bettering human society, planners generally deployed socio-technical agencies of rule – engineering systems that might regulate and moderate human behaviour, dispensing of the need for more directly coercive and personal forms of policing and control. They thus proposed to replace cesspits, outhouses, and other disposal systems that depended on human initiative with plumbing and sewers, systems that would run themselves.[19] By contrast, the Party governed through charismatic and coercive mechanisms. Rule over people, not rule through technical system, was the Party's area of specialization. These two modes of rule could complement one another, of course. Experts depended on the state's funding and organizational capacity, and the state benefited from experts' social management systems. Nonetheless, their visions of how to craft a vibrant society clashed.[20]

These differences resulted in what Charles Maier would call the defeat of Taylorism by Fordism. The former, affiliated with Frederick Winslow Taylor, proffered the expert, particularly the engineer, as the heroic figure who might resolve modernity's zero sum game, whereby the rich prospered at the expense of the poor. To resolve this tension, the engineer rationalized workplace organization in order to lower the strain on workers while raising their productivity, thus ensuring contentedness and prosperity for all.[21] By contrast, in Fordist systems, authorities sought to overcome shortages and potential economic crisis by repressing small producers, functionally reorganizing and centralizing the economy, and asserting political and managerial authority in the workplace. Increasing workers' purchasing power was part of this Fordist strategy. In the Soviet context, Fordism would equate to the collectivization of agriculture, the centralization of economic power through the repression of private trade and production, and the imposition of one-man management on the shop floor. In this system, engineers did not arbitrate production relations, as Taylor had envisioned. Instead, as in Stalin's Russia, they became extensions of managerial rule, and they deployed psychological measures, not rationalized production, to diffuse workplace tensions.[22]

Despite the rise of Fordism, the Party continued to embrace scientific management, of which Fordism and Taylorism were just two strains. In this regard, the Party retained a strong affinity for the ideas of Alexei Gastev, whose Central Institute of Labour conducted experiments designed to discipline human movement, infusing it with machine-like efficiency. Although arrested in 1938, Gastev trained many of the Stakhanovites of the 1930s – those individuals who earned economic privilege and political fame by arranging for record-breaking work outputs that challenged managers, directors, and fellow workers to raise production norms.[23] In the Stakhanovite movement, individual will, enthusiasm, and discipline dominated over system.

Despite such conflict between expert and Party views of governance, Ivanitskii worked feverishly and faithfully on behalf of the new Soviet regime, seeking always to advance the cause of science as an apolitical and *perceptive* tool, a technology of knowledge rooted in observation and experimentation.[24] Much like constructivist architect Moisei Ginzburg, Ivanitskii believed that urban design could be objective because it was scientific.[25] Although Ivanitskii deferred to the Party's political decisions, such as whether to prioritize heavy or light industry, he refused to modify or distort the scientific process to suit the Party's desired results. In seeking to understand Soviet life, he worked with observable trends only. Thus, in gathering, assessing, and synthesizing data on Nizhnii Novgorod, Ivanitskii conducted a careful study of the city's long-term regional growth patterns, dismissing the astounding but momentary growth rates of the First Five-Year Plan as an aberration.

Ivanitskii's commitment to independent, method-driven science would eventually run headlong into conflict with Stalinist city planning, particularly with the transition in the mid-1930s to planning on "industrial lines." As of 1931, the new State Institute of City Planning (Giprogor) favoured large professional teams in which individual specialists answered for narrow, well-defined aspects of the plan. Ivanitskii himself directed one of these teams under the auspices of Mosgiprogor (Moscow State Institute of City Planning), but in so doing he remained directly involved in all aspects of planning work. He also refused to corrupt the scientific process for the sake of meeting deadlines, despite pressure to do so. Deemed an artisan by his opponents, who blamed the failures of local city planning on Ivanitskii's methods, Ivanitskii found his scientific ethos and persona to be strangely outdated. In the Soviet Union of the 1930s, outcomes and speed mattered more than careful research or even human welfare.[26] Having spent years combatting underfunding and the harassment of specialists, as well as political intervention into planning itself, Ivanitskii wearily resigned, following other specialists of his generation to Moscow, where he – like they – accepted a bureaucratic post insulated from explosive shop-floor and urban politics.[27]

Ivanitskii's departure marked the arrival of the Stalinist era in local city planning. Trained in Soviet schools and lacking Ivanitskii's breadth of experience, Ivanitskii's successor – Nikolai Alekseevich Solofnenko – drafted plans with an eye to pleasing political elites. To achieve this, Solofnenko altered the scale and aesthetic of Ivanitskii's plans, sacrificing the very scientific integrity, economic realism, and professional pragmatism that had marked Ivanitskii's work. Under Solofnenko's watch, planners based their calculations of the city's economic and demographic future on "Stakhanovite" norms, although this measure of worker productivity was aberrant, temporary, and destructive to the overall production process. Solofnenko also promoted the Stalin cult, representing himself and his work as the embodiment of "Stalinist care" (*Stalinskaia zabota*). Against Ivanitskii's desire to raise science above politics, Solofnenko grounded his authority as a scientist in political performance. In a circular manner, he used his authority as a scientist to legitimate state goals, however questionable they might have been, because such political subservience promised to protect his status as a Soviet expert. His very authority as a

Soviet expert was thus recast, founded on a distinctly Stalinist performance of power.

Soviet City Planning and Its Historians

Historians often reduce this story to a tale of victimhood or collaboration, set against the backdrop of proverbial Russian backwardness, on
which the failures of plans such as those of Solofnenko are frequently
blamed. However, as this book demonstrates, the Nizhnii Novgorod plan
of the 1930s did not run amok on backwardness, but on politics, and
complaints about backwardness in the planning profession were themselves political and strategic, not factual.[28]

The concept of victimhood also fails to apply, for although Ivanitskii
and his avant-garde friends suffered demotion, marked in particular by
their removal from provincial posts, they generally forged a working relationship with the state, securing power and influence in the capital.[29]
Although ousted from his post by local officials, Ivanitskii retained his
professional prestige and status, continuing to play a role in determining
the procedural norms to which provincial planners such as Solofnenko
would submit. Similarly, his constructivist peer, Moisei Ginzburg, would
receive the prestigious commission for the planning of Sevastopol after
the Second World War, despite the state's rejection of Ginzburg's earlier
constructivist avant-garde design.[30]

Solofnenko's story likewise resists a simple reading in terms of victim
and victimizer. As a *vydvizhenets* (a beneficiary of affirmative action for
the lower classes), Solofnenko's promotion to the head of the Gorky city
planning team represented a revolutionary promise of social mobility
realized. Nonetheless, his city plan failed to earn official status. First, the
Second World War disrupted the approval process. Second, the postwar
period witnessed a retreat from the monumental vision typical of the
1930s, including Solofnenko's plan. Despite this failure, Solofnenko,
too, would remain an integral part of the local planning community.

Because experts such as these forged a productive relationship with
the Soviet state, scholars have also erroneously cast them as figures will-
ingly complicit in the Stalin cult, if not marionettes of power.[31] The truth,
however, is far more complex. Planners, engineers, and architects tended to be hybridized figures, both within the state and yet outside of it.[32]
None could be autonomous scientists or professionals, as would befit the
Western ideal, for all depended on the Soviet state for employment.[33]
At the same time, they generally shunned Party membership. They

became agents of the Party program, even as they resisted many of the trappings of Marxist ideology. In this sense, Ivanitskii, the avant-garde, and Solofnenko were located "*vnye*" (inside and yet outside of) power – that is, within the discourses and ideology of Soviet modernization, yet in a distinct position that was not perfectly defined by the state's original intentions or goals.[34] Even when officially upholding the aesthetic of Socialist Realism in 1934, planners and architects took advantage of its hazy parameters to cast ideas carried forward from the 1920s as part of the Party's new Socialist Realist canon.[35]

To understand these complexities, one generally needs to step away from Moscow and assume a provincial perspective on the aesthetic politics of these years. Far from Moscow, the lines between centre and locality, loyalty and disloyalty, as well as victim and victimizer blurred. In Nizhnii Novgorod, for instance, most members of the engineering community remained firm Ivanitskii supporters, even if they were Party members. They conspired to encourage a self-designated spokesman for the common people to criticize Solofnenko's work for its putative formalism, a terrible accusation in Soviet aesthetic circles. Yet, not only did Solofnenko's work withstand this attack, but neither the engineers nor this spokesman suffered retribution for their impudence, although in Soviet society at the time, a single well-placed denunciation could bring about the arrest, trial, and incarceration or even execution of the one denounced. All involved in this affair – no matter what their generation, class background, or particular specialty (architecture or engineering) – remained firmly *inside* the story of urban development, as equals engaged in a delicate contest for power, security, and authority.[36]

The view from the provinces also highlights the fact that Soviet architects and planners were not primarily men of ideas, as literature on avant-garde design and theory too easily suggests. In focusing on professionals' abstract debates, as conducted in Moscow and recorded in journals and conference proceedings, scholars distract from the complex social and economic context in which planners' arguments were formulated, defended, applied, and sometimes reworked.[37] Soviet urban planning was inherently political. It involved the distribution of resources, as well as a conceptual and bureaucratic battle for power. As men of science, architects might claim to transcend such politics, simply by virtue of their putative objectivity. However, as Boris Groys would argue, any such claim to stand above subjective taste was an act of deceit. Planners had a vision that they wished to impose on society, and they were arbiters of real spaces, occupied by material resources and flesh-and-blood people.[38] Their actions called forth resistances, which their words, deeds, plans, and politics sought to overcome.

Understanding precisely who planners were and how their work functioned matters for all Soviet scholars, because planners served as mediators of ideological discourse. As such, their work directly concerns Stephen Kotkin's thesis that socialism was a discourse-bound civilization, a way of speaking and defining self, as imposed by a hegemonic Party apparatus. For all practical purposes, by Kotkin's understanding, the Soviet Union was a discursive house, a conceptual edifice with its fissures and cracks, but nonetheless one in which Soviet citizens made themselves at home. Whatever their "little tactics" of survival, they took place within this discursive space of socialism.[39]

Yet, as this study indicates, although instructed to build socialism, Party leaders and Soviet city planners generally failed to produce anything more than the likeness of a socialist house, whether physical or conceptual. The lines of the Soviet conceptual edifice were never sufficiently clear and stable. Identities and meanings were too pliable to form a bounded civilization.[40] Even the mechanisms for building such a world – science, planning, policing, and ideology – were repeatedly shuffled, reorganized, and then restructured yet again. The very definition of such key concepts as kulak, worker, friend or enemy, ethnicity, and citizenship changed repeatedly. In any case, imposed discourses merely mediate the perception of the world; they cannot fix meaning, which is always fluid and relational.[41] The process of building socialism, not a finished conceptual edifice, defined city planning and city life from the start.[42]

The concept of Soviet society as a cohesive entity was itself a product of the political economy of power. As an idea, it was seductive, forceful, and even violent, but it captured only the image of socialist life, not its substance.[43] Planners themselves sought to sustain this myth, for they had a vested interest in generating and maintaining the concept of the state as a centrally directed, planned, and administered power. With Ivanitskii, they worked to achieve a coherent, highly centralized planning apparatus. They identified themselves with the state as a modernizing and progressive force. The image of Soviet society as a planned regime animated and legitimized their existence as professionals.

Yet, Soviet authorities could not produce "fiat socialism," or socialism according to plan, because ideas morphed when applied to the real spaces of human life. The act of city planning resembled literary translation, as analysed by Walter Benjamin. As Benjamin notes, the very act of rendering a word or idea from one linguistic system into another displaces its meaning; not only does many a word change nuance in a new language, but when read in this new context, the meaning of the original text is also transformed.[44] Soviet urban planning involved such dual alienation, whereby both the ideal image of the socialist city (the original language) and the actual space of the city (the receiving language) were changed.[45]

As Soviet professionals discovered, urban planning involved living spaces, people, and practices, not just ideas and images scrawled on sheets of paper. Planners did not have the luxury of dealing with abstract plans and ideas alone. They dealt with a city of actual people, events, and materials. They *lived* in this city, a space of Party members and common citizens who often resisted their ideas and actions. Against the "represented city" (i.e., the city as depicted in map or text), urban space posited what Henri Lefebvre calls "absolute space," which encompasses those aspects of life that cannot be neatly seen, described, or captured in an analytical, textual, or visual frame.[46] Such absolute space posed a constant challenge to Soviet city planners, who struggled to bind its complexity into analytically defined, rational functions that they might manipulate scientifically. Unfortunately, the light of scientific analysis illuminated only select aspects of urban life, covering other areas in shadow.[47] Planners and authorities discovered the content of these shadows, or "blind fields," only when they stubbed a toe on the unforeseen consequences of their actions.

Stumbling through the dark was necessary, however, for planners' goals were not achieved in the abstract. They had to be brought to life in the messy space of the absolute, on an urban stage where the instructions of the Party stage-director, the response of the Soviet audience, and the behaviour of other actors gave meaning to the Marxist-Leninist script. Indeed, given the contested nature of urban space, planners' work should be assessed primarily in terms of performance. It should be viewed not only as visual art, but as dramatic act. Even planners' scientific and theoretical models belonged not only to the world of visual representation, but also to what Lefebvre calls "the zone of politics," for these models asserted opinion, power, and authority.[48] They *scripted* power, being designed to give agency to planners who dwelled in a world of living beings, a place much more complex than they could perceive, represent, or understand, but in and upon which they nonetheless had to act.

From the Ivory Tower to the World Below: Planners in Action

Planners such as Ivanitskii did not present themselves as actors, political or otherwise. They aspired to authentic status as transcendent authorities, untainted by petty struggles for power. Like omniscient narrators of a novel, they ascribed certain actions, emotions, and needs to the citizens of the city. Their attempt to view the city scientifically, as if from above, denied the fluidity of the city as a stage. It denied the stage itself, although the very act of climbing into the ivory tower of science was itself a performance – a form of political posturing meant to garner authority over the contested space of the city below.[49]

In stepping out of the ivory tower, the post-Ivanitskii generation appropriated techniques that Ivanitskii and his cohort would have deemed unacceptably political, such as charismatic posturing, aesthetic dilettantism, and symbolic consultation with the public. Through these, the stance of the apolitical and transcendent scientist was subsumed within an elaborate system of professional ritual designed to sustain the image of Soviet democracy. In this new world, Ivanitskii's claim to authentic and independent vision had no place. Solofnenko's generation carefully fulfilled the roles that the state deemed necessary, even when such on-stage actions undermined the sort of authoritative stance adopted by the earlier generation. Echoing the transition from Taylorism to Fordism, Solofnenko's work served to transmit socialism as an image and psycho-social force, often at the expense of pragmatic and effective technical work.

Stalinist City Planning: Professionals, Performance, and Power discusses these games of power, as played out through planners' attempt to create the socialist city. Addressing both the "zone of politics" and "the absolute" of the city, this work discusses the tensions between technological (expert-led) and sociological (class-driven) transformation, as complicated by the *long durée* of Russian cultural practice, belief, and power. As it shows, socialism was not a discourse-bound civilization, but a drama whose threads of action and meaning encompassed the Russian past, the Communist future, and a present too complex to capture in any two-dimensional image or word. In it, the cityscape both facilitated and resisted Soviet power, being both object and agent of a drama larger than anyone in the city, larger even than planners themselves.

Chapter 1 opens by exploring the city's symbolic landscape, the world that set the stage for planners' work. This symbolic cityscape voiced the very challenges that planners would face: the resilience of tradition, the internal tensions in Marxist Soviet thought, and the contested nature of the cityscape in material, historical, and cultural terms. As the chapter notes, Russian authorities had long appropriated the city as a stage for the display of power, whether that be imperial power, Orthodox faith, or the Soviet claim to have produced a new, revolutionary self. As symbol, the Soviet cityscape served as both a platform for the display of power and as a palimpsest, a site in which old memories and beliefs remained ever present, shaping the very space of performance.

Soviet leaders' attempt to redesign this stage is the focus of chapter 2, which discusses "visionary planning," the avant-garde's iconoclastic attempt to rip away the foundations of the old world.[50] Seeking to transcend the particularities of custom and location, visionary planners climbed into the ivory tower of academic and theoretical science. From there, they re-envisioned the city as a constellation of factory towns, each organized along industrial lines, as if all of human production, even home life, could be turned into a vast assembly line. Its architects argued that such rationally administered cities would liberate the human individual from the servitude of tradition, including the bonds of family. Implicit to this model was a society where scientific expertise and scientific management governed society systematically, without need for more direct police or administrative intervention.[51] As this chapter notes, such models flourished only until planners set foot in the city itself.

Chapter 3 turns to Ivanitskii's attempt to plan the historic city of Nizhnii Novgorod. As readers will discover, Ivanitskii's belief in the objectivity of science did not obscure his savvy understanding of urban politics. Although he believed that science could transcend petty politicking, his work nonetheless took the city council's political and economic limitations into account. Unfortunately, Ivanitskii's scientific peers would challenge such pragmatism by insisting that the science of Ivanitskii's projects was incomplete. Like shrewd politicians, they used demands for further research to delay planning decisions that posed a political risk.

Chapter 4 discusses Ivanitskii's departure from Nizhnii Novgorod, exploring how this launched the era of Stalinist urban planning. The consolidation of charismatic rule under Stalin witnessed the rise of a new state-approved vision of the city, which fostered an "iconographic" approach to urban planning. Unlike visionary planning, which celebrated the visual prowess of scientific expertise and artistic creativity, iconographic planning followed the methods of icon painting (iconography), whereby iconographers (i.e., planners) copied sacralized models articulated elsewhere (i.e., in the Moscow city plan) onto their own palette (i.e., the cityscape). In imposing a standardized aesthetic on the Soviet city, the iconographic denied the variability and complexity of the world beneath its monumental vision, being violent in what E.A. Dobrenko calls the "de-realization" of Soviet life. "Empirical reality," Dobrenko notes, was "irrelevant to it," something denied and displaced.[52] Proud of scientific objectivity, Ivanitskii could not be the figure to usher in such planning; that chore went to his successor, Solofnenko, who deftly wove this new image of the city into his own scenario of power.

Chapter 5 explores planners' attempts to project this iconographic image as lived ritual, an act performed within the three-dimensional space of the city. We witness here Solofnenko's mastery of Stalinist aesthetics and ritual, as he found security and status in compliance with Stalinist authorities. In this chapter, we also glimpse rituals and practices usually associated with later periods of Soviet history, including professional consultation with the public, a professional middle class seeking privilege in return for dedicated service, as well as the discontented voices of engineers who sought a return to functionalist design. All posed a challenge to Solofnenko.

The last two chapters explore planners' attempts to fill the "absences" produced by Socialist Realism's otherworldly plenitude. Such "absences" were discursive constructs – or, as Lefebvre would emphasize – spotlights that illuminated some social and administrative problems while covering more substantial problems in shadow. As noted in chapter 6, planners construed illegal and uncontrolled construction as a sign of backwardness and a lack of culture, although such problems derived from the very structure of Soviet modernization. As seen in chapter 7, these concepts served a strategic purpose – namely, to script the collective performance of "culturedness," to be realized through the mass beautification of the city.

Put together, these chapters outline the drama of building socialism. Chapter 1 sets the stage, while chapter 2 discusses attempts to remake this stage. Chapters 3 and 4 examine how political and social forces mandated a rethinking of both stage and script, and chapters 5 through 7 explore the script in action, as well as in perpetual reinvention. Building a city involved rethinking socialism in its totality. From stage set to script writing, and then to active performance, this book explores urban planning as a lived and creative event – always socialist, always scientific, always personal, and always an act whose impact and message would be incompletely understood.

As a study of city planning in Nizhnii Novgorod in the 1930s, this work cannot capture all the complexity of Soviet urban life, of course. It does nonetheless present the challenge of projecting power into space, whether that space be physical or perceived. Towards this end, it explores attempts to sculpt the cityscape in such a way as to shape memory, promote modernization, foster optimism, bolster the Stalin cult, and mobilize citizens behind planners' planning goals – always from the standpoint of provincial architects as agents and objects of power, acting on and in urban space. As readers will discover, although the Soviet state might echo Humpty Dumpty of Lewis Carol's *Alice in Wonderland* in saying, "When *I* use a word, it means what I choose it to mean – neither more nor less," in fact, the Soviet state found its plans, concepts, and words to be frail and "crackable." The challenge of turning words and plans into lived socialist experience, tangible and understood, would be met on the Soviet urban stage.

Chapter One

From Nizhnii to Gorky:
Setting the Stage of Socialism

It is not the work of a moment for a society to generate (produce) an appropriated social space in which it can achieve a form by means of self-presentation
and self-representation – a social space to which that society is not identical and
which indeed is its tomb as well as its cradle.

Henri Lefebvre, *The Production of Space*[1]

Symbolic Inversions: Occupying a Conceptual Landscape

The year of revolution brought both celebration and destruction to
Soviet cityscapes. Workers took control of factories, even as the supply
of input materials ran dry, forcing those same factories to close.[2] As the
poor moved into the dwellings of the rich, economic breakdown, war,
and hunger drove much of the urban population to the hinterland. In
the midst of this, the Bolshevik Central Committee not only tore down
monuments to the tsarist past and raised statues, posters, and monuments to the Revolution, but also invited leading artists to preserve
historic architecture. Meanwhile, Party propagandists and the Russian
avant-garde joined together to organize street festivals that might both
inculcate and represent the mass enthusiasm on which Bolshevik legitimacy rested.[3]

Despite such celebration, appropriation, and destruction, the cityscape remained largely unchanged – worn by war and poverty, but not
dramatically transformed. Revolutionary festivals momentarily changed
city squares into sites and symbols of revolution, but they did not alter
the urban infrastructure, which remained the legacy of a supposedly
bygone era. This offended leaders who believed, in nineteenth-century

fashion, that architecture must express the spirit of a particular people and epoch. The historic cityscape also proved cause for consternation on the part of Soviet designers who felt that the environment could shape selfhood – being not a product of rational action, but itself an organizer of the human psyche. As designer Alexei Mikhailovich Gan asserted in his book *Constructivism* (1922), the existing Soviet urban fabric was a "staunch ally of counter-revolution."[4]

Attempts to overcome the past notwithstanding, the cultural ideas, codes, and semiotics of the pre-revolutionary heritage endured, shaping the expression and realization of the Bolshevik project in both conscious and unconscious ways. Although the revolutionary project called for the eradication of tradition, so that a new and progressive society might emerge, the very imperative of mass politics, coupled with enduring traditions of thought and culture, conspired to ensure that the future would be built on the foundations of a past that was denied, masked, and elided, but never fully or truly eviscerated.[5] As Karl Qualls might say, "agitation" (the symbolic framing of space) combined with "accommodation" (respect for local needs and memories) in the Soviet attempt to foster spatial identification with Soviet rule.[6]

As such appropriation indicated, place is a palimpsest, not a slate that can easily be wiped clean. Not only would old infrastructure set the foundation of the new, but the potent symbols of place often gave rise to what John Czaplicka calls "the contested archaeology of the local."[7] Historic identities, etched into geographic space, offered alternative ways of being, available for appropriation as cultural valuables at any time.[8] In localities such as Nizhnii Novgorod, one found the subtle resistance of inherited cultural codes, which were not necessarily opposed to Soviet power, but which nonetheless shaped the formulation and reception of Bolshevik ideas.[9] They became, as Katerina Clark might suggest, a part of the Soviet "cultural ecosystem" of power.[10]

The layering of history, memory, and culture in the cityscape made it impossible for the new leadership to craft an impenetrable world of discourse, impervious to older ideas and values. Far from imposing a new discourse, the symbolic language of Bolshevism embedded itself into ideas and modes of understanding much older than itself.[11] The stage on which Bolshevik authorities sought to enact socialism and the very language through which they articulated their ideological narrative were influenced by a set of symbols alien to and yet appropriated and redefined by Party members. In this, Nizhnii Novgorod's material and semiotic form foreshadowed the challenges that planners themselves would face, including inherited ideas and practices, self-contradicting strands within revolutionary thought, and centuries of unplanned or partially planned growth.

The Pre-Modern City: A Spiritual-Material Terrain

In its history, Nizhnii Novgorod represented many things – Orthodox culture and faith, economic prowess, military ambition, provincial modernization, and revolutionary development. Yet, it began as a fortress – or *kremlin* – overlooking the mouth of the Oka River.[12] Located at the junction of the Volga and Oka rivers, this kremlin housed the prince and his retinue, who laid claim to the territory's vital trade routes. Although originally independent, in 1389, the region and its prince fell under Moscow's control. The existing fortress, a relic of the sixteenth century, thereby signifies not the lost power of an independent prince, but rather Moscow's growing prowess. Built by an architect from what is now Italy, this kremlin was designed to protect the city from raiding tribes, as well as to provide a launching point for Moscow's assault on the khanates to the east and southeast.

As the boundaries of Muscovy shifted eastward in the 1550s, Nizhnii Novgorod became a location where East met West for the purpose of commercial exchange. Transformed into a vital trading post, it developed a firm and lasting identity as a commercial hub.[13] Powerful merchant families such as the Stroganovs emerged, leaving their imprint on local life and architecture. As a means of asserting power and buying divine pleasure, many of these patronized religious movements, including the Zealots of Piety, a seventeenth-century community that sought spiritual revival in Muscovy.[14]

These religious and mercantile forces also gave rise to the city's distinct soterioscape – that is, a landscape in which buildings and monuments were arranged in such a way as to narrate and celebrate religious belief. Soterioscapes were narratives in space, telling a story of salvation. Infusing the everyday with cosmic import, such soterioscapes invited spiritual reflection by inhabitants as they went about their daily affairs. A common element of medieval cityscapes, these religion-inspired city spaces set the stage for the religious and political rituals that were ubiquitous in Europe at the time. As Lewis Mumford says with regard to the medieval city:

> The medieval city was a stage for the ceremonies of the Church. If in an industrial age the imagination soars to its highest level in a railroad station

or bridge, in medieval culture practical achievement reached its peak in the service of a great symbol … No sedentary student, viewing this architecture in pictures … is in a state to penetrate this urban setting even in its purely aesthetic aspect. For the key to the visible city lies in the moving pageant or procession: above all, in the great religious procession that winds about the streets and places before it finally debouches into the church or the cathedral for the great ceremony itself.[15]

In keeping with such medieval practice, Nizhnii Novgorod's soterioscape bound the spiritual and material worlds, encoding belief in space, where it would become a lasting challenge to Bolshevik thought and power.

Nizhnii Novgorod's soterioscape was organized as a west-to-east pilgrimage through the city from Annunciation Monastery in the southwest to Pecherskii Monastery in the northeast. Although both monasteries and the kremlin were administratively distinct entities, each with its own religious, residential, commercial, and defence functions, all were bound by a single road, which served as the physical and soteriological link between the three. Architect N.F. Filatov has argued that these three sites also formed a single defence zone, with the two monasteries providing the first line of defence for the kremlin, which lay between the two, but the soteriological bond between these three was arguably stronger and more relevant in day-to-day terms.[16]

The city's soteriological story began to the south of Annunciation Monastery, at Yarila Hill, which was named after a pagan Slavic god and reputedly a site for pagan rites of spring. In making their way to the kremlin-city, travellers turned their backs to this site, the symbol of a fallen world.[17] Moving towards Annunciation Monastery, they figuratively turned their hearts towards the hope of redemption, as represented by the Messiah whose birth announcement the monastery honoured. Then, as travellers moved past the monastery towards the kremlin, they were soon greeted by the sight of Nativity Church. Dedicated to the nativity of Mary, the God-Bearer, this edifice celebrated the human womb that made possible the nativity of the Messiah, whom Orthodox believers embraced as God Incarnate. (See figures 1.1 and 1.2.)

The kremlin represented the world of Christ's life on earth, for one entered it through John the Baptist Gate, which feted the baptism that marked the beginning of Jesus' ministry, with its teachings, parables, and many accounts of miracles. From this gate, travellers walked up a veritable *via dolorosa* – a steep hill approximately a hundred metres in height – until they reached the climax of their trek: the Cathedral of the Transfiguration. Although Western Christians place relatively little

1.1. Annunciation Monastery. Photograph by A.O. Karelin, n.d. A.A. Semenov and M.M. Khorev, eds., *Andrei Osipovich Kare-lin: Tvorcheskoe nasledie* (Nizhnii Novgorod: Arnika, 1994), 102.

1.2. Church of the Nativity. A.A. Semenov and M.M. Khorev, eds., *Andrei Osipovich Karelin: Tvorcheskoe nasledie* (Nizhnii Novgorod: Arnika, 1994), 132.

emphasis on the event of the Transfiguration, to Orthodox Christians it not only testified to Christ's divine nature, but also symbolized the cosmic dimension of salvation, the power of the divine spirit to transfigure, or glorify, the material world. From here, travellers who turned to enjoy a spectacular view of the Oka might reflect on their journey, both physical and spiritual.

In moving past this cathedral and exiting the kremlin, visitors and inhabitants symbolically came to the end of Jesus' life. Outside the kremlin's walls, they stumbled upon the Chapel of the Exaltation of the Cross, a small edifice honouring Jesus' death.[18] From there, a road led down the slope to Pecherskii Monastery, whose name – as given by its founder Dionisii in the fourteenth century – refers to Kiev's Pecherskii Monastery, named in honour of the cave (*peshchera*) where its founder once dwelled. Given this monastery's place in the city's religious and symbolic landscape, the name can also be understood as an oblique reference to the catacombs of ancient Rome, where first-century believers met, worshipped, and prayed. Thus, travellers' journey through the life of Christ ended with the rise of the Church, viewed as a living symbol of Christ's resurrection, an event at the heart of the Orthodox faith. (See figures 1.3 to 1.6.)

Surprisingly, this spatial-religious configuration was not designed by any single individual, but rather emerged haphazardly over time. The monasteries were built soon after the city's founding in the thirteenth century, and the kremlin dates to the early sixteenth century. Nativity Church and the Chapel of the Exaltation of the Cross were built in the late seventeenth century, around which time the Cathedral of the Transfiguration was renovated. Both this renovation and the construction of Nativity Church were sponsored by Semen Zadorin.[19] Insofar as Zadorin completed the soterioscape, he might be credited with authorship. Yet, his only serious contribution was to build Nativity Church, for all other objects in this soterioscape preceded his building efforts.

Because this soterioscape emerged haphazardly, lacking a clearly defined plan or author, this configuration has escaped the attention of local historians, including experts in architecture. Perhaps, the historians who lived within this soterioscape viewed it as commonplace, or as a matter of interest to ethnographers, not to historians. For Soviet thinkers eager to stress secularization and modernization, not the appropriation of an Orthodox heritage, it probably appeared to be an inconvenient relic, reminiscent of "the sacred city" so often equated with the East. Besides, it was not a premeditated structure.

Yet, as a space of society – its tomb and cradle, as Lefebvre would say – this soterioscape both represented and fostered Orthodox identifica-

Нижній-Новгородъ.—Nijni-Novgorod. № 7.
Ивановскій съѣздъ и ворота.

1.3. John the Baptist Gate. Photograph by M.P. Dmitriev, n.d. V.P. Mashkovtsev and T.P. Vinogradova, eds., *Tsarstvenno postavlennyi gorod: Nizhnii Novgorod v staroi otkrytke* (Vladimir: Posad, 2000), 162.

Нижній-Новгородъ.—Nijni-Novgorod. № 40.
Кремлевская стѣна и Ивановская башня отъ Мининскаго сада.

1.4. Kremlin road. Photograph by M.P. Dmitriev, c. 1890. V.P. Mashkovtsev and T.P. Vinogradova, eds., *Tsarstvenno postavlennyi gorod: Nizhnii Novgorod v staroi otkrytke* (Vladimir: Posad, 2000), 160.

1.5. Cathedral of the Transfiguration. Photograph by M.P. Dmitriev, 1911. V.P. Mashkovtsev and T.P. Vinogradova, eds., *Tsarstvenno postavlennyi gorod: Nizhnii Novgorod v staroi otkrytke* (Vladimir: Posad, 2000), 153.

1.6. Pecherskii Monastery. Nizhnii Novgorod postcard, n.d. V.P. Mashkovtsev and T.P. Vinogradova, eds., *Tsarstvenno postavlennyi gorod: Nizhnii Novgorod v staroi otkrytke* (Vladimir: Posad, 2000), 24.

tion.[20] For the most part, movement through this space would have been mundane, a part of citizens' everyday movement in and through the city. Its power was latent, invoked only when some casual passer-by or trades-man took the time to note and reflect upon the message implicit to the city's layout. No special ritual or Orthodox feast day was required for this space to remind the common citizen of the Orthodox belief that humanity's earthly journey had spiritual implications or that a divine presence witnessed their day-to-day travails and victories. In this sense, this soterioscape was, as Mumford might have suggested, the clothing of a culture – its identity and ornament, as well as its sheltering outer skin.[21]

Imperial Cities: Symbolic Power

This medieval soterioscape endured to the very end of the imperial period, although it lost much of its potency over time. The tsars spon-sored construction that interfered with its narrative coherence, and modernization gradually reshaped the city, so that patterns of daily movement no longer overlapped with this soterioscape. As a result, the soterioscape became a symbolic terrain distanced from everyday experi-ence. Although it would still have made a suitable path for pilgrimage, we have no record of such an event taking place.

Peter the Great undid the power of the Nizhnii Novgorod soteri-oscape almost immediately (and perhaps unintentionally) by ordering the construction of a new Annunciation Cathedral between the kremlin and the Chapel of the Exaltation of the Cross – an utterly inappropriate location, if one considers the narrative order of the symbolic cityscape. Then again, the Nizhnii Novgorod soterioscape failed to place the tsar at the centre. Insofar as Peter I subordinated church to state, turning the former into the handmaiden of the latter, his decision to found a new Annunciation Monastery at the highpoint of the city, the pinnacle of power, seems suitable. Through this act, Peter the Great proclaimed his "divine mandate" to remake Russia, transfiguring the material world.

Like his predecessors, Peter the Great deployed the urban landscape as a stage for the dramatization of his imperial power.[22] Partly for this purpose, he decreed the building of the new capital city of St. Peters-burg, whose planned streets and classical architecture displayed Peter's commitment to the wholesale importation of European technological, aesthetic, social, and diplomatic traditions. His "revolution in Russian architecture," as James Cracraft calls it, marked the dawn of rule by sys-tem and reason, rather than solely by tradition or through arbitrary personal decree.[23] Not that this tsar accepted any legal or institutional limits on his power or succeeded in subordinating the arbitrary to the systemic. Law remained an extension of his personal will. Nor did he reject Orthodoxy.[24] Nonetheless, with the formation of the Senate, the institution of planned urban development, and the Europeanization of elite culture, Peter I launched the modern era in Russian history.

As part of this urban display of power, Peter the Great ushered in what Mumford has called the "baroque" in European architecture. As the architecture of imperial authority, the baroque turned the city into a realm for the exercise of visual prowess. The city's wide boulevards, all lined with classical architecture, produced repetitive visual lines that delivered a sense of aesthetic power and pleasure to any figure galloping through the city.[25] To achieve this effect, this tsar ordered homeowners to build flush with the road, with front entrances facing the street.[26] Inadvertently, his new designs also turned provincial cities into the wooden antipode of his stone Petersburg. For in his eagerness to finish his eponymous new capital city, a symbol of victory over the Swedes, Peter I ordered all stonemasons to St. Petersburg.[27]

Unlike St. Petersburg, medieval cities such as Nizhnii Novgorod celebrated discovery, not display. Privileging the native and the local over the national, their winding and narrow streets, despised by imperial rulers, offered aesthetic surprise and self-enclosed community. The curves of these streets sheltered local residents from the wind, even as their many dead ends made the city difficult for outsiders to navigate. Because crooked streets offered no long-distance views, churches tended to be covered with ornate detail, for up-close viewing of their hand-carved designs.[28] Urban dwellings were entered via the courtyard, not from the street, because the courtyard sheltered the home from outside noise and dust.[29] Riverfronts, as in Nizhnii Novgorod, might be lined with sheds, storage areas, and the back views of buildings. The beauty of such a city could not be enjoyed at a gallop or by boat.[30]

In reshaping the city, Peter the Great not only recast city streets, but also the direction and nature of elite perception. As Chris Otter notes, the European liberal subject was identified with certain visual practices, including attention to detail (perception) and sight at a distance (objectivity).[31] In place of tactile intimacy and private enclosure, Peter I's city offered visual command, something only fully accessible to the elites who cantered down its wide boulevards on horse or in carriage. The very architecture of space, which might be viewed as an architecture of (European) perception, helped define and even forge the new elite. Not only that, but it represented the first stages in the *objectification* of the city, its measuring through scientific time and space.[32]

Although until his death construction outside of St. Petersburg stagnated, Peter the Great also began to drape his robes of imperial authority over the Russian interior through the imposition of a homogeneous architectural style.[33] This imperial aesthetic power expanded only gradually, because authorities could not afford to tear down existing cities – a fact that meant that fires, not plans, became the primary agent of change. Still, little by little, the heart of provincial cities developed what became known as the "capital section," so named because it replicated the classical grandeur and order of St. Petersburg. The capital section came to represent a city's claim to economic and political significance, not to mention civility.[34] Ironically, this same "civility" displayed a city's provinciality, for such architecture was derivative, a distant echo of the beauty of the nation's capital.[35]

Most changes to the Nizhnii Novgorod cityscape came at the turn of the nineteenth century, largely thanks to the improved stretch of imperial power. Not only did Catherine II designate Nizhnii Novgorod as the capital of the newly formed Province of Nizhnii Novgorod, but also her administration began providing the engineers required to turn destruction from fire and flood into opportunities for planning and rationalizing the cityscape. The crooked streets, high fences, side entrances, empty spaces, and irregular façades of the medieval city disappeared, even in the outer rings of the city, where wooden architecture continued to predominate. From the late eighteenth century to the early nineteenth century, engineers filled ravines, levelled roads, and straightened streets.[36]

Such trends arguably reached their pinnacle under Nicholas I, who sponsored the most dramatic of imperial-era changes to the cityscape. Eager to facilitate commerce in the wake of his predecessor's decision to relocate the Makariev trade fair to the left bank of the Oka River opposite Nizhnii Novgorod, he reconfigured the entire urban landscape to ease the movement of commercial traffic through the city. Because the kremlin road could not accommodate the large caravans travelling to the fair from Kazan and Arzamas, Nicholas I decreed the construction of four new boulevards around the kremlin, ordering all non-pedestrian traffic to follow one of these four routes. Showing his affinity for engineering (in which he was trained prior to taking the throne), Nicholas I also arranged for the construction of a pontoon bridge over the Oka River, to join historic Nizhnii Novgorod to the fairgrounds.[37]

Moreover, Nicholas succeeded in a task first begun by Peter the Great

– namely, the functional rationalizing of the city. Before Peter I, the kremlin served as the centre of religious, military, and economic activity, all intermingled in a most irrational and "unenlightened" way. With Nicholas I, however, the Nizhnii Novgorod kremlin became a purely administrative unit bereft of homes and commerce, its road reduced to a pedestrian walkway.

Eager to indulge the pleasure-seeking eye, Nicholas I turned the riverbanks of Nizhnii Novgorod into sites for visual pleasure. He ordered the construction of two wide roads, or embankments, along the Oka River slope, so that residents and visitors might gaze at the hustle and bustle of the fair, located on the far bank of the Oka River. In the spirit of Peter the Great, to beautify these slopes, Nicholas I decreed that all buildings along these embankments face the waterfront, so as to offer a pleasing façade to sightseeing boaters. In reviewing all these changes, one might say that the stage for the demonstration of enlightened imperial power was finally complete.

In opening the cityscape to visual pleasure and commercial traffic, however, Nicholas I unwittingly fostered forces that would challenge autocratic rule. To oversee the construction of the trade fair, his predecessor Alexander I turned to an engineer recruited from France just after the signing of the Treaty of Tilsit: the Spanish-born Augustin de Béthencourt y Molina. Invited by Alexander I to establish Russia's new Institute of Transportation, Béthencourt introduced French-style polytechnical education to Russia. Compelled to offer preparatory courses to entrants of varied, often weak education, this school became the sole source of professional education for a whole cadre of engineers, as well as a channel through which both French engineering knowledge and Saint Simonian ideas were transferred to Russia. Although French technical skills were welcomed, Saint Simonian ideas troubled Tsar Nicholas I, who opted to limit such international information transfer by banning Russians from studying in France.[38] Although well aware of the value of expertise (indeed, he sponsored the research that paved the way for the Great Reforms of his successor), Nicholas I viewed the ambitions of Saint Simonians as a threat. He rejected their utopian view that technology and communications could and should transform society, making it more dynamic and democratic.[39]

Still, in sponsoring engineering as a profession, Nicholas I laid the foundations of a new Russia. Although Russian engineers generally supported state-led modernization, their ethos of service readily turned them against tsars who proved resistant to their ideas.[40] At the tsars' behest, moreover, they laid the infrastructure for modernization and industrialization, forces that would, in turn, contribute to the ultimate collapse of the Romanov dynasty.

Eager to stave off revolutions of the sort that convulsed the countries to the west, Nicholas I carefully grafted his new administration onto old values and practices. He thus promoted a new, anti-Enlightenment ideology known as "official nationality," which enshrined Orthodoxy, autocracy, and *narodnost'* (nationality or "peopleness") as hallmarks of Russia's unique, particular way of life. Through this formulation, Nicholas I rejected supposedly universal Enlightenment values, embracing instead national distinctiveness, a decision that also launched the search for a uniquely Russian style in architecture.[41] Showing similar concern for the power of tradition, when re-engineering Nizhnii Novgorod roads he ensured that all continued to begin and end with a church, as in the past. Wherever engineers disrupted holy springs in their efforts to prevent uncontrolled groundwater from eroding the slopes of the Oka River, Nicholas I ordered that they sacralize the man-made outlet for such springs, building a wooden chapel to preserve their "holy" status.[42]

Nicholas I's co-optation of tradition was not only strategic, but also necessary. The Romanov dynasty's power and authority was born of the Orthodox past, not only of the Russian empire's modernizing prowess. Besides, the past was resilient, even in physical terms. Behind the modern façade of the nineteenth-century city, the wild spaces of the older city remained – the ravines, the dilapidated homes with side entrances and high walls, and the crooked streets. Many new boulevards followed the lines of long-standing ravines, and the kremlin's now-decayed inner and outer fortification lines demarcated the boundaries of capital section and city, respectively.[43] Everywhere, along out-of-the-way streets, the medieval world of dead ends and low-lying, puddle-covered pathways persisted.

The Industrial City: A Nation Is Born

The years following the reign of Nicholas I would witness yet another remaking of the city, this time largely thanks to the self-destructive dynamics of capitalism itself. As an important commercial centre, the city's trade fair invited investment into port facilities and a railway depot, which, in turn, attracted industry to the region. Soon, mills and ship-building yards radically altered the region's economic profile, reducing the importance of petty trade. By 1897, only one-third of residents would identify themselves as traders, and 50 per cent would consist of newly urbanized peasants eager to find work in local industries.[44] Seasonal industrial labourers would rise in number to 227,000 by 1914, causing severe housing shortages.[45] Thanks to improved credit, telegraphs, and railways, as well as new rules for joint-stock companies, by the end of the century, Russian traders ceased to rely on fair-based buying and selling, operating out of permanent warehouses and shops instead.[46] Although the fair would continue to lure two to three hundred thousand visitors annually (quite a number for a city with a population of 94,000),[47] the fair ceased to be an important national economic force.

Local merchants and industrialists welcomed these changes, becoming boosters of urban growth and development, pushing aside the state and nobility in stepping forth to act as agents of modernization. They eagerly invested in new infrastructure, banks, stock exchanges, cultural institutions, and churches.[48] Meanwhile, growing concern for urban public health and local development spurred the formation of more effective, self-administering local governments in both city and village.[49]

Because the government reforms of 1864 and 1870 gave local authorities greater power to define their city's architectural aesthetic, local merchants and industrialists indulged in the construction of grandiose mansions whose architectural styles varied from avant-garde modernism to the classical and the eclectic.[50] Responding to the imperatives of newfound Russian nationalism, architects turned to folk art, not to the nation's capital, for aesthetic inspiration. Acting in this same spirit of "people pride," in 1869, the local elite arranged for a new city plan that included a minor toponymical revolution – that is, the renaming of city streets after local and national heroes, including Minin, Pozharskii, Suvorov, Kutuzov, Dobroliubov, Gogol', Mel'nikov, Rukavishnikov, and Stroganov.[51] The urban landscape came to celebrate local and national prowess, not the "enlightened" power of the tsars.

The All-Russian Industrial and Art Exhibition of 1896 gave Nizhnii Novgorod's merchants, intellectuals, and richer nobles an opportunity to flaunt their city's progress.[52] The exhibition grounds were situated immediately next to the trade fair, on the left bank of the Oka River. In preparation for the event, the duma and local luminaries (with financial aid from the tsar) outfitted the city with electric streetlights, paved roads, a drama theatre, a temporary courthouse, a new business exchange, public gardens, and a tramline that linked historic Nizhnii Novgorod to the exhibition grounds via a pontoon bridge over the Oka River. They also completed the restoration of the kremlin's Dmitriev Tower, in which local historians placed their new Museum of History and Art.[53] In the words of native-born writer Maxim Gorky, historic Nizhnii Novgorod became a "city of lights" on the hill that overlooked the exhibition, which was situated on the opposite bank of the Oka River.[54]

Opening that summer on a patch of terrain located to the southwest of the annual trade fair, the exhibition brought thousands of national and international visitors, allowing the city to showcase the economic and cultural potential of the Russian state, particularly its provinces. The event included exhibits on avant-garde art, modern medicine and agriculture, the colonization of Siberia, and the latest in industrial production and communications, as well as the most recent developments in sanitary technology. As a central attraction, it also featured a water tower from which one might survey the fairgrounds, enjoying the spectacle of the fair's visitors and displays below.[55] In all of this, the exhibition also served as an educational forum for enlightening the population about the wonders of the modern age.[56]

In showcasing economic and technological progress, the All-Russian Industrial and Art Exhibition proposed new ways of being and thinking, not the least of which was the notion that a stereotypically backward Russian provincial city could be radically modernized. The exhibition provided the opportunity for self-creation, defining the Russian province as a site of culture, education, and international entrepreneurship, not a site of cultural and economic backwardness. In this way, the exhibition served as a structure for spacing (*espacement*) as defined by Jacques Derrida: although it did not yet redefine local life, the event opened up new ways of seeing and perceiving local experience.[57] The exhibition's bright lights and tall displays cast a dark shadow over the underdeveloped sectors of the city.[58] Its new, avant-garde designs stood in stark contrast to Nizhnii Novgorod's annual trade fair, a world of Eastern merchants, petty traders, mounds of wholesale and retail goods for redistribution, bawdy popular entertainment, and widespread poverty. By juxtaposing the old (the trade fair) against the new (the exhibits), the exhibition may have helped to produce the *perception* of the need for urban services, infrastructure, and housing, provoking what Michael Hamm has called a "crisis of modernization."[59]

Indeed, with its water tower, its exhibits of technology, and its absence of bawdy entertainment and dingy booths, the All-Russian Industrial and Art Exhibition arguably encouraged a *desire for perception*, particularly for the open, clean, and elevated spaces that would permit this. Its water tower, a feat of engineering, offered a clear, unfettered view of the fairgrounds, being a symbol of that power of vision that marked the elite gaze. Its steel construction and technology-celebrating exhibits foreshadowed the coming transformation in architecture, as steel, glass, cement, and plastics would not only be put to functional use, but would also come to define modern architecture's aesthetic style. Thanks to these new materials, after the Revolution, Russian architects would reject old rules of design. Seeking visual clarity and "authenticity," they would reject ornamentation and symmetry, instead pursuing design that expressed a building's interior structure, materials, and use.[60]

Although a temporary event, the exhibition permanently altered the cityscape. After most of the newly built exhibition pavilions were sold, a wealthy local merchant transported the tsar's pavilion to the city centre, where it was renovated to become the new city duma building.[61] A few years later, the exhibition grounds became a city park.[62] The Moscow city council's pavilion on urban affairs became a permanent collection for the Moscow Museum of Urban Management (today's Museum of the History of Moscow), perpetuating the exhibition's educational mandate, which had been to instil appreciation for modern improvements.[63] Most importantly, the new drama theatre, tramlines, electric streetlights, paved roads, and cultural facilities built in preparation for the exhibition became fixed features of the urban landscape. The very performance of modernization and progress, in this case, reshaped the material city.[64]

Symbolic Occupation: Towards a New Soteriology

The Russian Revolution of 1917 ushered in dramatic changes to the cityscape, although initially most were confined to the world of representational space. Having seized power, Bolshevik Party and cultural leaders sought to recode city space, replacing monuments to the Orthodox faith and the Russian tsar with allusions to their own pantheon of Marxist, Bolshevik, and revolutionary heroes. In effect, the Bolsheviks went to war with their past, violently uprooting an earlier sense of place and time through their assault on the urban landscape.[65]

Yet, Soviet representational space incorporated imperial and tsarist symbols, indirectly perpetuating pre-existing systems of discourse and ritual. The Bolsheviks grafted the new message of Revolution onto the old world of political and cultural understanding, even as they borrowed the tsarist world's more innovative technologies of rule. These inherited spaces, discursive and institutional, served as convenient vehicles for communicating revolutionary ideals. Yet, they were not only co-opted by Soviet leaders, but also influenced their actions, ideas, and sense of revolutionary self.[66]

The Bolsheviks' symbolic occupation of the city began with the literal and figurative expropriation of the old elite. The merchants' Commercial Club became the Theatre for Youth (TIuZ), the Rukavishnikov mansion became the Museum of Local History, and the archbishop's residence became a music conservatory. They turned the Nobles' Meeting House into the Sverdlov District House of Culture, and the city duma building into the House of Labour. They also renamed Prison Square as Freedom Square and – almost a decade later – designated Maxim Gorky's childhood home, the Kashirin House, a museum, something to be cherished by the local population.[67]

Many of these changes had a specifically religious focus, inverting the symbolic and cultural power of Orthodox sites. Local leaders placed the pedagogical institute in the seminary building, substituting secular for religious education. They turned Peter and Paul Cemetery, named in honour of two founding fathers of the Christian faith, into Kulibin Park, named in honour of a local inventor, a native-born founding father of science.[68] The city's Monastery of the Exaltation of the Cross became a labour camp, possibly an oblique reference to Bolsheviks' belief in the redeeming power of labour.[69] Finally, church buildings were confiscated and turned into museums and libraries, which the Bolsheviks viewed as a more authentic means of effecting spiritual and moral renewal.[70]

Nizhnii Novgorod's authorities also memorialized local and national heroes, thereby writing their city into the story of Soviet revolution.[71] Like all cities, Nizhnii Novgorod therefore came to have a Soviet Square, a Lenin Square, and an October Square.[72] Houses of Culture sprouted up in working-class districts, to gift the masses with quality education and entertainment.[73] In addition, in October 1932, local authorities renamed the entire city "Gorky," in honour of city-born hero Alexei Peshkov, whose rise to international acclaim under the pen name Maxim Gorky represented the self-creation and success to which local officials aspired.

The city's new name featured prominently in local Soviet propaganda, as "From merchant Nizhnii to a socialist Gorky" became the leading slogan of urban development. Although faulty construction, delay, ill-repair, poor services, and poverty remained pervasive realities, authorities dismissed these as *otstatki*, or vestiges of the past. They were viewed as temporary blemishes destined to disappear together with old "merchant Nizhnii," which local authorities described as a long-dying organism into which the "narcotic" of capitalism had once injected the mere semblance of vitality. Every new sidewalk, paved road, sewer pipe, electric line, and apartment building became a sign that their socialist city-child, their "little Gorky," was maturing and growing healthily. The city's new designation was not simply a name, but a mandate and identity.[74]

In the process of articulating this new identity, Soviet authorities destroyed the old soterioscape and imposed their own spatial narrative of human salvation. They placed a planetarium in Annunciation Monastery, substituting a scientific explanation of the universe for a monastery that had celebrated the annunciation of Christ, whom Orthodox believers regarded as the Logos, or ordering force, of the cosmos. Nativity Street, which paid tribute to the birth of Christ, became Mayakovsky Street, named after a radical avant-garde poet whose works celebrated the regenerative force of Revolution.[75] Nativity Church became, for a time, a municipal museum, a substitution that imputed redemptive power to technology.[76] The Cathedral of the Transfiguration, which had symbolized the unification of the divine and human spirits, was torn down to permit the construction of the House of Soviets, a symbol of the power of working-class unity.[77] (See figures 1.7 and 1.8.) The Chapel of the Exaltation of the Cross ceased to exist, but the Monastery of the Exaltation of the Cross, as noted above, became a site for confining real and perceived opponents to Bolshevik rule.[78] Finally, Pecherskii Monastery became a recreational area, as if to suggest that health, rest, and vitality no longer lay in religious community and spiritual healing, but in physical relaxation.[79]

This Soviet soterioscape, like the medieval soterioscape, existed only tentatively, being an ephemeral and unstable narrative in space. Nativity Church only briefly served as a site for the promotion of municipal development, whereas the planetarium was not built until the 1940s and outlived the Soviet collapse.[80] Appearing in fragments, along a path that no longer defined the city's traffic patterns, this representational landscape – like the medieval one – did not emerge at the behest of any particular institution or individual. Rather, it testified to the resilience of tradition, to the power of old symbols to invoke new ideas, and of old spaces to outline the form of the new.

This Soviet soterioscape captured many of the tensions that would riddle the world of Soviet planning. The presence of planning materials in Nativity Church could be read as a tentative celebration of the redemptive power of technology, whereas the House of Soviets celebrated working-class prowess. Suitably staged, the tension between these two dimensions of Soviet socialism – the technocratic and the populist – would plague

1.7 and 1.8. Nizhnii Novgorod House of Soviets (Alexander Z. Grinberg, 1929–1931). Olga Orel'skaia, *Arkhitektura epokhi sovetskogo avangarda v Nizhnem Novgorode* (Nizhnii Novgorod: Promgrafika, 2005), 91.

the Soviet Union of the 1920s and 1930s. Indeed, as an a-cartographic and a-technical system of representing the city, the entire soterioscape represented a non-scientific approach to social representation and to locating oneself in time and space. Although it celebrated Marxist revolution, which purported to be science, the soterioscape did not advance a scientific way of seeing the city, but rather sought to win the hearts and minds of the resident population. In it, the die was cast for conflict between planners, administrators, and ordinary urban inhabitants.

Certainly, these spaces of the past, both physical and cultural, exercised and enabled defiance. The physical and symbolic landscape, in retaining the outline of historic cultural codes, offered a source of alternative moral identities and practices. Even as street, city, and bridge names changed, memories of earlier, alternative designations lingered.[81] Thus, in 1936, the city's main newspaper, *Gor'kovskii rabochii*, made reference to "Trinity Lane" and the "Neapol'" hotel, both of which had officially ceased to exist.[82] Many Soviet citizens deliberately malformed Soviet toponyms, while others clung to pre-revolutionary names as a matter of moral duty, as a way to preserve an alternative truth or identity.[83] Still other usages of older names were circumstantial, prompted by the simple need to communicate using long familiar terms.[84]

The Bolsheviks' own ideological and political struggles encouraged the misnaming of streets, for the Soviet leadership's ever-changing policies and incessant purges repeatedly altered the Soviet pantheon of heroes and, with that, the city's configuration of toponyms. In 1934, with the regime's self-proclaimed success in "building socialism," local authorities seemed to hope for toponymic stability. They therefore ordered local officials to assign a single official name to each street, alley, and square in the city.[85] Yet, street names continued to change, as a renewed wave of Party purges again disturbed the list of "acceptable" Soviet heroes. The entire toposcape remained in flux.[86]

Constructing Place: An Incarnate Imaginary

Despite such problems, Bolshevik leaders did their utmost to redefine the foundations of Soviet city and community. Bolshevik thought, like all modern conceptual edifices, attempted to delineate a base that could be defined as the source from which Bolshevik thought and power naturally sprang forth.[87] Seeking to present themselves as the inevitable product of historic class struggle and the march towards justice, Soviet leaders worked diligently to ground revolutionary history in local spaces. Plac-

ards to local revolutionaries, together with history books and revolutionary monuments, sought to make the Revolution legitimate, inevitable,
and also local. In effect, these staged power, providing a set where the
past was clothed in darkness and sadness, and the future shone brightly
from some point to the left of the stage.

Nevertheless, as every ruler from Peter the Great onward had discovered, space produces resistances, only some of which might be co-opted.
Unlike Nicholas I, the Bolsheviks did not wish to guard Orthodoxy's
churches and holy springs. Yet, they necessarily appropriated its cultural
valuables – not just icons, money, gold, and gems, but also its symbolic
systems. Place, as physical and moral code, proved resilient, compelling
the Party to dialogue with an existing social and spatial terrain. Nor was
this problem unique to the Party, for – as the next chapters show – the
state's architects and engineers faced similar challenges.

Chapter Two

Visionary Planning: Confronting Socio-Material Agencies

We have become like metal, our souls are at one with the machine.

Vladimir Kirillov, "We"[1]

Constructivism, Fordism, and the Socialist City

In 1928, when Ivanitskii arrived in Nizhnii Novgorod, many specialists aspired to use technology to help forge the citizenry of the future, a vision perfectly in sync with the soteriological narrative imbedded in the Soviet cityscape. In the city's symbolic landscape, technology played the role of the nativity, the force that would make the transfiguration of the human self possible. In keeping with this message, avant-garde architects looked to the space of the city as the means through which to reshape society.[2] The constructivists among them theorized the "social condenser," a living complex whose techno-social organization was to produce a healthier, more productive, and socially engaged citizenry. To figures such as Ivanitskii would go the task of extending this model to the entire city, so that its overall design would serve as the infrastructure of a new Soviet society.[3]

With a goal that encompassed the construction of over two hundred new factory towns, the Soviet First Five-Year Plan offered vast scope for these ambitions.[4] The relatively vacant lands on which such towns were placed permitted what S. Frederick Starr called "visionary planning," in which architects used their creative skill to rebuild society from its very foundations. Offering what Richard Stites would have called a "techno-utopia," such plans turned Frederick Winslow Taylor's visions of scientific management into much more than a means to improve workplace efficiency.[5] Applied to the home, in the form of a housing combine, Taylor's vision became a means of rationalizing social reproduction by replacing the woman's role in the home with specialized state-provided services, such as child care, laundries, factory kitchens, and the like.[6]

To theorists, such housing combines merged art and life through the medium of machine-like efficiency. Although many avant-garde artists, designers, and writers criticized the housing combine as a rather crude mechanism for societal control, many of these individuals nonetheless embraced the machine as a model for art and society. To them, the machine *was* art, design, science, and possibility, all wrapped into one, and Alexei Gastev's attempts to infuse human movement with machine-like rhythm were poetry.[7] Together with the American automotive giant Walter Chrysler, they might have proclaimed, "There is in manufacturing a creative job that only poets are supposed to know."[8] To many, the machine and the factory were ideal models for the design of both home and city.[9]

S. Frederick Starr was correct to refer to such avant-garde planning as visionary, for its cold objectivity consisted of rethinking society from afar, using the tools of scientific *perception* to dissect the functional aspects of human activity before redesigning the city with an eye to facilitating the very rationally analysed activities that experts had categorized and scrutinized.[10] Such projects fashioned human society in the designers' image, as an extension of planners' science, reason, and analytical order. The very mode of observation that undergirded such design drew attention to society's rational aspects, ignoring the place of spontaneity, unpredictability, and cultural patterns that might not conform to experts' vision. As Boris Groys emphasizes, such design laid claim to power and, as such, would be prone to challenge from political authorities.[11]

Although the Party wished to exploit the avant-garde's skill, it could not help but challenge the avant-garde both for its ambition and for the highly abstract nature of its vision. Visionary planners' man-as-machine ideal for the city lacked realism. Economic upheaval, weak control over construction, changing political attitudes to both experts and functionalist models of human life, and the technological complexity of the combines would preclude the realization of the visionary. Avant-garde planning, lost as it was in utopian vision, not only denied and overlooked the daunting economic and technical challenges of building socialism, but also it ignored the threat posed by the Soviet leadership's competing, more Fordist approach to social management. The Party under Comrade Stalin wished for architecture and design that would provide a platform for the representation and consolidation of centralized political power, exerting a psychosocial impact on the general population. Avant-garde design, born of a desire for functionalism and technocratic authority, did not serve this purpose.

Building the Socialist City: The Ford Factory Town of Avtozavod

Nizhnii Novgorod became the location of one such experiment in avant-garde design when Soviet authorities opted to erect a facility to produce Ford vehicles just a few kilometres up the Oka River from the city. The site hosted nothing more than a few small huts and leafy willows not far from the river, making it the ideal "blank slate" onto which to sketch visionary plans. It also appealed because the grounds were dry, and the factory could exploit the labour, industry, and communication systems of Nizhnii Novgorod city and province, regions noted for their leatherwork, pottery, metalworking, rope making, and shipbuilding. These skills did not exactly prepare workers for automobile manufacturing, but at least such skilled workers had some knowledge of fabrication and design.[12]

Although the factory remained outside city boundaries until 1936, the new plant's vast size and its multiple auxiliary facilities were a catalyst for industrial development throughout the Nizhnii Novgorod region. A turnkey operation, the contracted plant was to produce a hundred thousand vehicles a year. As part of the deal with Henry Ford, Soviet authorities agreed to purchase Ford parts and product designs, and Ford arranged to train fifty Soviet engineers per year at his Detroit plant.[13] Although Ford couched the deal in terms of facilitating development abroad (an almost charitable matter), the deal actually served to alleviate the Ford Motor Company's business woes, for competition from Chevrolet, a "Don't-Buy-American" campaign in Europe, and the early years of the Great Depression had led to a significant drop in its profits.[14]

In closing the deal with Ford, Soviet authorities were not only buying a car, but also solidifying their faith in assembly-line production. At first blush, the repetitive, body-tiring, and mind-numbing nature of assembly-line work would appear to be utterly unsuited to a self-proclaimed socialist state. However, Soviet authorities viewed the assembly line as a technology that would enable them to mobilize the country's vast pool of unskilled labour, while disciplining peasant bodies to the regularized movement of industrial production. Determined to integrate workers and former peasants into the industrial process, state authorities strove to break peasant forms of association and labour, in order that state-controlled means of recruitment, training, organization, and sociability might predominate.[15]

As a Ford facility in all but name, the new site offered an ideal stage for the conflict between Party and professionals over the use of technology, which was somehow deemed to be apolitical, meaning not only that it could be imported from the West (in the form of Ford production, for instance), but also that avant-garde architects and engineers, as its masters, could claim supra-political status. The Party and professionals approached engineering technology differently, however. Whereas scientists and artists embraced Taylor's approach to scientific management, the Party favoured Fordism, whereby political leaders and managers wielded predominant authority in the workplace.[16] Even as the avant-garde worked to design the factory town, the Party under Stalin achieved Fordism by consolidating power, centralizing the economy, removing small producers (such as peasants), and asserting greater political and managerial control over production.[17]

The avant-garde did not foresee this outcome, but rather engrossed itself in disputes over the design of the socialist city of the future. On this question, its members roughly divided into two schools, somewhat inaccurately labelled "disurbanist" and "urbanist." The former, led by Mikhail A. Okhitovich, desired to scatter settlement along state communication networks and energy grids. Within this school, one could find Nikolai A. Miliutin, who theorized the linear city model of growth whereby each city became a row of three strip-shaped zones of residential, recreational, and industrial growth that stretched along roads, rivers, and rails.[18] The alternative "urbanist" school promoted the garden city ideal first articulated in England by Ebenezer Howard. Built in the midst of agricultural lands, Howard's factory towns offered an escape from urban congestion, access to fresh food and clean air, and small populations (under 50,000 people) with the right to self-rule. Not unlike "disurbanist" schemes, the garden city model rejected the big city as alienating and undesirable.[19]

Insofar as Party leaders viewed cities as a vital component in the battle against old ways of being, particularly against "peasant mindsets," Avtostroi (the state agency responsible for the construction of the factory) favoured the garden city, as envisioned by Leonid M. Sabsovich.[20] Modifying Howard's initial vision to suit the Soviet Union's socialist mandate, Sabsovich proposed the construction of housing combines that substituted the collective for the family as the primary unit of social organization. To facilitate such collective loyalties, Sabsovich applied the principle of assembly-line production to domestic life. Established to emancipate women from household drudgery, rendering the family obsolete as a site of reproduction, his collectivized facilities assigned responsibility for various domestic chores (e.g., cleaning, child rearing, cooking, and dining) to specialized industrial facilities such as factory kitchens, industrial laundries, cafeterias, daycares, and schools. These also confined individual activities to the sleeping cell, forcing residents' waking hours into public space.[21]

Although embraced for its putative efficacy as a social condenser, or engine of a new society, much of the appeal of Sabsovich's combine lay in its promised economic rewards. By releasing women from the burden of domestic chores, Sabsovich's plan theoretically achieved the employment of two adults per household, thereby reducing the number of dependents per industrial worker. Sabsovich calculated that this would decrease the number of required tertiary workers in the factory community, which would further reduce the cost of providing housing and services for the factory town. That the Ford plant would deploy assembly-line production only enhanced the appeal of Sabsovich's proposals, for this form of production permitted the factory to utilize unskilled labourers, including women, who tended to have less education than their male counterparts.[22] As a result, Sabsovich's idea garnered high praise from both the chief economist of the First Five-Year Plan, Stanislav G. Strumilin, and the Commissar of Enlightenment, Anatolii V. Lunacharskii.[23]

From the beginning, these social condensers faced criticism for the compulsion inherent in them. Experts such as Sabsovich defensively argued that combines, with their modern services and freedom from family life, would appeal to Soviet citizens. But even within the avantgarde, many felt that the housing combine offered too little individual scope for human development.[24] Only the sleeping cell offered some element of private life. Dismissing these concerns, Sabsovich argued that true selfhood could only be forged through the collective.[25] Referring to survey reports, he also claimed that workers welcomed both communal spaces and state-supported domestic services – which may have been true, but was not quite the same thing as wishing for housing combines.[26]

Sabsovich's emphasis on collective selfhood highlights the fact that these combines were not meant to foster what scholars call "liberal subjectivity." Liberal subjectivity relies on a series of vision-related qualities: volition (the freedom to look), distance (perception), objectivity (tied to distance, or the ability to step outside and view), and thought (understood, in metaphorical terms, as "seeing").[27] If the combines had been designed to foster these qualities, then the sleeping cell would have emerged as a central feature of design, being essential to carving distance from self and other, as required for the development of insight. Yet, in Sabsovich's designs, such cells appeared as somewhat of an afterthought, attracting little discussion, except when specialists voiced concern about their "isolationist" quality.

At the same time, although Sabsovich's housing combines denied citizens the right to a private life, they cannot be considered panoptic. The sleeping cell provided shelter from the "stranger's gaze."[28] Even had this cell been eradicated, the sort of mutual, collective surveillance produced by the combine's design was too symmetrical and mutual to be panoptic. Although police and Party surveillance recognized no right to privacy, such surveillance did not penetrate the workers' world everywhere at all times, being specific in structure and means. It was, in this, more "oligoptic" than panoptic.[29] Besides, the combines were not designed to foster policing, but rather to create self-regulating communities that would not require such modes of social control. They were meant as a techno-social system in which the very design of the structure would sustain a desired form of community, without requiring the intervention of Party or government controls, except to maintain the housing combine as the infrastructure of socialist society.

These ideas, it should be stressed, did not exclude older notions that human society was, in essence, an organism. The man-as-machine aesthetic did not entirely destroy concern for human beings as biological organisms who were prone to fatigue, weakness, and ill health. The biological sciences compelled technocrats to consider the inconstant nature of human energy levels.[30] Soviet planners often compared society to a garden, reflecting the lingering impact of nineteenth-century greenhouse systems on planners' models of the city.[31] Concerned for workers as biological entities, not simply as cogs in the wheel of production, Avtostroi demanded that all plans for the new factory town provide seven square metres of living space per person, much higher than the three square metres that was the average in nearby Nizhnii Novgorod.[32] Avostroi also required that all factory housing be placed "on the meridian," meaning along a north-south axis, so that an abundance of morning and evening sun could flood working-class apartments. Whatever the tensions between progress and nature, Avtostroi and Soviet planners had not entirely forgotten the latter.

Sabsovich's model initially appealed to both authorities and architects, because it suited the collectivizing spirit of the age. Combines adhering to Sabsovich's ideas were built at a time marked by the forced collectivization of agriculture. As long as the drive to collectivize production, both agricultural and social, dominated state policy, Sabsovich's designs retained their appeal. But when, in March 1930, Stalin gave his "Dizzy with Success" speech, demanding a halt to forced collectivization, Sabsovich's model lost official support.[33] Applying Stalin's condemnation of forced collectivization to urban design, in May 1930 the Central Committee of the Communist Party denounced the housing combine, referring to it as a "semi-fanatical" attempt to leap through history to socialism.[34]

Just as Stalin's speech did not fully bring collectivization to a complete stop, so the Central Committee's ruling did not bring the construction of housing combines to an end. Rather, it fostered the proliferation of "transitional combines," which permitted a modicum of family life. In many of these, individual cells were designed to be joined or separated at will, allowing for the creation or disaggregation of social units as needed. In the early years, planners expected families to live together, conjoining several sleeping cells to form small apartments. Over time, the combine's domestic support systems and collective social events were to weaken family loyalties by fostering identification with the working-class collective. At that point, architects argued, these small apartments would revert to individualized sleeping cells.[35]

Judging the Socialist City: Visions of the Socialist Future

In the midst of this transition from total to partial collectivization, Avostroi invited students from the Soviet Union's premier architecture and engineering institutions to submit designs for the new factory town. The students who participated in Avtostroi's competition represented all the major scholars of Soviet design, including the Union of Contemporary Architects (OSA), which was the theoretical home of constructivism, as well as the Association of Architects-Urbanists (ARU) and the Higher State Art and Technical Institute (Vkhutein), both of which sent students of a more "rationalist" bent.[36] The more traditionalist Moscow Architectural Society (MAO) entered, as did students from the Moscow Higher Technical Institute (MVTU), a bastion of constructivist teaching.[37] Participants from this final school, however, hailed from the All-Union Association of Proletarian Architects (VOPRA), an up-and-coming group of provincial and younger architects who challenged the authority of the avant-garde, even their own constructivist teachers.[38] The Central

Municipal Bank (Tsekombank) also sent a sketch, although it had not received a direct invitation to do so.[39]

While an incredibly wide range of proposals should have been expected, given the variety of competitors, Avtostroi limited contestants' scope of creativity by demanding that all participants submit a plan for a Sabsovich-style factory town, with enough combines to house fifty thousand workers. These criteria precluded any disurbanist scheme for eliminating the city as a settlement form, focusing all attention on the socialist city as a social condenser. Within these narrow confines, students offered an impressive array of ideas, which will only be briefly and incompletely discussed here.[40] For our purposes, what is most striking is the purely theoretical nature of these proposals, which displayed more concern for the socialist city as an abstract visionary ideal than as something to be realized in a specific place and time.

In keeping with the constructivist appreciation for linear cities, OSA students offered a variation on Miliutin's three-strip approach to linear settlement, whereby the city expanded laterally, as three continuous strips of residential, recreational, and industrial land.[41] Thinking in terms of dynamic growth, the OSA team also proposed two separate stages of development. The first stage respected popular commitments to the family, as voiced in citizens' responses to questionnaires distributed by constructivist theorists. The OSA therefore proposed six-storey dormitories, each with its own cooking, sports, and social areas, linked by and to two-storey communal buildings. The communal buildings were to foster collectivism, but did not compel it.[42] For stage two, they proposed both higher buildings and an elevated level of collectivism in the form of sixteen-storey dormitories bereft of cooking and cleaning areas in order that all residents might be forced to spend their time in the settlement's central community buildings. In this second stage, they also proposed to separate children from their parents, handing responsibility for the children's upbringing to specialists in early childhood development.[43]

Vkhutein students, who focused on provoking discussion, offered not one design, but an entire series of one-author suggestions.[44] Most displayed a strong rationalist influence, perhaps garnered through the Basic Course that all Vkhutein students took (and which was run by a rationalist theorist). Deeply concerned with the psychological impact of colour and form, these students – with the rationalists – rejected any single approach to urban design, emphatically demanding that architects grace the cityscape with a variety of urban forms.[45] Of this group, the most notable design came from Viktor P. Kalmykov, who proposed a

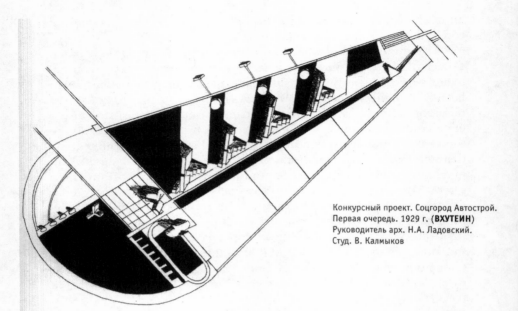

Конкурсный проект. Соцгород Автострой.
Первая очередь. 1929 г. **(ВХУТЕИН)**
Руководитель арх. Н.А. Ладовский.
Студ. В. Калмыков

2.1. Design for the socialist city of Avtozavod (Viktor P. Kalmykov, 1930). Olga Orel'skaia, *Arkhitektura epokhi sovetskogo avangarda v Nizhnem Novgorode* (Nizhnii Novgorod: Promgrafika, 2005), 37.

parabola-shaped town that wrapped the zoning strips of the OSA's linear city around the town's cultural centre. Modelling the rationalist concern for aesthetics, Kalmykov proposed that a variety of housing structures, from bungalows to skyscrapers, be placed in a "stepped" manner, with the tallest buildings at the centre and the bungalows on the outskirts. Like the OSA, his second-stage construction separated children from adults.[46] (See figure 2.1.)

Unlike the OSA and Vkhutein, the ARU team sought to provide multiple levels of community at all stages of construction. Every apartment building, even in the latter stages of community development, featured single (seven square metres) and double (fourteen square metres) rooms, which could be combined to create two- to three-room apartments. Because the endurance of family life would require space for food preparation, all corridors ended with a small kitchen – something that an Avtostroi engineer, S.M. Liubimov, called a "gift to a dying way of life" (*dan' otmiraiushchemu bytu*).[47] Rather than force residents to mingle in a single cultural zone, the ARU turned each building in the combine into a small community-in-itself. Every residential building featured a middle floor dedicated to communal activities, including dining. These second-floor communal areas linked via second-storey corridors to child-care facilities, granting parents easy access to their children. To encourage "higher" forms of collectivism, the ARU linked every two residential buildings (a total of 8,000 people) to a shared community building via an above-ground corridor. In addition to the services offered in the smaller buildings, this facility offered medical services. Each of these two-building communities included a kindergarten, which was squeezed into the space between the two buildings. Major administrative buildings serving the entire settlement were located in its centre.[48]

Although highly innovative, all of these entries were marred by technical errors. OSA students had apparently erred in placing housing on future factory and railway locations, and they had unthinkingly slotted the construction of the hospital for second-stage, not first-stage construction. Many commentators objected to plans to remove small children from parental care in second-stage growth. OSA also drew criticism for placing a mere twenty children in each of its crèches – a laudatory idea, given how smaller numbers would facilitate individualized care, but nonetheless rejected as too costly. The Russian Commissariat of Health (Narkomzdrav RSFSR) recommended fifty to sixty children per facility, a number that commentators favoured. As for ARU designs, many dubbed the commune "strange" – too large, with too much opportunity for old-style family living in second-stage construction. Moreover, as the Commissariat of Health and the State Sanitary Institute noted, the ARU plan situated children's institutions in the cramped space between buildings, where foul air from nearby collective buildings could contaminate the children's living space.[49]

Criticisms such as these not withstanding, these constructivist and rationalist designs offered a level of creativity unmatched by the remaining two teams. MAO students, trained by the Vkhutein professor, Ivan V. Zholtovsky, remained staunchly loyal to the old Grecian laws of form and proportion. A theorist of "harmonized constructivism," Zholtovsky incorporated new building materials into what were classically shaped, symmetrical designs.[50] Extending this conservatism to city planning, the MAO team proposed to arrange the city around old-style city quarters with rectilinear road grids. MAO's plan failed to provide for the future communalization of its apartments. Insofar as housing quarters and individual apartments would soon become the Soviet norm, MAO students arguably "enjoyed the last laugh." But, at the time, meridian construction and transitional combines were the norm.[51]

The final plan, submitted by MVTU, became the model for the Ford plant's factory town, because of its superior regional planning. Unlike other contestants, these students outlined a highly cost-effective means of linking the city to the factory and park, as well as to the nearby cities of Nizhnii Novgorod and Dzerzhinsk.[52] In this, the plan showed the strong influence of a particular MVTU instructor – namely, Alexander Platonovich Ivanitskii, who was busily finishing his plans for nearby Nizhnii Novgorod. Like Ivanitskii's plans for Nizhnii Novgorod, MVTU's design allotted nine square metres of living space per person, foreshadowing the soon-to-be approved federal norm. Structurally, it also paved the way for the merger of the factory district (Avtozavod) and the City of Nizhnii Novgorod, as desired by Ivanitskii. No wonder, then, that Ivanitskii declared the MVTU proposal to be *zhiznennyi*, or dynamic.[53]

In the spirit of public debate and discussion so cherished by the architectural community, Avtostroi arranged for a two-week meeting of the jury, which included representatives from a wide array of vested government agencies, including local factories, unions, the Communist Youth League (Komsomol), the All-Union Tractor and Automobile Association (VATO), and the Supreme Council of the National Economy (VSNKh). Experts in design, aesthetics, and public health descended on the area to pronounce judgment on each design.[54] In addition, Avtostroi welcomed non-voting viewers and commentators, including delegates from the Russian Commissariat of Health and the Russian Commissariat of Internal Affairs, the Society for the Protection of Motherhood and Youths, and local and national newspapers, as well as from Magnitostroi and Stalingradstroi, two agencies involved in the construction of similar factory towns. The Nizhnii Novgorod provincial government boycotted the event in protest of the fact that it was held in Moscow rather than in Nizhnii Novgorod.[55]

The outcome of the jury debates highlighted the disjuncture between the competition's goals and its use. Avtostroi's selection of such a large, diverse audience reflected the typical role of such events – to facilitate the exchange of ideas. Ever since the first such competition was organized by the Moscow Architectural Society in 1867, such gatherings had served to inspire creativity.[56] Assuming this to be the purpose of the entire endeavour, Vkhutein contestants had been content to submit incomplete but dramatic designs. However, because Soviet authorities suddenly announced that the construction of the factory town was to begin on the first of May, the discussion focused on the technical aspects of the plans – their accuracy, preparedness, and ready feasibility.

The focus on practicality benefited the students of the Moscow Higher Technical Institute (MVTU), whose plan featured rather boring rectangular housing. Without any ornamentation or variation in the size, shape, or design of buildings (despite the fact that, in dismantling the family, they assigned a specific age group to each building), their residential boxes loomed as ugly hulks. A row of them might have offered a sense of visual rhythm if they had been situated diagonal to the road, as was the housing in several other proposals, but MVTU contestants failed to exploit this possibility. MVTU students tried to break this monotony through the strategic placement of kiosks and small decorative structures between the buildings, but the overall aesthetic nevertheless remained weak.[57] Such boxes hardly lived up to the creative expectations of their peers, but their simplicity would make them easy to complete quickly.

Given that MVTU team members belonged to the infamous All-Union Association of Proletarian Architects (VOPRA), one might be tempted to attribute their success to architectural politics. As a group consisting mostly of lower-class, provincial architects, VOPRA had formed the first all-Soviet architectural union (the avant-garde had made little headway in the provinces), gained a reputation as the "newest thing" in architecture, and launched a purge of the state's leading architectural bodies. Many of the MVTU's opponents in the Avtostroi contest would suffer from this onslaught.[58] VOPRA's dominance was brief. Already in 1932, Stalin forced all architects into the newly formed and state-controlled Union of Soviet Architects. But, at the time of the contest, VOPRA was poised to become the new leading school of architecture. (See figure 2.2.)

Jurors made no mention of this broader dispute – perhaps, because the debate centred on the technical and practical elements of the designs, largely by-passing the question of aesthetic or abstract ideals. Although some participants objected to this, the jury's decision to focus on selecting the simplest and most effective plan, not the plan with the boldest ideas, may have averted a more volatile and politicized dispute over design preferences. Besides, Ivanitskii himself had advised the MVTU team, which possibly precluded such bold politicking. After all, Ivanitskii had been a friend and strong supporter of constructivists, and he by no means allied with VOPRA's cause, which opposed so much of what Ivanitskii represented. As an expert trained in the tsarist era, with mastery of foreign languages, not to mention an extensive travel record, Ivanitskii fit all the criteria of a "rightist" class enemy or an "old school" teacher

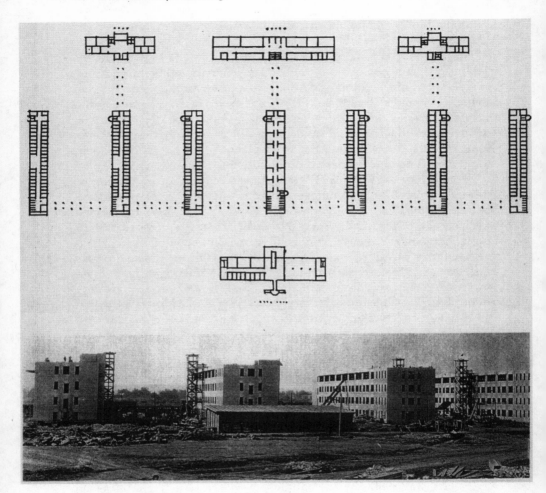

2.2. MVTU design for the socialist city of Avtozavod (with a photograph of its construction). Olga Orel'skaia, *Arkhitektura epokhi sovetskogo avangarda v Nizhnem Novgorode* (Nizhnii Novgorod: Promgrafika, 2005), 61.

destined for replacement by a new, truly Soviet generation. Whatever the situation, the politics of the debate focused on the technological strengths of each plan. If this was a cover for aesthetic politics, then the printed record certainly gives no indication of this.

The Accidental Radicals: American Capitalists Build the Socialist City

The rush that facilitated MVTU's victory resulted from the curious fact that Avostroi had contracted with an American firm, the Austin Company of Cleveland, Ohio, to undertake construction beginning that summer.[59] Famed for its ability to erect industrial plants in record time using wide-span steel trusses that facilitated the construction of pillar-free buildings ideally suited to assembly-line production, the Austin Company embodied all that the Soviet Union found alluring about the United States – its industrial prowess, its technological capabilities, and its penchant for size and speed. Despite ideological hostilities, such collaboration was encouraged by authorities, who sought to exploit the best global technologies, long since identified with America.[60] For the Austin Company to begin its work as planned, however, it needed to receive its instructions within two weeks of the jury's deliberations, leaving too little time in which to radically rework the winning proposal.[61]

Naively, Soviet authorities assumed that they could effectively appropriate American techniques, practices, and designs directly, despite differing cultures, languages, and measurement scales. The difficulty of translating technical terms, measurement systems, and building and management practices would prove daunting, offering plenty of scope for frustration and adventure on the part of the Austin representatives about to arrive in Nizhnii Novgorod to oversee the construction of factory and town. They did not foresee the shortage of equipment, the limited food supplies, or the simple challenge of getting things done without strongly placed political connections.

Moreover, as alarmed jury members noted, Austin initially seemed baffled by the Soviet concept of the socialist city – something apparent already in March 1930, as jurors discussed the various entries to the competition. In its initial submission, the Austin Company submitted a design that promised to fulfil the American dream, not the Soviet one. In it, each apartment had a small nursery, a laundry, and a kitchen, as well as a private entry through a (private) car garage. Misunderstanding the Soviet concept of working-class community, Austin placed communal facilities at the factory, reserving residential buildings for intimate familial activities. Such a plan, perfectly sensible for a Ford plant, assumed that the Soviet Union would offer a separate apartment, kitchen, and car (with garage) to working-class families.

Even when Austin submitted a second plan (after having been corrected in its errors), it persisted in economizing space, as if unable to recognize that the Soviet Union lacked a property market. In the United States, where real estate markets drove up the cost of land, particularly in the city centre, planners naturally sought to economize. Soviet authorities, however, sought to lavish space on their workers, and no market constraints interfered.[62] Having been placed in a swampy region, the factory lacked extensive land on which to build without first installing drainage and flood protection facilities, but Soviet planners showed little concern for this. To them, Austin's economizing – like its lingering confusion of a House of Soviets (a government building) with a House of Culture (a cultural centre) – marked the company as inept.[63]

Unfairly dismissive of such natural errors on the part of an American company, many reviewers called the Austin Company's submission a "primitive" and "ignorant" plan. One architect scornfully remarked, "If a student in grade two submitted a project of this sort, we would say that he lacked talent."[64] Many demanded that Austin's contract be abrogated, while others suggested that Austin be forbidden to draft plans in the United States, far from Soviet experts' eyes. Although Ivanitskii emphasized that Austin's designs would be realized according to sketches finalized by Russian engineers, no matter where the company worked, anxiety remained. In late March, then, Soviet leaders set up a Soviet-run design body within Avostroi to complete Austin's sketches. Although this design body was officially subordinate to the Austin Company, as an "auxiliary" or "assisting" body, it was clearly designed to exercise control over Austin's work. Avtostroi also assigned oversight roles to Ivanitskii and two other Soviet consultants.[65]

Despite such scepticism, the Austin Company remained in charge of bringing a highly modified MVTU plan to life.[66] The sketches for the House of Culture, the House of Soviets, the factory kitchens, schools, bathhouses, and other distinctly socialist facilities were drafted by Soviet agencies, but Austin assumed responsibility for building enough housing for twenty-five thousand people in the initial stage of construction.[67] Working with surprising speed, Austin completed plans for the overall layout and first-stage construction by mid-April, enabling construction to begin on 2 May 1930.[68] Thus, an American capitalist firm with staunchly Methodist owners and team leaders launched the construction of a model socialist city for an atheist regime opposed to church, family, and free economics.

The final housing plan, as finessed by the Austin Company, clearly bore the MVTU imprint. As in the MVTU plan, each housing combine consisted of five dormitory buildings, a club, and two nurseries, all linked by heated second-storey corridors. Austin had been instructed to convert MVTU's ideas into a "transitional combine," which it did by borrowing design elements from other entries. Its five dormitory buildings alternated single and double rooms on the first three floors, with nine square metres per room. The fourth floor offered larger rooms (the size of the double and single combined) to serve small communes of three to four people. All rooms, even singles, included a wardrobe and washbasin, and there were lounges and a small hotplate on each floor. Every building also included a red corner, a physical space dedicated to the veneration of the Party and its leaders (particularly Lenin). The settlement also included a House of Culture with postal-telegraph services and areas for study, exercise, and relaxation.[69]

Less celebrated and, yet, also essential to Austin's work were the family apartments, to which two-thirds of all buildings were dedicated. In these apartments, which were typical of Soviet residential facilities, several families – each in a single room – shared a kitchen and bath. These buildings did not link to a clubhouse or kindergarten for cost-saving reasons.[70] Cramped, uncomfortable, and with little privacy, these inadvertently proved a boon to the secret police in its search for informers.[71] However, such apartments were not specifically designed for surveillance purposes. Rather, they were born of shortages – from the need to expropriate living space from the former elite after the October Revolution and, in this case, from the need to provide housing at minimal cost, without the expense of public services. Soviet planners officially viewed such apartments as an inconvenient fact, not as an ideal.

Implementing the Plan: The Agency of the Material

The MVTU's designs would prove utterly impractical, something foreseen by many who attended jury discussions, but were powerless to prevent their construction. Klavdiia A. Zimina, the recently elected chair of the Nizhnii Novgorod city council, proved to be the most vocal and perceptive of these non-voting attendees. Noting the paucity of discussion about the sleeping cell, she asked why jury members failed to consider how the combines would be *experienced*. As she presciently remarked, workers would likely spend a great deal of their time in these cells – something apparently not considered by designers, who expected residents to frequent communal areas in their leisure hours. She also noted that planners ignored the fact that Soviet children's institutions generally charged fees for their services, which dissuaded workers from using them. She then questioned the proposed reliance on factory kitchens, given that factory kitchens in places such as Moscow could not cope with demand. Drawing attention to other impracticalities, she proposed that the housing combine be treated as an experiment. In this regard, she advocated the construction of just one housing combine, not an entire city of them.[72]

Zimina proved correct. Although excitingly efficient and rational in theory, housing combines proved to be politically and operationally unviable. Embodying the worst of "high modern vision," as defined by James C. Scott, their design rested on the assumption that human society could be functionally and economically read, assessed, and reorganized.[73] In many ways, they reflected the visionary preoccupations of architects too long deprived of practical work. Throughout the 1920s, in the absence of major commissions, the avant-garde had stewed in its own artistic and theoretical juices. Such impotence, marked by limited opportunity in which to realize their ideas, had apparently fed the illusion of total visual-technocratic power – that is, the notion that their vision could, at a time of rapid development, be made real by fiat.

Inevitably, it was the Austin Company that discovered these facts, not the students who participated in the competition. Thanks to problems in procuring reliable labour, equipment, and personnel, the Austin Company would remain in the Soviet Union a year longer than intended, completing only a portion of the promised first-stage construction, which was to come to a total of twelve combines, or housing for twelve thousand people. Of these, only the first combines (i.e., the first five buildings) would feature the original plan's "bells and whistles," including covered second-storey corridors between buildings and facilities for dining, recreation, and child care, none of which would be operative before Austin departed in December 1931. As for the remaining combines, in early 1931 their designs were simplified, so that they had pitched (not flat) roofs and were built of wood and stucco rather than brick.[74]

Some of Austin's problems began even before they arrived on the construction site. Thanks to poor communication between Avtostroi (responsible for building and design) and Metallostroi (responsible for labour and supplies), Metallostroi's work on preparing the grounds actually inhibited construction.[75] At its request, over five thousand workers arrived in April 1930 to cut trees and bushes, dig ditches, fill ravines, build a harbour, and lay roads and a railway line from Kanavino to the local (Doskino) railway station. To serve their own needs, these work-

ers installed water lines and electric cables and erected several temporary stores, bathhouses, and shelters. Because housing and services were
inadequate, no one dared to remove these "temporary" edifices. So, they
remained where they were, placed without regard for future city plans.[76]

More problematically, the Soviet government could not provide the
specialists, quality materials, organizational know-how, or institutional
stability required to realize either the factory or the factory town. The
Austin Company complained that the experts assigned to assist (and
oversee) their work were both undertrained and inexperienced. Translators, too, were in too short supply. Construction supervisors lacked the
staff required to coordinate the distribution and delivery of supplies,
and the construction site was deficient in electric energy, excavators,
trucks, and heavy transport equipment. Often, construction materials
were dragged by horse, and workers were hired to dig foundations with
shovels. Because building materials were both costly and scarce, the
Soviet Union purchased construction materials on the European market rather than on the higher-priced American market, a switch that
required modifications to Austin's designs. Meanwhile, institutional
wrangling between Avtostroi, Metallostroi, and the Austin Company over
hierarchies of authority, materials, money, and priorities only further
complicated matters.[77]

Labour shortages proved a persistent problem. Partly because it
lacked mechanized construction equipment and equipment operators,
Metallostroi had a bottomless need for bricklayers, cement pourers, car-
penters, and diggers, many of whom had to be trained on the worksite.[78]
Metallostroi tried to recruit collective farmers, but farm administrations
resisted the loss of their own workers.[79] Authorities also tried to compensate for labour shortages through mass mobilizations, which brought
tens of thousands of provincial workers to the construction site. Unfortunately, such events neither resulted in quality work nor solved the problems posed by too few workers on site.[80]

Skilled and experienced workers proved difficult to retain because of
the site's unappealing living and working conditions. Despite the shortage of labour, Metallostroi and Avtostroi could not provide for the workers that they did have. By late 1931, thirty thousand permanent workers,
service workers, and engineering and technical staff had arrived on site.
Initially, officials had hoped to avert housing shortages by recruiting
workers from nearby villages.[81] Although most workers did, indeed, commute from Kanavino or Karpovka, a village located between Avtozavod
and the City of Nizhnii Novgorod, transportation to and from the con-

struction site remained inadequate. Hours were long, roads were poor, and public transport was nearly non-existent, with the exception of the railway line from the construction site to a nearby factory. In any case, neighbouring settlements could not accommodate the full sum of workers. Many workers therefore lived on the construction site in barracks and endured little or no pay, inadequate food, unsanitary conditions, and too little heat in winter months.[82] In response to such poor conditions, skilled labour generally left, seeking better pay and housing elsewhere.[83]

Because of these catastrophic housing shortages, workers eagerly took up residence in unfinished buildings, again obstructing progress on realizing the modified MVTU plan. By the end of summer 1930, just months after MVTU won the competition, entire families had moved into the single-room/single-person units of the first combine. By May 1931, all fifteen buildings in the first row of three combines were occupied, although all buildings in the settlement (including the first combine) lacked running water and heating, as well as child care and food services. Rather than demand such facilities, workers moved into the spaces designated for factory kitchens and boilers. Partly because of this, Austin did not finish the first factory kitchen until later in 1931.[84]

By this time, the socialist city of Avtozavod had become a massive camp, an ad hoc city with poor living conditions and few public services. To fill the gap produced by the combines' inability to provide the promised services, small kiosks selling clothing, soap, and building materials sprouted up between the buildings of the combine, along with storage sheds. Given the number of unfinished and crude residential buildings lacking running water, outhouses and cesspits also dotted the urban landscape, undermining experts' attempt to provide lush clean air and open space. Without proper waste removal services, the construction site threatened to become a public health catastrophe, especially during the spring thaw.[85] As for the residential units of the housing combines, they were the sine qua non of cramped domestic inconvenience, offering too little space and equipment with which to shelter, feed, clothe, and nurture a family. Rather than liberate women, they condemned homemakers to overcrowded, underserviced living.

Early in 1931, then, Avtostroi put an end to combine construction, opting instead to build small, standardized, two-storey, wood-framed buildings with stucco exteriors. Low-rise housing, both planned and unplanned, rapidly occupied the lands formerly allotted for multi-storey combines, together with a cheaply built movie theatre, a temporary

House of Soviets, and a temporary printing office and boilers.[86] Across
the Soviet Union, the collapse of the Soviet housing program meant that
80 per cent of all housing remained in the form of small, wooden dwellings, generally with no running water or sewer provisions. Two-thirds of
this belonged, in practice, to individuals – a vision that was a far cry from
the collectivist modernity that visionaries had set out to achieve.[87]

Avtozavod was hardly the only experimental socialist city to fail. Magnitogorsk, in the Urals, faced similar shortages of living space, followed
by the same popular response, which was to turn housing combines and
barracks into a collection of minute and uncomfortable family units.[88]
In nearby Nizhnii Novgorod, too, experiments with socialized housing
folded, as co-operatives sponsored by various enterprises or their workers suffered from inadequate funding and services. They proved too
costly to run without extensive volunteer labour on the part of residents.
Besides, co-operative buildings were ill adapted to the ever-changing
nature of the family structure. Families grew and shrank, but their living space remained unchanged.[89] Perhaps for this reason, in June 1931,
the Central Committee again condemned "excessive experimentation in
housing," deeming family housing to be the desired norm.[90]

Avtozavod remained a window through which the world might peer at
Soviet socialism, but it offered a very different view of the Soviet experiment than architectural visionaries had predicted. The defeat of combines and the spread of low-rise housing illustrated how Soviet socialism
(like Western capitalism) had pursued industrial modernity through an
exploitative version of capital accumulation, modernizing at the expense
of the common people. The consumer and agricultural sectors of the
economy suffered extensively. Many surely accepted such collective sacrifice for communal well-being, embracing the new factory as a symbol of
victory; nevertheless, everyday life in Avtozavod testified to the extreme
hardship and distress wrought by the First Five-Year Plan.

How Visionary Planning Failed

The failure of the housing combine evidenced the agency of the material – that is, the prevalence of technological and economic problems
that were, to no small degree, the by-products of misguided Soviet modernization.[91] The experiment with the housing combine collapsed in
the face of an economic and social crisis wrought by the Soviet Union's
rapid-fire industrialization. Severe shortages of shelter not only compelled residents to move into unfinished buildings, but also compelled

the Soviet leadership to call a halt to new construction in cities such as Nizhnii Novgorod. Whether or not the housing combine might have enjoyed greater success in more prosperous conditions is a moot question, for given the social and economic conditions of the period, the housing combine simply could not be realized.

The avant-garde nonetheless shared some of the blame for the failure of the housing combine. Born in subtle arrogance, the housing combines were – as Nizhnii Novgorod's Zimina noted – always designed for others, not for the architects themselves.[92] As men of art, most architects demanded an above-average allotment of personal space, which precluded their living in such high-density residences as the housing combine.[93] While workers crammed into unfinished boiler rooms, Avtozavod's architects, engineers, foreigners, and managers settled in the local administrative centre or, in some cases, in the Antei Hotel in the nearby district of Kanavino, a part of Nizhnii Novgorod.[94] Some young specialists, not yet married or ready for their own family life, may perhaps have welcomed the family-less combine, but most clearly designed these structures for workers, not for themselves.[95]

Broader Soviet politics also undermined the housing combines, for the Sabsovich combine represented the power of technological systems. It represented professionals' claim to stand as agents of a higher scientific or aesthetic truth that might be applied to the reorganization and improvement of human society. The elitist, theoretical outlook that inspired the avant-garde ultimately challenged the authority of the Party, which did not govern primarily through technological system, but through the direct conquest of hearts and minds. In banning housing combines, the Party denied to the avant-garde the technocratic privilege of fashioning society in the expert's own image. Rejecting such authority, the Party directly subjected designers to the watchful oversight of both people and the Party apparatus.

Frankly, the housing combines' aesthetic failed to suit Stalin's political needs. The MVTU–Austin design reproduced the small-community inwardness that had been rejected by Russian leaders since Peter the Great.[96] Not unlike housing prior to the reign of Peter I, MVTU's housing featured construction in which the side, or "exposed seam," of the building faced the street and the main entrance faced the courtyard, where it was sheltered from the dust, debris, and noise of the street. By orienting all housing on a north-south axis (along the meridian), the MVTU plan prioritized residents' access to light over the ornamenting of the streetscape. This interiority, coupled with plans to limit settlement size, theoretically ranked locality over nationality; after all, as noted in the previous chapter, bans on courtyard entrances originated with Peter the Great's decision to turn city streets and plans into manifestations of his personal power, authority, and beneficent rule.[97] One might even argue that MVTU's design showed traces of the anarchist thinking of Peter Kropotkin, whose writings had inspired Ebenezer Howard.[98] Such inwardness and locality did not suit the Stalin era.

To Stalin, as to Peter the Great, the city served as a stage for the display of power. In the name of fostering state patriotism, Stalin naturally rejected meridian construction and revived the practice of building flush with the street, so as to grace the public face of the city and the nation with streets lined with tall, classical, and monumental buildings. As the aesthetic equivalent of the "Great Retreat," the rise of the monumental marked the search for a symbolic system that might unite the country.[99] Having declared the victory of socialism, the Soviet state sought a shared heritage around which all social groups could rally. As a result, the language and ethos of state-based patriotism gradually edged out the language of class war.[100] In this environment, the iconoclastic anti-traditionalism of the avant-garde became passé. Eager to assert itself as the repository of historic human progress, the Soviet government embraced the traditions of the Russian imperial past, particularly its classical and monumental architecture.[101]

Avant-garde theorists might have foreseen this, for distaste for their iconoclastic design predated Stalin's rise to power at the end of the 1920s. Vladimir Il'ich Lenin had voiced his affinity for realist, non-modernist art as early as 1922, and the Commissar of Enlightenment, Anatolii V. Lunacharskii, rejected constructivist design already in 1926.[102] Even Nikolai G. Chernyshevsky, the iconoclastic hero of many Party members, had demonstrated a strong preference for monumental design.[103] Perhaps more importantly, workers voiced a powerful dislike for constructivist, avant-garde design. When given an opportunity to vote for their preferred architectural style, workers opted for classical, monumental buildings, not the latest and newest in avant-garde art.[104] Modernist-style housing combines held little appeal beyond the small circle of engineers and architects who first conceived of them, and even these individuals declined to reside in them.

The failure of the housing combine also reflected the Party's weak commitment to women's emancipation, which such edifices were supposed to achieve. The Russian Communist Party had long since ranked women's liberation as a secondary priority, to be realized *after* the consolidation of a workers' state.[105] In the 1920s, male-dominated unions conspired to keep women out of the workplace. When women finally entered industry en masse during the First Five-Year Plan, they entered a gender-segregated industrial sphere, where women obtained the messier and poorer paying posts. At the same time, because the state could not afford to provide the social services that might alleviate women's domestic duties, the state passed legislation to strengthen the family as a legal, social, and economic unit. Soviet women thereby attained full employment, something for which they had fought for years, without winning either emancipation from housework or a renegotiation of traditional gender roles.[106]

In any case, by the 1930s, the family not only served as an essential socio-economic unit, but also as a symbol of patriarchal and traditional authority. As a male-centred, hierarchical institution, the family symbolically bolstered the centralization of power. Stalin could pose as father to the socialist motherland precisely because the family remained a core element in Soviet society, providing the living embodiment of the metaphor through which he represented the political realm.[107] In embracing fatherhood and family, of course, the state did not abrogate its right to intervene in private affairs, something made clear by the persistence of concepts such as "living space" and the "sanitary norm."[108] Indeed, Stalin's place at the helm of state and citizenry in many ways destabilized and undermined the place of the father at home.[109] Nonetheless, the family served as a convenient prop for the new conceptualization of the Soviet state as a familial unit.

Conclusion

The assault on housing combines and avant-garde design did not represent the final demise of constructivist architecture. Figures such as Moisei Ginzburg would continue to make vital contributions to Soviet architecture and design. As a member of the Typological Section of the Committee for Construction, Ginzburg was responsible for the design of standardized apartments and even – for a time – of a transitional model for communal housing. Such research enabled him to further pursue his study of form and function, focusing on the production of efficient homes.[110] Younger, less experienced architects would also show an affinity for functionalist design, even if classical design was said to be a simpler challenge for them to master.[111] Besides, the Party needed a skilled aesthetic and engineering elite, including members of the former avant-garde.

Despite the flaws in the MVTU design, Ivanitskii also scored a minor victory, for the MVTU's plan for roads, particularly the link between the factory town and the nearby city of Nizhnii Novgorod, would endure. Moreover, the defeat of the avant-garde's socialist city did not directly impinge on Ivanitskii's work, which focused on historic Nizhnii Novgorod. There, Ivanitskii carefully considered the economic and political needs of city administrators, not just the theoretical organization of the city. Although he apparently remained committed to techno-social systems of managing and bettering society, and even to science as the objective arbiter of truth, his vision for Nizhniii Novgorod could be (and was) readily adapted to suit the Party's new vision of a centrally managed society – an endeavour that he supported as long as he, as expert, could work with some degree of autonomy and freedom from political interference.

Perhaps ironically, Ivanitskii's work, at least in the early 1930s, would suffer not from political authorities' meddling, but from political wrangling within the planning community. Terrorized by the Cultural Revolution, which was marked by populist attacks on "bourgeois specialists," many scientific professionals sought refuge in the ivory tower of scientific objectivity. Rather than use research to guide professional action, they used research – or rather, endless calls for more of it – to forestall concrete action of any sort. Unfortunately, such attempts at self-preservation did nothing to enhance scientific authority. If anything, as the next chapter shows, this political game invited the state directly into the ivory tower to arbitrate scientific disputes and drive architects out of this tower and into the world below.

Chapter Three

From Ivory Tower to City Street: Building a New Nizhnii Novgorod, 1928–1935

Insofar as a scientific statement speaks about reality, it must be falsifiable; and insofar as it is not falsifiable, it does not speak about reality.

Karl Popper, *The Logic of Scientific Discovery*[1]

Planning the Historic City: Science, Ideals, and Praxis

Assigned the task of planning Nizhnii Novgorod, Alexander Platonovich Ivanitskii operated in a scientific and political milieu that differed greatly from that of the factory town, where the factory dominated all aspects of local life, including all decision making. By contrast, in places such as Nizhnii Novgorod, a range of rival institutions served to extend the state's operative capacity beyond the capital. These not only competed for resources and power, all in the name of building socialism, but also they represented specific needs and programs to be accommodated in Ivanitskii's work. To plan a city such as Nizhnii Novgorod, Ivanitskii could not simply draft ideas from afar; instead, he had to acquaint himself with local needs, concerns, and interests, in order that he might mediate competing claims to energy, land, and transportation.

A graduate of the St. Petersburg Institute of Civil Engineering in 1904, Ivanitskii belonged to a pre-revolutionary cohort that rejected direct involvement in politics. Together with such architects-planners as Alexei V. Shchusev and Vladimir N. Semenov, Ivanitskii preferred to leave political decision making to the state.[2] Keeping his focus on the social and economic needs of the city before him, Ivanitskii's approach to urban planning was not visionary. Although he incorporated avant-garde ideas, Ivanitskii's strategies remained "concrete," rooted in site-specific studies and goals. Whereas plans for Avtozavod theorized an ideal city, Ivanit-skii's plans grappled with the political and economic challenges of an existing settlement. Scientific and planning theory influenced, but did not dictate, the content of Ivanitskii's work.

For all its pragmatism, Ivanitskii's approach to urban planning would soon be challenged. As Ivanitskii discovered, his fellow scientists desperately sought to avert the political risk inherent in proposals crafted to accommodate a specific city's political and economic needs. Manipulating the interpretation of Ivanitskii's scientific findings in such a way as to defend their own institutional concerns, they denounced Ivanitskii's pragmatism as "poor science." They insisted that Ivanitskii conduct further research, although further research could never have yielded more conclusive, less politically controversial results. Such stonewalling undermined Ivanitskii's credibility as a man of science, for it underscored science's inability to arbitrate what was, in effect, a political dispute over institutional responsibilities and development priorities. Even scientists had their institutional biases.

To better understand this conflict, this chapter explores the nature of Ivanitskii's work, the thoughtful political and economic compromises that he forged, and the details of the ensuing struggle within the scientific community. Contrary to other studies, which suggest that Soviet planning in these years suffered primarily from understaffing and weak institutions, this chapter argues that Soviet city planning stumbled on the politics of the planning community itself. It also suggests that state intervention into the world of city planning should in many ways be attributed to the errors of Soviet specialists, who walled themselves in the Soviet equivalent of the ivory tower, from where they issued endless calls for research and debate – not in order to advance the building of socialism, but in order to shelter themselves from the messy "absolute" of urban life.[3]

Greater Nizhnii Novgorod: The Challenge of Coordinating Fragmented Growth

The Province of Nizhnii Novgorod's leaders recognized their desperate need for a Nizhnii Novgorod city plan in December 1927, when the Fifteenth Party Congress ruled in favour of aggressive industrialization. Carefully considering the Nizhnii Novgorod region's economic potential, they noted (with delight) that provincial production had tripled since 1913. The population living near the mouth of the Oka River had risen from 94,000 people in the 1890s to an impressive 249,000 inhabitants. To their dismay, most of these newcomers (141,893 people) and their industrial employers had settled on the left bank of the Oka River, across from Nizhnii Novgorod. Here, in the vicinity of the recently incorporated cities of Sormovo and Kanavino, public services such as running water, sewers, schools, parks, pavement, and other urban amenities were all too scarce.[4]

Living conditions in the large, industrialized region of Sormovo, home to the region's shipbuilding facilities, were emblematic of problems throughout this newly industrialized zone. Its streets lacked pavement, street lights, public transit, and trees or grass. Its housing tended to have neither running water nor sewer connections. Throughout the whole of the Nizhnii Novgorod urban region, only 10 per cent of all buildings offered indoor plumbing, and these were concentrated in the oldest and most historic sections of Nizhnii Novgorod. In Sormovo, where small wooden homes predominated, even cesspits and outhouses were too few in number. Although Sormovo was incorporated as a city in the early years of Soviet power, all of its public services came courtesy of local factories, which not only offered too little in the way of such service infrastructure, but also polluted the region's air and waterways.[5] To officials concerned with health, productivity, and the ways in which population growth would strain the area's limited water, plumbing, transportation, and energy systems, Sormovo offered a dismal picture.[6] (See figure 3.1.)

The first decade of Soviet power did little to ameliorate these problems. In the mid-1920s, on the left bank of the Oka River, the provincial government sponsored the construction of a small model settlement named "Little Lenin City," with running water, plumbing, and other amenities.[7] In 1925, provincial authorities also funded the construction of a tramline linking Nizhnii Novgorod to the cities of Kanavino and Sormovo. The tram offered a valued service to cities on the left bank of the Oka River, but the City of Nizhnii Novgorod generally profited from the fees paid for its use, a fact that underscored the inequities of local growth. Unlike left bank settlements, where factories provided all housing and services, the City of Nizhnii Novgorod offered its own public transportation, energy, water, and housing, all of which generated significant revenue.[8]

Seeking a solution to underdevelopment, particularly on the left bank of the Oka River, in 1928 provincial authorities amalgamated the City of Nizhnii Novgorod with the fifty smaller settlements located at the mouth of the Oka, including the small cities of Kanavino and Sormovo.[9] They

723. СОРМОВО.   Шоссейная улица. Большая дорога.

Изданiе фотографа М. Дмитрiева въ Н.-Новгородѣ. 1911 г.

3.1. Sormovo, early twentieth century. Photograph by M.P. Dmitriev, 1911. V.P. Mashkovtsev and T.P. Vinogradova, *Tsarstvenno postavlennyi gorod: Nizhnii Novgorod v staroi otkrytke* (Vladimir: Posad, 2000), 314.

designated the new entity "Greater Nizhnii Novgorod," forcing all of its constituent cities and towns into a single municipal administration, to which responsibility for coordinating development across the region was soon to be delegated. In theory, this would ensure equitable development, extending historic Nizhnii Novgorod's wealth to the working-class regions on the left bank of the Oka River, while outfitting former "merchant Nizhnii" with a more suitably industrial identity. Amalgamation would also facilitate coordinated, rational growth throughout the city, whose constituent settlements were already economically interlinked.

To strategize this growth, provincial authorities launched work on a new city plan. According to Soviet procedure, which was still being developed and formalized at this time, this process had to begin with *planirovanie*, which involved the careful calculation of the new city's demographic and economic potential, given the socio-economic goals of the Soviet state.[10] Based on these calculations, planning experts could proceed to draft a zoning plan (*planirovka*) that would designate areas for housing, recreation, and industry. Once this was complete, experts could progress to stage three – namely, devising a general city plan (*general'nyi plan*, or *genplan*) that would organize housing, transportation, architecture, and services within their respective zones. Once approved by authorities at the highest echelons of the Soviet Union, planners could commence with the production of "detailed plans" (*detal'nye plany*), or projects for individual roads, monuments, housing, and more.[11]

State regulations specified that all aspects of this planning process should be based on hard scientific research, a ruling that compelled the Province of Nizhnii Novgorod Department of the Municipal Economy (Nizhgubkommunotdel) to seek the assistance of specialized scientific agencies. The contract for surveying urban lands went to the Map Section of the Russian Commissariat of Internal Affairs (NKVD RSFSR), from whose large and experienced staff the province hoped to recruit experts for its own administration. Although the NKVD, being associated with the secret police, might seem like an inauspicious choice, in 1928 the NKVD had not yet assumed control of the notorious United State Political Administration (OGPU), the state political police. The NKVD's policing therefore consisted of such benign activities as enforcing fire codes and maintaining public order. With long experience in conducting surveys, the NKVD RSFSR readily outbid such competitors as the Geodesical Commission of the Supreme Council of the National Economy (VSNKh SSSR).[12]

For work on the plan itself, Nizhgubkommunotdel turned to a group of Nizhnii Novgorod scholars who had come together to form the Industrial Commission, a body committed to the economic development of the region. Affiliated with the Nizhnii Novgorod Mechanics and Machine-Building Institute (NMMI), the members of the Industrial Commission offered expertise in energy systems, public health, hydrogeology, local history, economics, demography, botany, geology, and architecture. Evacuated to Nizhnii Novgorod together with the Warsaw Polytechnical Institute during the First World War, many of these scholars proved to be strongly committed to popular education and local growth, helping to form the Nizhnii Novgorod People's University in 1918. Although this attempt to educate the masses did not succeed, it testified to their strong, almost infectious commitment to bettering the lives of their less privileged fellow citizens.[13] This same spirit apparently transferred to their students, who volunteered to assist in surveying the city's housing stock, as well as its traffic and wind patterns. For the next few years, these students could be seen trudging up hills and down side streets, braving summer's humidity and winter's cold winds as they worked to complete their task.[14]

The Industrial Commission lacked an expert in urban planning per se, however, and it therefore turned to one of the most experienced planners in the Soviet Union, Alexander Platonovich Ivanitskii, to lead the newly assembled planning team. A man of wide experience, Ivanitskii had advised the planners of Yaroslavl after the First World War and personally developed city plans for Arkhangel'sk (1924), Baku (1924–8), and Gus' Khrustal'nyi (1927). He was an active member of the Scientific-Technical Council of the Russian Commissariat of the Municipal Economy, the government body responsible for reviewing and approving all preliminary city plans in the Russian Republic. He was also known for his efforts to foster collaboration between city planners and public health experts.

Committed to the emergence of city planning as a profession distinct from both architecture and engineering, Ivanitskii helped draft Soviet planning regulations and translated foreign books about urban planning into Russian. He also established faculties for training future urban planners at both the Leningrad Institute of Civil Engineering and the Moscow Higher Technical Institute (MVTU). In 1931, he would create his own planning studio within Mosgiprogor (Moscow State Institute of City Planning). He would also prove deeply committed to recruiting young, inexperienced planners to work at his side throughout the planning process, in order that they might master the craft of urban planning.[15]

Between Ivanitskii and the Industrial Commission, Nizhnii Novgorod's planning team suffered no shortage of appropriate expertise, dedication, or skill – no easy feat in the years of the First Five-Year Plan, when experts were in short supply. Large planning institutions such as the State Institute of City Planning (Giprogor) had begun to hoard specialists, keeping them permanently on staff, lest the state increase these institutions' production targets.[16] Moreover, young and experienced planners alike generally shunned work in the provinces, where pay, living conditions, and food tended to be poor. All the same, Ivanitskii readily accepted the Industrial Commission's challenge and successfully recruited such renowned specialists as A.N. Sysin, a locally born specialist on sanitation.[17] In Nizhnii Novgorod, at least, the future failings of urban planning could never be attributed to a shortage of talented professionals.

The Sources of Pragmatic Idealism: Landscape, Politics, and Financing

Because of the pressures of the First Five-Year Plan, the Province of Nizhnii Novgorod Department of the Municipal Economy required the Industrial Commission to complete its task by 1931, an incredibly ambitious deadline, given the uncontrolled and massive urbanization and economic growth generated by the First Five-Year Plan.[18] Yet, the Industrial Commission's challenges extended far beyond the chaos spawned by the state's socio-economic program. The very nature of Soviet governance and administration, coupled with the complex hydrogeological structure of the city, made their task exceptionally difficult. Inadequate funding and political support posed further challenges. Completing a general city plan by 1931 would prove impossible.[19]

Of all these hurdles, the greatest was the Soviet system of governance, in which no private interests were acknowledged and yet institutional and social conflicts abounded. Although, in theory, Soviet central authorities controlled the entire economy, ensuring a coordinated statewide program for building socialism, in fact the state's refusal to acknowledge non-state interests merely forced all the plurality of competing interests typical of any modern society into the corridors of the state bureaucracy itself. The result was "disjointed monism," defined by extensive competition within a single state apparatus.[20]

This intra-state competition was encouraged by authorities, who granted industry, households, and other economic actors vast scope for autonomous action. Officials expected these economic units to be creative in uncovering the resources that they required when state-promised goods were insufficient in quantity or quality.[21] As various agencies and interests within the state thus competed for the resources and operational capacity that they needed in order to realize Party-imposed mandates, they "resisted" one another, evading any state-sanctioned rules, regulations, and official procedures that might benefit their rivals.[22] Such activities were technically illegal, but they permitted local institutions and individuals to compensate for the excessive abstraction of state planning. Left to their own devices, these bodies could exploit local knowledge and resources.[23] Although in many ways beneficial, however, such autonomy meant that state agencies legally compelled to obey planning by-laws "resisted" planners, too.

Such intra-state competition advantaged heavy industry, which not only controlled the bulk of the state's resources, but also had a vested interest in upsetting planners' work. Anxious to meet annual production targets, such bodies cared little about a city plan that looked twenty-five years into the future, particularly when it threatened to constrain construction, impose pollution controls, or drive polluting factories from the city altogether. Although every municipal budget allocated a significant portion of the burden of paying for the city plan to industry, local industry generally refused to pay planning-related taxes. To extract these funds, local planners and the city council petitioned the Russian Council of People's Commissars and the Russian Commissariat of the Municipal Economy to intervene by *ordering* industrial agencies to pay, but this did nothing to solve the problem.[24] Besides, local government depended on industry's good will, because central authorities frequently channelled resources for local development through industry, without setting a minimum percentage or quantity that should go to local government. This enabled industry to retain most, if not all, of these materials for its own use. Although local authorities filed complaints against this practice as early as 1933, the problem lingered, limiting the city council's abilities to extract funding or compliance from industrial bodies.[25]

Being a cash-strapped entity, local government tended to worry more about meeting short-term construction targets than about city planning.[26] In 1931, Nizhnii Novgorod's provincial officials allocated the bulk of funding for urban development (i.e., a total of 73,800 rubles out of 113,070 rubles) to short-term construction – that is, to designs for buildings, roads, and other physical infrastructure, not to work on the city plan.[27] Although the provincial Department of the Municipal Economy (Nizhgubkommunotel) had the authority to reallocate funds from construction to city planning, it never did so. In fact, in 1931, it did the opposite, cutting planners' budget in response to the national currency crisis by combining several research projects (i.e., the study of urban trade and the planning of roads and bridges) and demanding fewer sketches.[28]

Without adequate funding, the Industrial Commission's work suffered. Its members failed to receive their wages in a timely manner, in part because their contract stipulated that payment would follow the completion of their task. Insofar as the Commission failed to complete its assigned task, its members went without pay. Although a money-saver for the government, the lack of wages prompted many experts to accept wage-paying work on the side, further delaying progress on the city plan. Thankfully, after their contract term ended in November 1931, planners could negotiate better wage-payment and funding agreements.[29] Even so, resources never proved abundant, for authorities understandably prioritized the construction of housing, which remained of desperately low quality and quantity.

Such difficulties alone would have sufficed to delay the Industrial Commission's work, but they faced a problem that compounded these issues: the city's hydrogeological structure. Greater Nizhnii Novgorod (like many cities in the region) rested on clay and sandy soils riddled with small rivulets and streams. This substructure was inherently unstable and had caused many landslides on the right bank of the Oka River, as well as flooding on the left bank (see figure 3.2). The devastating flood of 1926 provided vividly remembered evidence of this danger. Even without flooding, the left bank suffered from high groundwater levels and swampiness, which provided optimal breeding conditions for malaria-infested mosquitoes.[30] Excessive groundwater also jeopardized building foundations, and all of these problems restricted industrial and residential construction on the left bank to the city's most elevated terrain, which dotted the left bank region.

Planners had been well aware of these issues, but had predicted quick solutions, such as the construction of a dam along the Oka River's embankments. Further study under Ivanitskii quickly demonstrated that the city's hydrogeological problems were more complex, however – not simply caused by the overflow of the river, but also by the swelling of the region's many underground streams. As winter melt engorged the Oka and Volga rivers, these underground streams filled beyond capacity, flooding the region on the left bank of the Oka. No dam wall along the riverfront would solve this problem. Rather, the city required a vast, complex, and very costly left bank drainage system. To further complicate matters, Soviet authorities proposed the Great Volga Project for constructing hydroelectric dams along the Volga River, something that threatened to raise the average water levels in the Volga River. If this brought about a permanent increase in regional groundwater levels, this would exacerbate flooding, destabilize right bank slopes, and increase the amount of swampland. Research into the design of the dams had only begun, meaning that local scientists had no concrete information on which to base their study of the potential impact of the Great Volga Project.[31]

The problem of hydrogeology, or the "melioration" of soil to prepare for construction, loomed large in planners' minds. Without a viable, cost-effective melioration plan, high groundwater levels, swamps, peat bogs, and springtime flooding threatened the structural integrity of industrial and residential buildings, not to mention public health. In theory, of

3.2. Left bank flooding, c. 1896. Photograph by M.P. Dmitriev, n.d. Maksim Dmitriev, *Fotografii* (Moscow: Planeta, 1996), 63.

course, planners could simply opt for right bank industrial and residential growth. But, the existing economic infrastructure on the left bank proved too valuable to move. Planners had no choice but to devise a means of resolving these water problems, despite their lack of resources.

As with the city survey and planning itself, the question of melioration (*ameliorizatsiia*) was a matter in which locals required outside assistance. By 1931, they had passed responsibility for designing an anti-flood system to a more specialized agency. Such melioration work would nonetheless continue to suffer, because reports related to either the Great Volga Project or regional hydrogeology were dispersed among a number of institutions, many of which refused to share information.[32] The challenge of coordinating research, especially given inadequate information on the interplay of soil, underground water, and river levels throughout the area, would remain an enduring challenge.

Strategizing a Solution: The Zoning Plan as a "Working Hypothesis"

In response to these problems, Ivanitskii proposed to invert the planning process. As noted earlier, a zoning plan (*planirovka*) was supposed to determine the placement of housing, industry, and parks. Normally, it would be based on extensive melioration research, but Ivanitskii proposed to reverse the order of planning, so that an approved zoning plan would guide – and thereby limit the scope of – research into melioration. Since the same plan could also coordinate short- and long-term construction plans, a pre-approved zoning plan appeared to be an efficient and cost-effective approach to planning and development.

Although a shrewd proposal, winning local support for a vision that necessarily required some institutions to compromise on their priorities was no easy feat. As already noted, too often in the years before and after Ivanitskii's zoning plan won approval, institutions withheld supposedly sensitive data, although planners needed this information.[33] To elicit the requisite commentary and support, the Industrial Commission organized a series of broad public discussions, which served to elicit local feedback and, ultimately, forge consensus. Readily accommodating institutional concerns and needs, the Industrial Commission repeatedly modified its proposals, seeking to satisfy as many of its "clients" as possible. Thus, by late 1931, the Industrial Commission won broad support for a zoning proposal known as the "star-city" settlement plan.[34]

Ivanitskii's success in garnering local approval should not be attributed to his savvy approach to public relations, however. In late 1931, both the City of Greater Nizhnii Novgorod and the neighbouring District of Avtozavod faced crisis conditions. Years of unregulated economic development, coupled with inadequate investment into the city's infrastructure, had produced a severe shortage of housing and services. Tramlines broke down, and street lights burned out. The city's water and sewer systems were not equipped to service a growing population. Thanks to the violent turmoil of collectivization, even food was in short supply. Famine stalked the land, particularly in rural regions, although belt-tightening affected urban areas, too.[35]

By late 1931, this growing calamity spawned a powerful albeit delayed state response. Local authorities appealed to central officials for a moratorium on industrial growth.[36] Provincial leaders then formed the Association for Urban-Municipal Construction, designed to coordinate and promote municipal development throughout the province, particularly in Greater Nizhnii Novgorod.[37] Soon after, the Politburo itself intervened to ban further industrial expansion in all major urban centres, including Nizhnii Novgorod. At the same time, the Central Committee of the Communist Party (TsK KPSS) and the Supreme Council of the National Economy (VSNKh SSSR) allocated funds for municipal services and instructed officials in Greater Nizhnii Novgorod to build sufficient housing and infrastructure for an additional five hundred thousand people in just five years.[38]

Although the new decrees compelled local officials to take city planning more seriously, their heightened concern for the fate of city planning would be brief.[39] By 1932, Ivanitskii would once again find himself begging municipal and provincial authorities for funds. In response, the Russian Commissariat of the Municipal Economy (NKKKh RSFSR) suggested that Ivanitskii solve this problem through propaganda. Although Ivanitskii thereafter appeared before the city council, trying to convince its members of the urgent importance of city planning, the problem of underfunding and weak political support persisted. In 1935, the College of the Russian Commissariat of the Municipal Economy resorted to ordering the city council to provide greater financial support to urban planners. When this failed, its president personally paid a visit to municipal leaders. There is no evidence that such intervention made a difference.[40] In 1931, Ivanitskii's "window of opportunity," if indeed it was a window, would be fleeting.

Pragmatic Vision: Ivanitskii's Approach to Urban Planning

Displaying his savvy ability to combine science, pragmatism, and ideological correctness, Ivanitskii's star-city zoning plan was more than a strategy for tackling the city's catastrophic living conditions. Mixing aesthetic brilliance with practical knowhow, his proposal offered a do-able, highly inexpensive means of planning the city. In it, Ivanitskii incorporated both green and garden cities, which were the "rage" of the moment. To achieve this, Ivanitskii conceptualized Greater Nizhnii Novgorod as a constellation of small garden cities, stars to be bound by roads and parks. Conveniently, these parks consisted of low-lying swamplands that would be costly to develop, but which could nonetheless be embraced as valuable "air filters," able to remove industrial pollution.[41]

Insofar as Greater Nizhnii Novgorod was, in essence, already a smattering of pre-existing factory towns surrounded by green space, the star-city proposal conveniently permitted the city to remain what it was. Full realization of the plan would require the construction of another bridge over the Oka River opposite the Ford motor plant, the removal of a few industries from densely settled zones, and perhaps also a high-speed metro line or railway to more effectively link the city's dispersed nodes of settlement.[42] Overall, however, the plan required no radical remaking of the city. A more cost-effective yet ideologically astute plan could hardly be imagined – which explains, of course, why it garnered so much support. As one of the city's engineers said, the star-city plan "squeezed city planning into necessarily realistic limits."[43]

This star-city zoning plan appealed in much the same way as the MVTU plan discussed in chapter 2. It was practical, immediately realizable, and it linked the city's interior organization to that of the space around it. Presenting the star-city proposal together with a scheme for regional planning, Ivanitskii recommended that the Nizhnii Novgorod city-constellation be extended outward, incorporating the surrounding region. Outlying areas such as Pravdinsk, located on the Volga River above Sormovo, would become new stars in this expanded constellation.[44] Such a regional vision, popular both in the early 1930s and again in the 1960s to 1970s, offered a means of reducing metropolitan congestion by pushing a large segment of the urban population into satellite locations.[45]

This regional structure also enabled Ivanitskii to incorporate another idea in vogue at the time: the Green City. Like Sabsovich's housing combines, this plan showed the influence of Ebenezer Howard's concept of the garden city, in which a small factory town benefited from the food and leisure provided by a surrounding green area. To achieve this, Ivanitskii proposed to establish a "Green City" between Nizhnii Novgorod and Kstovo, located to the city's southeast. Possibly inspired by the 1929–1930 competition for Moscow's Green City, Ivanitskii's Green City consisted of a 500-hectare space for rest and relaxation, with enough untouched wilderness to grant each visitor (up to forty thousand at a time) a thousand square metres of escape from urban civilization.[46] Intended to provide a healthy alternative to city grime and congestion, this Green City would include a children's camp, sports facilities, a co-operative dacha-farming settlement, open fields, sites for botanical and zoological research, and small houses with running water, electricity, and sewer connections.[47]

Competing Visions: The Other Three Zoning Options

For all the strengths of Ivanitskii's proposal, three other zoning possibilities lurked in the background. Because the choice of zoning plan depended on a complex set of political, economic, and scientific considerations, any plan was subject to question on a wide number of bases. To complicate matters, all plans had to pass through multiple levels of review, from the city and the province to various Russian and Soviet commissariats. As a result, an agreement forged at one level of governance could be rejected at the next, forcing the plan to be reworked and renegotiated from the beginning. This indeed occurred in 1932, largely undoing Ivanitskii's hard-won victory on the star-city proposal.

In 1931, the least loved of the four possible zoning plans drafted by the Industrial Commission was the plan for *zarechnoe rasselenie*, or "across the river settlement." This zoning proposal envisioned extensive development on the left bank of the Oka River, the centre of regional growth since the nineteenth century. The term "across the river" highlighted the newness of the area, which lay opposite historic Nizhnii Novgorod on the far side of the Oka. According to the plan, the bulk of the city's industry, population, and government offices would be relocated to this area, from which swamplands would be removed through melioration. Municipal bodies would be moved to this left bank area, whereas provincial institutions would remain on the right bank, in the kremlin. Continuous settlement, unbroken by parks and swampland, would give the entire left bank region a developed, unified appearance.[48]

This zoning plan appealed to "cost crunchers," for if realized it would achieve extensive *long-term* savings on transportation and infrastructure, much more than any other zoning proposal. In developing the "wasteland" that divided the many villages and workers' settlements of Greater Nizhnii Novgorod, this plan decreased the total urban area to be supplied with public services and transportation. Although the immediate cost of such extensive melioration would far outpace the short-term cost of other plans, most economists believed that the plan's long-term savings would firmly offset these initial losses. However, in 1931, the factory town model remained popular, while large urban centres of the sort envisioned in this plan were deemed to be alienating. Moreover, swamp clearing seemed impossible to guarantee without a melioration plan and, by extension, without a completed Great Volga Project. This plan was therefore cast aside.

The next zoning plan featured *nagornoe rasselenie*, or "hilltop settlement," in which residential housing was limited to the city's highly elevated right bank plateau, where neither flood nor swamp threatened. Only a small emergency force of about a hundred thousand workers would remain in the vicinity of left bank industry, where malaria-infested swamps and floods threatened. This variant appealed greatly to public health officials because of its adherence to the linear-city structure. They praised the way in which this variant turned the Oka River into a green strip that insulated right bank residences from left bank factories.[49] Although its realization would require the construction of an extensive transportation system linking right bank residents to left bank workplaces via bridges over the Oka River, scientists and public health officials felt that the expense of such a structure was a political and public health necessity. Besides, this option abolished the city's latent class structure, whereby the elite lived on the right bank and working-class districts were concentrated on the left.[50] This latter perk never received mention, although the plan did meet the state's promise for truly equitable development throughout all city regions, including outlying working-class areas.

The high cost of realizing the hilltop settlement plan ensured that industry and local government rejected it. The plan did not eliminate the need for left bank melioration, because industry was too expensive to remove from the left bank.[51] Moreover, the transportation costs incurred by this plan would be enormous. To move one to two hundred thousand workers over the Oka River to and from industrial jobs on a daily basis, the city council would have to expend roughly 65 to 70 billion rubles per year. Although workers would theoretically enjoy improved living conditions on the right bank, they would face a much lengthier commute to work.[52] Besides, the hilltop variant offered no feasible way to harmonize short-term with long-term construction. In 1931, the city lacked a permanent bridge over the Oka River. The first of such bridges would not be completed until 1932, and yet this plan depended on the construction of a whole series of bridges. Unable to launch right bank construction without such bridges, the city would be forced to expend scarce resources on the construction of purely temporary left bank housing and services. Members of the Industrial Commission argued that such temporary construction would not proceed, for local officials would perceive such expenditures as a waste of valuable funds. Instead, all construction would come to a halt.

Yet another variant proposed *promezhutochnoe rasselenie* ("interspersed settlement"), or the construction of a "dispersed city" (*rassredotochennyi gorod*). This variant differed from the star-city zoning plan only insofar as it excluded Avtozavod, the district hosting the Ford motor plant.[53] As early as 1931, however, all industrial leaders and planners supported the full incorporation of Avtozavod, which had become the city's economic powerhouse and for which the City of Nizhnii Novgorod provided workers, entertainment, and education, as well as services. The third variant hardly merited serious discussion.

The star-city zoning plan, the fourth of Ivanitskii's variants, retained more appeal than the first three alternatives, for it not only incorporated the best ideas of the time, from green cities to garden cities, but also recognized the place-specific needs of the city that the Industrial Commission had set out to redesign. The Interdepartmental Committee for the Construction and Planning of Inhabited Territories, an agency under the Russian Council of People's Commissars (Sovnarkom RSFSR), therefore welcomed the star-city plan, urging other government bodies to extend their support.[54] The Nizhnii Novgorod Provincial Party Bureau (Nizhkraikom) likewise embraced the model, hurrying the plan through phases of local review and approval, so that it could be forwarded to the Russian Commissariat of the Municipal Economy (NKKKh RSFSR) for further consideration. Confident of its approval in Moscow, local government and city planners based the annual construction program of 1932 on the star-city plan's schema for long-term growth.[55]

From the Science of Politics to the Politics of Science

Yet, Ivanitskii's politics of compromise and consensus were soon to be derailed. As his star-city proposal advanced to a higher stage of review, it faced daunting opposition from the Scientific-Technical Council of the Russian Commissariat of the Municipal Economy (NTS NKKKh RSFSR), whose responsibility was to ensure that the proposal met the regulations and standards of the Russian Commissariat of Internal Affairs (NKVD

RSFSR).[56] Because the Scientific-Technical Council answered only for the plan's scientific merits and public health provisions, its members paid little heed to Ivanitskii's demand that Greater Nizhnii Novgorod's economic and social crisis be taken into consideration. As its comments made clear, the Scientific-Technical Council much preferred the hilltop zoning plan, which neatly separated residential from industrial areas. The fact that this plan lay beyond the city council's fiscal reach was of no concern to this body.

The conflict that resulted consisted of an irresolvable political dispute waged under the guise of a debate over scientific fact. Determined not to condone left bank settlement, whose public health provisions could be called into question, the Scientific-Technical Council deliberately skewed and misrepresented the Industrial Commission's data to suggest that the entire star-city proposal was scientifically flawed. Being an agency for scientific review, not an agency responsible for the city's *existing* economic and public health problems, the Scientific-Technical Council remained firmly stuck on abstract ideals. Although somewhat valid, from a purely scientific perspective, the Scientific-Technical Council's actions ultimately compelled the intervention of political figures who insisted that economic concerns and priorities, not just "the science," be taken into account.

As its published responses to Ivanitskii's star-city proposal made clear, the Scientific-Technical Council viewed conditions on the left bank of the Oka River, in Greater Nizhnii Novgorod's newly incorporated industrial districts, as unfit for human habitation. Its reviewers condemned the area's flooding, malarial swamps, and high groundwater levels as impediments to development, particularly in the absence of an effective melioration plan. Although Ivanitskii and the city council argued not only that a zoning plan could be approved without a completed melioration proposal, but also that its approval was *necessary* in order to narrow the scope of research related to melioration, the Scientific-Technical Council refused to offer even tentative approval of left bank settlement without a complete melioration plan.

The debate over the risk and consequences of left bank flooding captured the nature of this prolonged dispute. Using data submitted by Ivanitskii, the Scientific-Technical Council repeatedly emphasized that the city's left bank terrain lay an average of only 72 metres above sea level – that is, *below* the levels of the devastating regional flood of 1926 (76 metres), as well as below the flood levels of the less damaging deluges of 1881 and 1929, when the city's waterways rose to a height of 74 metres.[57] Although the Scientific-Technical Council's data were correct, the Industrial Commission objected to its incessant concern with *average* left bank elevation. Although average land elevations on the left bank were, indeed, lower than flood levels, the city's *settled* points stood 72 to 80 metres above sea level. As the planning team emphasized, even in 1926, only 15 per cent of *developed* land was flooded, and most years spring waters rose to just 62 metres, leaving industrial and residential regions on the left bank untouched.[58]

Similar debate raged over data related to the left bank's groundwater problem. The Scientific-Technical Council presented the Industrial Commission's data in such a way as to suggest that the entire left bank zone consisted of water-saturated or sandy soil that offered no support for substantial construction. As evidence, they pointed to reports of damaged foundations in the region of the Ford factory. Ivanitskii's team readily marshalled evidence with which to counter such claims, such as the fact that the majority of buildings with damaged foundations lay in the former trade-fair region, an area well equipped with drainage systems (as provided by Alexander I in 1817), whereas buildings in the region of Sormovo, which boasted a mere 72-metre elevation, showed no evidence of groundwater having damaged man-made structures.[59]

Similarly, the Scientific-Technical Council tended to attribute the region's vast malarial swamps to its clay soils, which inhibited water drainage, when in fact one could attribute such swamps to man-made barriers (*pregrady*), embankments (*nasyp*), and dams that interfered with natural drainage. Dams on the Levinka River in Sormovo and the Moscow-Kursk railway line provided two ready examples of such swamp-producing blockages.[60] Where the city council observed a man-made problem with technological solutions, the Scientific-Technical Council preferred to see an insurmountable problem.

The science of Ivanitskii's plan again proved open to dispute when the two sides debated the potential impact of the Great Volga Project, whose dangers were hyped by the Scientific-Technical Council. The Scientific-Technical Council remained convinced that the proposed series of dams would raise water levels in the Volga River, which in turn would place pressure on the city's groundwater regime, causing greater backup and seepage onto the surface.[61] Unfortunately, with no concrete data on the project itself, the city council could not provide firm evidence to disprove this claim. Still, they argued that the hydroelectric dams would impact only *normal* water levels, meaning that they would not exacerbate springtime flooding. In fact, said Ivanitskii, melioration against spring floods would protect the left bank zone from any hydrogeological changes ushered in by the construction of the dams. The city council further argued that concern over the Great Volga Project was a red herring that distracted from the real issue – not the *whether or not* of left bank melioration, but rather the *how* of melioration. Since left bank industry could not be moved or discarded, the need for left bank melioration was a *fact*, not a distant possibility.

Data indicating that left bank mortality rates exceeded those of the right bank, where historic Nizhnii Novgorod stood, fuelled still further dispute. Whereas the Scientific-Technical Council attributed high sickness and mortality on the left bank to malaria and factory air pollution, the city council blamed elevated left bank mortality rates on the relative lack of left bank development. They noted that the provision of paved roads, housing, and other infrastructure had reduced the mortality rate in Sormovo, where mortality had dropped below the nationwide average.[62] To counter the Scientific-Technical Council's claim that the steep height of the right bank trapped factory air over the left bank region, they stressed that prevailing winds blew polluted air towards and beyond the Volga – a problem for neighbouring regions, but not for the workers of Sormovo and Kanavino.[63]

Not simply a scientific matter, the dispute came with high stakes for both sides, especially given that the state newspaper *Izvestiia* had drawn attention to the swampy conditions in nearby Avtozavod. For the Scientific-Technical Council, victory meant that its members would never risk taking the blame for the long-term consequences of the left bank's flooding, air pollution, and complex groundwater regime. As many noted during the dispute, the Soviet *Norms for Construction and Planning*, as passed in March 1932, stated that all city plans should include melioration plans, leaving open the questions of what constituted an acceptable melioration plan and at what stage of the planning process this should be provided.[64] Such ambiguity produced uncertainty and therefore risk. As a result, the Scientific-Technical Council asserted its own, self-benefiting interpretation of the *Norms* – namely, that a completed melioration plan had to precede an approved zoning plan.

For the city council, on the other hand, victory in this dispute would eliminate costly "remakes" of the cityscape, which would be required if short-term growth did not proceed according to a long-term plan. To city council members' chagrin, however, the Scientific-Technical Council not only threatened not to approve the star-city plan, but also to forbid the construction of permanent, capital-intensive buildings on the left bank until their dispute was resolved.[65] To Nizhnii Novgorod officials, such a policy was unacceptable, because temporary structures also required costly plumbing, electricity, services, and transportation. In addition, because temporary buildings were necessarily low-rise buildings, merely one to two stories in height, they would quickly exhaust extant lands. Even temporary construction would therefore require extensive melioration, in order to open new land for construction. For this, the city council had neither plans nor money.[66]

The dispute became intense as angry words were hurled about. To Ivanitskii's fury, the Scientific-Technical Council used a letter in which Ivanitskii appealed to the city council for melioration funds as evidence, from Ivanitskii's own mouth, of the importance of a fully researched and approved melioration plan, which Ivanitskii lacked.[67] The Council also maligned Ivanitskii's research skills, chiding his planning team for its "shocking" ignorance of the melioration question, although evidence of this supposed "research neglect" derived from the above-mentioned letter. Meanwhile, the Scientific-Technical Council's report lavished the hilltop variant with positive adjectives, such as "highly valued" (*otsennyi*) and "well-researched" (*izuchennyi i razobrannyi*), although the Industrial Commission had not seriously studied the hilltop plan.[68] Angered, Comrade Shikhodyrov, vice president of the city council, dramatically prophesied the city's coming fiscal insolvency, declaring that melioration research alone would drain the city's budget in eight months – at least, if the city council had to fund the study of all four zoning variants, as the Scientific-Technical Council suggested.[69]

Neither the Soviet Union's centralized governance and ideology nor the appeal to "the facts" resolved this dispute, which went on for three years. Intra-state squabbles over policies and resources were common.[70] In theory, science – either Marxist ideology or research into "the facts" – should have arbitrated this conflict. But since public health and urban development could both be claimed as socialist priorities and scientific research could be used to support the positions of both sides, the decision as to which program should take precedence was a matter of political choice. Although the Industrial Commission and the Scientific-Technical Council focused on "the science," masking their conflicting political needs in the guise of "scientificity," in fact they ought to have appealed to political leaders for resolution. But, as Catriona Kelly has noted, at times of uncertainty, scholars are more – not less – likely to insist on the "objectivity" and "neutrality" of science.[71] Such was the case here.

Because both sides insisted that the science proved them right, the city council finally demanded the formation of an independent scientific panel to arbitrate the dispute. The city council proposed that the panel include two to three members of the Scientific-Technical Council, a city council representative, a planning specialist, a group of hydrogeologists and hydrotechnicians, and a representative from the Moscow State Institute of City Planning (Mosgiprogor), to which the city council had awarded a planning contract in late 1931. It also insisted that Ivanitskii be included on the panel, for he had agreed to lead Mosgiprogor in its work.[72] However, the panel's report, as issued in November 1932, naturally failed to mediate the dispute, for it again focused solely on the science of planning. Because of its apolitical stance, the commission ultimately upheld the Scientific-Technical Council's demand for further study of all four zoning plans, making that decision official.[73] After all, the science remained indeterminate, because research related to melioration remained incomplete – and, frankly, would indefinitely remain so.

Ivanitskii's political success thus turned to failure, as the Scientific-Technical Council dismissed concerns for economic viability and political necessity as irrelevant to its review process. In this, the Scientific-Technical Council arguably acted in bad faith, for such non-scientific matters lay at the heart of city planning. All city plans necessarily theorize, making projections for economic and social development. In this sense, all plans are both "utopian" (envisioning a place-yet-to-be) and political (addressing the social, political, and economic issues of their time). But, the Scientific-Technical Council not only "saw like a state," carefully gathering statistics and assessing the science of the plan, but also "saw like a politician."[74] By demanding further research, its members avoided risky decision making, a tactic used so often by Soviet experts that they quickly developed a reputation for stonewalling.[75] To succeed, Ivanitskii needed to appeal to the Soviet State Planning Committee (Gosplan SSSR), as one shrewd member of the Scientific-Technical Council suggested at the time.[76]

Adjudicating the Dispute: Gosplan SSSR

The inherently political nature of the problem – and of its solution – revealed itself in 1935, when Gosplan SSSR decided that it wished to increase production at the Ford factory. To accommodate the enlarged workforce, Gosplan SSSR demanded a new city plan for Avtozavod. This soon led to the approval of left bank settlement, simply because local authorities had not yet arranged for the construction of a bridge over the Oka River to the right bank. Without such a bridge, authorities had no choice but to locate additional housing on left bank land. Gosplan SSSR's decree therefore became a de facto validation of left bank settlement and melioration, an opportunity upon which Ivanitskii seized to win long-desired approval for a zoning plan.

The Scientific-Technical Council did not concede without resistance, however. When Gorstroiproekt, which won the contract to plan the expansion of Avtozavod, proposed left bank development, both the Russian Commissariat of Health and the Scientific-Technical Council objected, drawing attention to the high rates of malarial infection as well as to the lack of a melioration plan.[77] Although Gorstroiproekt reported that workers generally caught their malarial infections elsewhere in the province, not in Avtozavod, health officials remained displeased – in part, because Gorstroiproekt's justifications for left bank settlement were almost entirely economic, showing little concern for public health and safety issues.[78] Although they could not reject left bank growth, given Gosplan SSSR's expansion plans, members of the Scientific-Technical Council nonetheless insisted that Gorstroiproekt provide for the construction of roads to the sites of the unbuilt bridges that would make right bank (hilltop) settlement possible.[79]

The entire episode highlighted the inability of science to make what were, for all practical purposes, political and economic choices. Except for the sheer force of Gosplan SSSR's desire, the Scientific-Technical Council would never have approved Gorstroiproekt's plan. But, as a powerful voice in both economic management and urban planning, Gosplan SSSR could not be opposed.[80] Science could and should have informed this decision making, of course, but scientific data could not substitute for moral evaluation and reflection. Nor could it transcend institutional disputes, particularly not if scientists could be found on both sides. Indeed, after the Second World War, scientists would seek political arbitration of this sort on a routine basis, even in matters of abstract scholarly theory.[81]

Nonetheless, the Scientific-Technical Council resisted any change in policy vis-à-vis the left bank.[82] The city council laid claim to the ruling on Avtozavod as a precedent for left bank development in Nizhnii Novgorod, but the Scientific-Technical Council treated its ruling on Avtozavod as an exception. On this occasion, however, the Council's arguments proved weak: Nizhnii Novgorod and Avtozavod were hydrogeologically connected, sharing underground and above-ground water systems. Melioration in one region (or the lack thereof) would neces-sarily affect the other. Besides, as the city council stressed, it could not afford hilltop settlement. Thus, thanks to the Gosplan SSSR ruling on Avtozavod, in February 1935 the Scientific-Technical Council approved Ivanitskii's new zoning plan, despite the plan's call for residential settle-ment on the left bank.[83]

Conclusion: The Pragmatics of Planning

At long last, in 1935, Ivanitskii won approval for a zoning plan that could serve as a blueprint for research and development. But it was a pyrrhic victory, for despite years of battle, Ivanitskii's victory did not rest on sci-entific or planning principles, but on the whim of Gosplan SSSR. Ivan-itskii's scientific research had always taken political considerations into account, working to accommodate the needs and goals of all agencies under Gosplan SSSR and Gosplan RSFSR. In this sense, the new ruling validated his pragmatic approach to rethinking the Soviet city. Yet, the purely political method by which the dispute was resolved was a portent of events to come.

The newly approved plan was no longer the star-city zoning plan, but rather a variant of the first "over the river settlement" plan of 1931. Although all sides involved in the planning dispute of 1932 had rejected this zoning plan as impractical in both economic and political terms, the rise of Stalinist hierarchy and monumentalism had augmented its appeal. In proposing a large, continuous cityscape unbroken by swamp and field, this "compact" plan (as the "over the river" plan came to be known) emulated the big-city image modelled in the Moscow City Plan of 1935, conforming to the state's new aesthetic taste. Unfortunately, this new aesthetic served as the backdrop for greater political intervention into the world of planning. Greater Nizhnii Novgorod, like other Soviet cities, would serve not only as the infrastructure of social development, but also as a stage for the display of imperial power, and this transition would impinge on Ivanitskii's methods, freedom, and career as a local city planner.

To Ivanitskii's credit, his star-city zoning plan of 1931 would exem-plify science at its best: based on a study of long-term trends, not short-term policies, the star-city plan accurately forecast long-term population growth. It predicted, correctly, that the city would not succeed in build-ing more than two bridges over the Oka River (not in the Soviet period), and it tentatively proposed the construction of a metro system, which was realized in the 1970s. In fact, despite then and future challenges to his plan, the star-city plan became de facto reality.[84] The Great Volga Project admittedly exacerbated groundwater problems: the territory where groundwater levels stood less than two-and-a-half metres from the surface expanded from 3,500 hectares to 8,500 hectares. Nevertheless, because Volga River levels fell and authorities invested in hydrogeological engineering, left bank settlement became an unproblematic element of city life.[85] In the long term, Ivanitskii and his star-city plan would enjoy the laugh that wiped away the bitter taste of defeat.

Chapter Four

Stalinist Representation: Iconographic Vision, 1935–1938

Modern man is consistently obliged to operate within an architectural environment. The architectural structures of a city, quite freely perceived, will have a direct impact on the feelings of a "consumer" of architecture and call forth specific perceptions of the surrounding world by their aspect and forms. *The Soviet State, which puts planned regulation first among its activities, must use such architecture as a powerful means for organizing the psyche of the masses.*

Association of Architects-Urbanists, 1928[1]

The state is invisible; it must be personified before it can be seen, symbolized before it can be loved, imagined before it can be conceived.

Michael Walzer, "On the Role of Symbolism in Political Thought"[2]

As the confrontation with the Scientific-Technical Council highlighted, science did not stand above politics, acting as an objective arbiter in institutional disputes. To the contrary, what constituted sound science, evidence, and fact was open to question. Although members of the Scientific-Technical Council sought to preserve the façade of scientific neutrality, they stonewalled in an effort to ward off the dangers of controversial choices. Far from protecting science from political threats, this tactic delegated real decision-making power to non-scientific institutions. Although scientists continued to make constructive contributions to Soviet city planning, their resort to inaction limited their ability, as professionals, to define the future of Soviet city planning, even before the complete "Stalinization" of the planning process.[3]

The Scientific-Technical Council's foibles may be viewed as both cause and consequence of political interference in scientific affairs. Although the Communist Party of the Soviet Union largely ceased to brand special-ists as "class enemies" after the Cultural Revolution, it further restricted expert autonomy. In 1932, the state imposed the Union of Soviet Archi-tects, banning all other architectural organizations. Then, in 1934, Stalin mandated Socialist Realism as an aesthetic principle, insisting on a mon-umental style to which constructivists in the Union of Soviet Architects naturally objected. In 1934 to 1935, the state followed by closing private design studios, which were deemed to be "artisanal," a capitalist and out-moded form of labour. Insofar as such studios also served educational purposes, the Party's action ensured that all knowledge transfer would thereafter take place under its close, supervisory eye.[4] Finally, with the approval of the Moscow City Plan in 1935, the Party apparatus asserted its authority over architecture and planning, demanding that all plans everywhere in the Soviet Union conform to the stylistic and technical elements outlined in the new project for the Soviet Union's capital.

Although Ivanitskii initially retained his private studio, authority, and seeming autonomy, these events boded ill for him. The state's new Socialist Realist aesthetic reshaped the very nature of the planning profession. Even as they closed private design studies, authorities demanded that architects and planners copy artistic and technical images crafted in and for Moscow onto local cityscapes. Henceforth, planners would no longer be the arbi-trating translators of state ideas, but rather extensions of the state's visual image, as embedded in their work and in their professional selves.

In this, Ivanitskii's sense of science, of public duty, and of professional pride were clearly being threatened. Although pragmatic, allowing sci-ence to serve political purposes, he nonetheless regarded the scientific method as autonomous, having its own rights and power. Ivanitskii rejected the idea that the city plan should serve as an image of power, transmitting state authority through its political aesthetic. The idea that city planning should prioritize the image of grandeur and success to the detriment of scientific process was unacceptable to him. Although he supported the creation of a regulatory state apparatus, Ivanitskii none-theless rejected Stalin's attempt to interfere with planning methods. Ends might be political, but to Ivanitskii, the methods and means of sci-ence had to remain untouched.

The Rise of Compact Planning: A World of Hierarchy

Ivanitskii's victory in February 1935 was a pyrrhic one, for although it marked the success of Ivanitskii's new zoning plan, it also foreshadowed the demise of Ivanitskii's approach to urban planning. Gosplan SSSR's desire for the expansion of the Ford factory of Avtozavod had forced the Scientific-Technical Council to extend grudging support to left bank settlement.[5] Although the Council sought to make this support conditional, suggesting that its approval might be withdrawn if Ivanitskii failed to produce a complete melioration plan before the year's end, the Council simultaneously issued a number of decrees that effectively turned compact *planirovka* into the new law of local growth. It thus banned right bank construction as well as development outside city boundaries, a ruling that enforced "across the river" settlement (now known as the "compact plan"), despite the lack of a melioration plan.[6] Compliance with state demands had come to define the Scientific-Technical Council's work. In fact, in years to come, the Council's edicts would advance ever more radical and ambitious urban plans, despite lingering questions abut the viability of left bank melioration.[7] Political pliability, not scientific rigour, guided many of its rulings.

The Scientific-Technical Council's newly conciliatory stance was brought about by a wave of signals from Moscow suggesting the dawn of a new political and aesthetic era. In neo-imperial style, Stalin had begun to extend a homogeneous structure over all cities in the Soviet Union, as a way to centralize authority in Moscow. Just as imperial St. Petersburg had inspired innumerable provincial cities to build their own "capital sections," so Moscow became the new icon, the aesthetic model to which all cities and villages in the Soviet Union had to conform.[8] Under Stalin, as under the tsars, architectural mimicry of the capital signalled provincial success, even as it affirmed the provinces' subordinate position in the socio-geographic hierarchy.[9] By imposing aesthetic unity on the state, while reserving the largest and most grandiose edifices for Moscow, the new aesthetic imaged the Soviet Union as a single land, a spatial unity defined by aesthetic sameness and continuity over vast tracts of territory.[10]

This neo-imperial architecture mimicked older classical and gothic styles, infusing these with grandiose proportions, as suited Stalin-era taste. Its buildings evoked the glories of Russia's past, as well as those of earlier world empires, laying claim to the whole of human history as the Soviet heritage. Architects suggested that this new aesthetic was practical, for classical and historic design were supposedly much simpler for a new generation of architects to master, not to mention more appealing to the common people. Yet, the new style clearly served to represent Stalin's authority. Like Russian imperial architecture, it used the landscape as a stage for the projection of state power.[11]

This image of power not only extended horizontally across the Soviet Union, but also vertically, shaping the way in which Soviet cities were structured. Echoing Moscow's assertion of central power, the factory town gave way to centralized, hierarchically organized urban centres. Like the Moscow city plan of 1935, which served as the model of this new design, all Soviet cities began to feature a neighbourhood-and-quarter structure, a defining element of Soviet city planning until the Soviet Union's collapse in 1991. In this system, the residential quarter became the basic societal unit. Here, residents could access necessary services: grocery stores, laundry and bathing facilities, children's institutions, schools, local clubs, and parks. Several of these quarters combined to form a district, whose cultural and administrative facilities served all neighbourhoods within its boundaries. At the apex of the system stood the city centre, which served the entire municipal area.[12] As practical as such a system of services may have been, it echoed and reinforced the broader shift towards administrative, social, and political hierarchy, echoing such verticality in the organization of the city.

As the city at the top of this statewide hierarchy, Moscow served as a dramatic stage of power. Its 1935 city plan tore open the cityscape, exposing it to wide-angled light, openness, and space for monumental design. The plan broadened Moscow's historic streets and placed a vast architectural ensemble along the Moscow River. Taking this vision of bright airiness into the space beneath the city, Moscow also became the proud host of a metro system that infused the light and lustre of the above-ground world into the earth below. The plan also proposed technical enhancements, such as added sewer and communications systems, but the science of function no longer defined the plan's aesthetic.[13]

Despite its utopian abstraction, this new approach to city planning was nothing like the visionary planning of the avant-garde. Whereas visionary planners had deployed the tools of scientific perception, treating the city as an object to scrutinize, research, and rationalize, the state's new approach to envisioning the city strove for a different form of visual transcendence. In it, the abstract representation of the Soviet socio-political order began to substitute for its realization. Images of the bright future filled the everyday with a sense of socialism-in-becoming.[14] In such images, the present melted away, defamiliarized and "de-realized" by visions of a radiant future. Such defamiliarization theoretically permitted citizens to engage their cityscape on new terms, for their minds had been exposed to different, fully Soviet ways of understanding urban life.[15]

Astute observers could have predicted the advent of the state's new political aesthetic as early as 1932, when the Soviet Council of People's Commissars (SNK SSSR) and the Central Committee (TsK KPSS) ruled on the preliminary draft of the Moscow city plan. In that approved draft, the Moscow city plan followed neither a star-city nor a linear structure (the forms initially preferred by the city council and the Scientific-Technical Council, respectively), but rather organized the city as a hierarchy of districts, with the main institutions situated in the city centre. In that same year, in the second round of competition for the new Moscow House of Soviets, not a single constructivist design won, marking a gradual transition towards the monumental in both that competition and in Soviet architecture as a whole. Over time, the design for the new House of Soviets became more a fantasy than an engineering project, a trait captured in its final sketches, which were covered with drawings of planes, clouds, and human beings, placed alongside the proposed building as a way to demonstrate its enormous, larger-than-life size.[16]

As early as 1932, hints of these changes could be glimpsed in Nizhnii Novgorod, too. Already in 1931, authorities condemned the housing combine, and Lazar Kaganovich deemed all Soviet cities to be "socialist" by virtue of their Soviet status. Embracing this socialist identity, in 1932, local authorities baptized the city "Gorky," in honour of renowned, city-born proletarian author Alexei Peshkov. At around the same time, the Expert Council of the Province of Gorky Department of the Municipal Economy (Kraikomkhoz) instructed planners to abandon meridian construction, wherein all buildings were situated on a north-south axis in order to allow interior rooms to catch both morning and evening sunshine. The new decree ordered architects to set buildings flush with the street, so that the beauty of the street front, not the angle of the light entering apartments, came to define how a building was situated.[17]

In retrospect, these changes may have fuelled the dispute between the Scientific-Technical Council and the city council, in 1932, provoking the former's reluctance to approve Ivanitskii's star-city zoning plan.[18] No planner or professional in the city explicitly referred to the still-incomplete Moscow city plan in the course of that dispute, possibly because both the city council and the Scientific-Technical Council rejected compact settlement, which best reflected the model being set by Moscow. Nonetheless, the aesthetic and scientific winds of change were clearly blowing, placing the future of constructivist and factory-town design in question. Perhaps the Scientific-Technical Council was wise to wait for the state to clearly define its preferred political aesthetic.

Ivanitskii's response to these changes was pragmatic. Pushing aside the star-city plan, whose aesthetic was now passé, he reintroduced the "across the river" zoning plan, for which he won the city council's support, in 1934.[19] No longer envisioned as a constellation of small factory towns, the City of Gorky now appeared as a hierarchical metropolis in which the most important cultural, economic, and political institutions were concentrated in the city centre. Swamplands would be developed, permitting for contiguous development throughout the city. As mandated, in 1932, the urban quarter also changed its appearance, as all housing came to face the street. The courtyard entrances of the MVTU plan, like those of pre-Petrine Russia, again gave way to the street as a site for the display of state grandeur and power.

In keeping with the new emphasis on crafting the city centre as a focal point for political and aesthetic influence, Ivanitskii applied a single architectural schema to the whole city. In his proposal, all roads on the left bank of the Oka River led to the arrow-shaped promontory (*strelka*) formed by the confluence of the Oka and Volga rivers. As the site of the only bridge across the river to the kremlin, the strelka was the city's transportation hub. To express this geo-social fact architecturally, Ivanitskii proposed that a Lenin monument be erected on the site, on the location of the soon-to-be decommissioned Alexander Nevsky Cathedral. Ivanitskii also suggested the annexation of Bor, which lay on the far side of the Volga, opposite the kremlin. Had the city taken possession of this territory, it would have encircled the strelka from all sides, turning this strelka into the city's geo-political heart.[20]

In developing this new zoning plan, Ivanitskii conceded neither scientific authority nor the principle of expediency. In keeping with his pragmatic bent, he promoted the compact plan as a way to grapple with the challenge posed by the lack of available left bank land on which to build. Such scarcity made left bank melioration, the elimination of swampland, and the merger of Avtozavod and Gorky not only aesthetically prudent, but practically inevitable. In the future, there would be no other vacant land. Granted, the city council still could not fund melioration, but Ivanitskii circumvented this problem by treating the now-abandoned star-city plan as a stepping stone towards compact development. In the short term, development would follow the star-city model. Later, as new lands for development were meliorated, construction would fully adhere to the provisions of the compact plan.[21]

As a pragmatist, Ivanitskii possibly felt that he could continue to work as he always had, accommodating political priorities without compromising the scientific method. Concern for *observable* economic, social, and political problems defined Ivanitskii's use and interpretation of research. Although he accommodated the state's desire for larger, more centralized cities, he did not concede the truth claims of science. Science's goals might be political and therefore subject to state oversight, but its ways of measuring, assessing, seeing, and defining "workability" were supposed to remain autonomous and intact. Indeed, Ivanitskii had devoted his life to promoting *scientific* planning as a methodology.

Towards the Iconographic: Ivanitskii's Departure

In February 1935, when his compact zoning plan finally won approval, Ivanitskii's political prospects must have appeared bright, for the city council had a new president – Radion Semenovich Semenov, a man with an expressed concern for urban planning.[22] In the past, Ivanitskii had pleaded for funds from local leaders, all to no avail. Assisting his cause, local newspapers had repeatedly attacked political leaders for their callous disregard for the *melochi* (details) of urban development and planning.[23] None of this had made any difference. Now, it seemed, Ivanitskii could hope for support from this new municipal leader.

What Ivanitskii could not foresee was the durability of the Soviet penchant for anti-systemic, highly individual, and rather Promethean approaches to development, as exemplified by Stakhanovism. In 1935, after Alexei Stakhanov broke records for coal hewing, an against-system, against-experts movement rippled across the Soviet Union. Ambitious individuals eager to break output records pitted themselves against factory administrators and co-workers. Disrupting production, their heroic endeavours generally proved detrimental to factory processes, yet the regime lauded their extra-systemic feats. As a celebration of individual strength, speed, and enthusiasm, the movement posed yet another challenge to engineer-led and science-defined socio-technological systems of administration, the very things that Ivanitskii cherished.[24]

The surge of Stakhanovism signaled the rise of a new cult of individual heroism, whereby "the little man" and the "manager" (*khoziain*) single-handedly combatted all the defects of Soviet economic and home life. Encouraging this spirit in urban affairs, in 1933, the Supreme Council of the Municipal Economy (VSKKh SSSR) imposed *personal* (*lichnyi*) responsibility for housing and municipal development on the deputy presidents of all executive governments – municipal, provincial, and sectoral (i.e., in industry and housing).[25] In 1935, this practice was extended to individuals at all levels of the state and production hierarchy, as the new city Party protocol made *individuals* responsible for any failure to implement Party directives with regard to transportation and housing.[26] In keeping with this new policy, the 1935 city council report on the state of urban construction and planning featured, in bold print, the names of the engineers, builders, foremen, and architects on whom success relied.[27] Those who succeeded would receive lavish praise and reward, whereas failure would be greeted with scorn.

Such practices threatened Ivanitskii on two levels. As a planner, he would find that such anti-managerial and disruptive individualism interfered with professional management, including attempts to regulate construction. As the head of a planning team, moreover, he would find himself under pressure to perform his own feats. No matter what the limits of funding, data, or time, he would be expected to meet his deadlines and achieve all planning goals.

Seemingly oblivious to these changes, in early 1935, Ivanitskii negotiated the sort of contract of which most professionals can only dream. He won the right to establish his own planning studio, select his own subordinates, set his own work deadlines, and seek out information from local agencies as required. The city council, together with the Russian Commissariat of the Municipal Economy, gained the right to vet Ivanitskii's choice of staff, but little more. The contract obligated "local institutions" to "cooperate" with Ivanitskii, an ill-defined clause that appears to have been designed to pin all blame for future planning delays and failures on inadequate support from Gorky-based institutions.[28]

Meanwhile, Ivanitskii moved to Moscow to establish a studio within the new Institute of Architecture and Construction in Moscow, thereby abandoning his earlier principle that all city planning should take place on site. Of poor health, without the spirit or energy to shuttle between Gorky and Moscow, Ivanitskii merely promised that his new studio would dedicate itself solely to the Gorky city plan, finishing an (approvable) general city plan before 1936 drew to its close.[29] With his handpicked team and his lengthy acquaintance with conditions in Gorky, he believed that he could assure fairly rapid progress to city officials. But, he refused any clause that might penalize him for the failings of the system around him.

Ivanitskii appears to have been under political attack, however, for the city council report of 1935 explicitly blamed *him* for all delays in city planning since 1928.[30] The report specified that the city council not only wanted planning deadlines met, but that it wished to make some individual – in this case, Ivanitskii – personally liable for any failures. The report thus committed the city council and city planners to complete the city's general city plan by 1 January 1936, setting a fixed deadline of the sort rejected in Ivanitskii's initial contract. Insofar as the report specified no extenuating circumstances, such as missing funds or data, the deadline became a non-negotiable end in itself.

The city council soon followed by altering Ivanitskii's contract to limit his autonomy and make him officially accountable for any and all possible failings in the city plan. In addition to imposing strict deadlines, it stipulated that if either the Institute or Ivanitskii's studio were shut down by government order, the onus for finding a new agency to work on the city plan would go to Ivanitskii. Then, despite having imposed greater responsibility on Ivanitskii, the contract restricted his authority, placing everyone in Ivanitskii's studio, with the exception of Ivanitskii himself, under the direct supervision of the city's new chief architect, Vladimir F. Grechukho. As Ivanitskii's new deputy, Grechukho became the plan's co-author.[31]

Ivanitskii vehemently opposed the contract, which undercut his authority even as it made him solely liable for the successful completion of the city plan. Ivanitskii complained that the contract placed him in "a false position" (lozhnoe polozhenie) with regard to his staff. Ivanitskii also expressed frustration with the council's proclaimed intention to place the entire burden of city planning on his shoulders, even though the council had diminished Ivanitskii's authority over his subordinates. Ivanitskii likewise objected to the strict deadlines imposed by the contract, pointing out (rather presciently) that such deadlines were pointless: deadlines could always be met formally, even if substantial progress did not take place, and the rush to meet such arbitrary deadlines would undoubtedly result in faulty and therefore less economical work.[32]

Unwilling to compromise on his authority, Ivanitskii resigned, bringing to an end the era of pragmatic scientific planning, in which "the facts" set the framework of debate, even if they could not dictate policy outcomes. Although the Scientific-Technical Council requested that Ivanitskii join the next Gorky planning team as an auxiliary member, he declined to do so.[33] Nikolai V. Malakhov, an engineer who worked on the city council's newly created Architecture and Planning Administration, argued that the city council should have offered better conditions to Ivanitskii, given his talent and skill.[34] Rapprochement was not in the air, however. The city council refused to change its offer, and Ivanitskii departed, refusing to be anything more than a occasional "consultant" to the planning team that succeeded him. Ivanitskii's local planning endeavours were over.

Lengiprogor: A New Culture of Planning

After Ivanitskii resigned, the city council handed the city planning contract to the Leningrad State Institute of City Planning (Lengiprogor), whose work would ironically embody all that Ivanitskii rejected, even as it benefited from the many institutional reforms that Ivanitskii had both promoted and formulated. Although brought about by Ivanitskii's rejection and defeat, Lengiprogor's contract was negotiated by the Scientific-Technical Council, of which Ivanitskii was a part. Seeking to ensure that planning proceeded smoothly, the Council brought the direct political interference to which Ivanitskii had objected to an end. It arranged for the Planning Administration of the Russian Commissariat of the Municipal Economy to review and advise Lengiprogor's work, thereby asserting its own right to supervise the planning process.[35]

The intervention of the Scientific-Technical Council testifies to the growing institutionalization and standardization of Soviet planning, something that Ivanitskii openly supported. Although scholars date the maturation of this system to the 1940s, its growth in the 1930s was impressive.[36] By 1939, the Russian Commissariat of the Municipal Economy had established architectural boards with project offices under each regional and city council, and it continued to set norms for the planning and construction of transportation, sanitation, and service facilities.[37] Ironically, such institutionalization may have spawned the showdown with Ivanitskii, for in 1934, the City of Gorky was given its own city planning department. This department was under the authority of chief architect Grechukho, to whom the offensive second contract granted all power over Ivanitskii's staff.

Hoping to forestall a new contract dispute, the Scientific-Technical Council forced the city council, together with Grechukho, to formulate a more moderate and just contract defined by *mutual* obligations. The new contract therefore excluded the most controversial and offensive elements of Ivanitskii's second offer. It limited Grechukho's supervisory duties to the submission of two reports on Lengiprogor's progress to the city council each month, along with organizing external reviews of Lengiprogor's work at the city council's expense.[38] Grechukho joined the Lengiprogor team, but his work was subject to the planning team's review and modification.[39] The city council also accepted responsibility for compensating Lengiprogor for loss of work if, by *government* action, the contract was delayed or cancelled. Finally, the city council agreed that deadlines could be renegotiated if the city council failed to supply the requisite money and research materials to Lengiprogor in a timely manner.

The new contract also specified mutual penalties for failing to fulfil the terms of the contract. It clearly outlined the city council's procedures for verifying Lengiprogor's work, for paying wages, and for seeking redress in case of a broken agreement. Lengiprogor agreed to help the recently formed city planning department select lots for annual construction – work to be completed on site in the city, provided that the city council offered Lengiprogor free housing, office space, transportation, food, and financial compensation. Because it was based in Leningrad, Lengiprogor also agreed to send visiting (*vyezdnye*) brigades to Gorky for the purpose of conducting on-site investigations.[40] To ensure an adequate degree of local voice and input, the agreement also permitted the city's own planning department to create a consultation bureau to review and advise Lengiprogor's work, ensuring that the plan met local needs. Sustaining Ivanitskii's practice of training new professionals to staff the city council's planning departments, the contract further compelled Lengiprogor to accept three young professionals from the City of Gorky into its ranks, making them leaders of Lengiprogor's planning brigades.[41]

At this point, the city council joined the Scientific-Technical Council in inviting Ivanitskii to take charge of the new planning team, or at least to join the team as a consultant. But, the recent tensions with the city council had strained Ivanitskii's health, and he remained firmly opposed to the concept of fixed deadlines to be met no matter what the obstacles that he encountered. Despite the Scientific-Technical Council's negotiation of a fairer contract with the city council, Ivanitskii preferred to remain in his bureaucratic post in Moscow, where he might formulate rules, regulations, and reviews. The risk of on-the-ground politicking and negotiating was something that he now wished to avoid. Ivanitskii would later review the plan produced by his successor, but he himself did nothing more to help develop it.[42]

Ivanitskii's departure represented the dawn of a new era, marked by the "industrial organization" of work.[43] Despite its respect for local input and the training of younger scholars, Lengiprogor ran its affairs much differently than Ivanitskii had. Under Ivanitskii, city planning had largely depended on the mind and skills of Ivanitskii himself, who served as

4.1. Alexander Platonovich Ivanitskii, 1881–1947. Olga Orel'skaia, *Arkhitektura epokhi sovetskogo avangarda v Nizhnem Novgorode* (Nizhnii Novgorod: Promgrafika, 2005), 177.

both the head administrator and the chief expert. Deemed to be "artisanal" by the state, Ivanitskii's planning teams had consisted of close-knit groups of experts who had been personally selected, supervised, and often trained by Ivanitskii. By contrast, Lengiprogor was a large organization consisting of five hundred experts, only a small portion of whom would work on the Gorky city plan. Those dedicated to planning the city would also organize their work on "industrial lines," each taking responsibility for one closely defined research task.[44]

The new team's leader embodied this transition, for he represented the rise of a younger, Soviet generation of professionals. Born in 1903, Nikolai Alekseevich Solofnenko received all of his professional training from Soviet institutions, starting with the Engineering-Construction Faculty of the Polytechnical Institute of Chernigov. He then studied at the Ukrainian Architectural Institute and the architectural faculty of the Art Institute of Kiev, from which he graduated in 1928, when Ivanitskii launched the planning of what was then Greater Nizhnii Novgorod. Unlike Ivanitskii, Solofnenko had not travelled abroad, and he certainly

4.2. Nikolai Alekseevich Solofnenko, 1903–1974. Olga Orel'skaia, *Arkhitektura epokhi sovetskogo avangarda v Nizhnem Novgorode* (Nizhnii Novgorod: Promgrafika, 2005), 183.

had no personal connection to the Scientific-Technical Council. When Solofnenko joined Lengiprogor in 1934, he had no prior experience as a city planner, for he had worked only as an architect. Moreover, as the child of petty white-collar workers (*sluzhashchie*), Solofnenko represented the social mobility that Soviet life encouraged and facilitated. He was a *vydvizhenets* – that is, a beneficiary of Soviet affirmative action policies, designed to form a new elite out of less-privileged groups.[45]

As a product of the Soviet Union, Solofnenko did not share Ivanitskii's understanding of the nature of science or scientific planning. Although he recognized the power of science as a process and method, he apparently accepted the state's belief that scientific authority was rooted in political compliance, not in abstract expertise. Whereas Ivanitskii had rejected strict deadlines, pointing to the errors that resulted from rushed work and to the way in which forced deadlines prompted "pseudo completions" of work, Solofnenko kept deadlines religiously, pleasing political leaders. Rather than emphasizing the need for scientific objectivity, Solofnenko accepted the Soviet principle of *engagement*. As an extension of this, conformist political display came to matter more to his work than accurate scientific perception.

As Ivanitskii had predicted, to meet contracted deadlines, Solofnenko's Lengiprogor often practised deception, making a show of completing work when nothing had been done. In December 1935, for instance, Lengiprogor wowed the city council with an impressive array of eye-pleasing sketches and charts, mere illustrations of Ivanitskii's ideas. To the city council, the visuals offered the illusion of substantial progress, garnering Solofnenko effusive praise for Lengiprogor's "marvellous" performance. With such razzle-dazzle, Solofnenko distracted the city council from paying close attention to his team's failure to provide a left bank melioration plan, as promised by Ivanitskii to the Scientific-Technical Council earlier that year.[46]

At times, Solofnenko outright deceived, plagiarizing the work of other expert bodies in order to generate the façade of success. For instance, responsibility for the melioration plan had been contracted to the Water Management Section (*Vodokhoziaistvennyi Otdel*) of the Leningrad Scientific Research Institute of the Municipal Economy (LNIKKh), to which Lengiprogor failed to send the requisite research materials until very late in the year. Determined to meet Lengiprogor's planning deadlines, which were jeopardized by its failure to equip the Water Management Section with the requisite data in a timely manner, Lengiprogor effectively stole the Water Management Section's tentative melioration plans, modifying them only slightly before submitting two melioration plans to the Scientific-Technical Council. Because the Water Management Section also submitted two plans, the Scientific-Technical Council received four proposals for melioration, none of which amounted to more than a preliminary sketch.[47] Nonetheless, Solofnenko declared the four proposals to be a success that would strengthen the city's bid for research funding.[48]

Solofnenko displayed similar political savvy in spring 1936, when Lengiprogor brought voluminous architectural sketches to a city council review of its work. Such sketches ought to have been reserved for the final stage of city planning, when the *detal'nye plany* (detailed plans) were produced.[49] In early 1936, planners had not yet decided on the location of the city's main squares and boulevards, let alone the nature of the architecture to be placed on them. Regardless, Lengiprogor arrived with a plethora of images. The proposed edifices were pompous and monumental, far beyond the fiscal reach of a provincial city.[50] From a purely academic standpoint, every one of these sketches was an inexcusable waste of valuable time and energy. However, local officials delighted in them, making them a public relations coup – no small feat, when those pesky melioration plans remained incomplete.[51]

As impractical as they were, Solofnenko's drawings offered the planners' version of Soviet Socialist Realism, for they were Potemkinist in their image of a pseudo-reality. They articulated socialism as a promise, as a reality-in-becoming that was, somehow, to be embraced as more "real" than everyday affairs.[52] In this particular case, the "Potemkinism" of these images lay not just in their depiction of a new world, totally removed from any scientific calculation of what was feasible and possible, but also in Solofnenko's drama of achievement. Through his surfeit of drawings, he substituted the image of scientific diligence for its substance, thereby protecting himself from political assault. This was, to use theatre parlance, a "representational" act – an overt and somewhat hyperbolized performance of a role, played in such a way as to please an audience that expected certain gestures and cues to be used to define the "correct" attitude, sentiment, and emotion for the part. In the highly ritualized world of Stalin's Russia, this sufficed to articulate loyalty, enthusiasm, and professional dedication.

New deadlines – and new dangers – always loomed on the horizon. After Solofnenko's "smoke and mirrors" of December 1935, the city council not only heaped praise on his work, but also charged Lengiprogor to exert "maximal force" on the general city plan, setting a completion date of 1 January 1937.[53] Solofnenko's success merely brought the next deadline nearer. To complicate matters, not everyone found his performance believable. Engineers in the city planning department fully disapproved of Solofnenko's sophistry. They exposed the premature nature of his sketches, noting the lack of serious progress on melioration. Still, director Solofnenko had been quite sensational. And thanks to renewed demands for performative brilliance, the drama would continue.

The Iconographic Stage: Towards the Representational

In 1936, this drama entered an entirely new act – with a new set and changed roles for planners. The old guard's ivory tower of science remained at the far back corner of the stage, overshadowed by a large new monument near the front, the site from which the unseen figure of Stalin cast a shadow over the stage. In crafting his own scenario of power, Solofnenko neither climbed up the monument nor gazed down from the tower. His power, however limited, would be determined by his performance on the stage. To him went responsibility for embodying the new Soviet man, including the new Soviet planner, in his actions. The reproduction of certain ritualized forms, not authenticity in his work, would determine his degree of success.

Central to this performance lay "iconographic planning," which deployed a technique central to Orthodox religious art. Like iconographers, planners forewent individual creativity, reproducing the sacralized forms enshrined by Moscow, which bore "iconic" status.[54] To use the Orthodox term, Moscow was "divinized," a material realm transfigured not through divine grace (as in Orthodox transfiguration), but through its identification with the person of Stalin and, through him, with Lenin. Just as iconographers faithfully copied sacred forms, displaying creativity only in their nuances of tone, colour, and brush stroke, so Soviet city planners had to faithfully reproduce the sacralized urban form of Moscow. Planners' only freedom lay in fitting this image to the city being planned – in this case, the City of Gorky.

As a first step in this process of disseminating Moscow's newly sacralized form, architects everywhere were instructed to collectively discuss the implications of the Moscow city plan.[55] Following orders, architects, engineers, industry managers, and planners gathered to discuss the plan with Party and state officials in October 1935. At that meeting, the new city council president "proposed" that Lengiprogor duplicate elements of Moscow's plan.[56] Likewise, the 1935 City of Gorky council report ordered planners to replicate as much of the Moscow plan as possible in their own work.[57] By reproducing key structural elements of this plan, they hoped to achieve some of the glories of the capital in their own city.

Iconographic design officially came to define the plan for the City of Gorky after March 1936, when the Russian Commissariat of the Municipal Economy imposed a Moscow-style, iconographic plan on Lengiprogor. That month, Lengiprogor submitted two variants of a general city plan. Although both variants elaborated the approved compact zoning plan, as outlined by Ivanitskii in February 1935, only the first variant retained Ivanitskii's pragmatism. The second, known as the radical variant, borrowed Moscow's larger-than-life style. In the spirit of iconographic planning, the Russian Commissariat of the Municipal Economy favoured the radical variant of the general city plan.[58]

The radical variant called for far-reaching changes to the cityscape. In it, Lengiprogor suggested the creation of a monumental parade ground on the left bank.[59] As in the Moscow city plan, Lengiprogor's radical variant proposed to dramatically widen streets to as much as fifty metres (from an original width of eighteen metres). Although such widening would involve the destruction of the city centre's high-quality stone and brick homes at a time when housing was scarce, promoters argued that the measure was necessary – not only aesthetically, but also because it would allow sunlight, traffic, and pedestrians to better penetrate central city streets. As part of the plan, Lengiprogor also proposed to build five-storey housing along all major streets, with special effort going to the roads that linked one city district to the next, in order to provide the illusion that the city was fully urbanized. Swampland and undeveloped zones would remain hidden behind this new housing's façade.[60]

Also following Moscow's lead, Lengiprogor made a river – in this case, the Oka River – the central feature of the city's architectural ensemble. Following the nineteenth-century tradition of investing national identity and pride in the landscape, the Oka River became the city's new *genius loci*, harbouring the "spirit of the place."[61] To focus attention on this "primordial" and "timeless" symbol of local identity, planners proposed to build a twenty-five kilometre architectural ensemble along both sides of the river from its mouth to Avtozavod. The ensemble would pair monumental buildings on the right bank with counterparts on the left bank, linking each pair via a bridge over the Oka. (See figure 4.3.) A total of five bridges, plus another railway bridge, would connect the two banks.[62] Rejecting Ivanitskii's former plan, the new proposal reduced the strelka to a mere gateway to the city. The Lenin monument would be placed elsewhere, and workers' housing, storage facilities, and a lighthouse would occupy the site.[63]

The radical plan also called for the realignments of major roads. On the left bank, the new plan envisioned the straightening of roads, particularly those linking Sormovo to the rest of the city. Not unlike street widening, this would involve the destruction of a large portion of the city's existing infrastructure and housing, a costly proposal at such a time of shortage. On the right bank, it called for the eastern wall of the kremlin to be torn down in order to make the Oka River visible from Soviet Square, the main square in the historic city.[64] A highly controversial and never realized proposal, this removal would have deprived the roads in historic Nizhnii Novgorod of their focal point, for all major thoroughfares in the old city radiated outward from the kremlin wall, which was the visual and architectural anchor of the whole. Removing this wall would not only remove a piece of history, but also pose a grand architectural dilemma.

On the whole, the radical variant promised an industrial, highly cen-

4.3. Sketch from the 1936 Radical Plan for the City of Gorky. Olga Orel'skaia, *Arkhtektura epokhi sovetskogo avangarda v Nizhnem Novgorode* (Nizhnii Novgorod: Promgrafika, 2005), 150.

tralized, and monumentalized city. If realized, it would have utterly altered the cityscape, offering public spaces of such vast openness and scale as to abolish the intimate privilege that had once been a defining feature of imperial city streets.[65] It also proposed streets too vast for the messy everyday human interaction typical of the nineteenth-century boulevard, including Nevsky Prospekt in St. Petersburg. In planners' new image of the city, public space as a site of spontaneous interaction disappeared, at least in theory. Designed as sites for the commemoration of state power, the city's new spaces were meant to foster public identification with the state. Ripping apart the old to make space for the new, the full realization of this plan would ultimately depend on popular appropriation of what these spaces represented. Under Solofnenko, in fact, planners strove vigorously to achieve this.

On a more troubling note, the technical success of this new plan depended on the construction of a vast melioration complex, something much more ambitious than anything suggested by Ivanitskii. In 1931, when the star-city model had dominated planners' thinking, experts had considered the use of localized drainage wells to control groundwater and flooding. Compact settlement, which forewent areas of swamps-turned-parkland, required more extensive melioration. To provide such drainage, in 1934, Ivanitskii proposed to utilize existing natural and man-made drainage systems, adding only two U-shaped canals around the inner portion of the left bank region. Modelled on the drainage system designed for the Nizhnii Novgorod Trade Fair in 1817, these canals were to double as transportation avenues.[66]

By contrast, Lengiprogor's radical variant of 1936 proposed to flatten the natural landscape, thereby enabling planners to impose rectilinear order. To this end, Lengiprogor planned to fill natural drainage systems, drain low-lying areas, and straighten large waterways.[67] The new approach to flood control raised serious alarm, for its attempt to redirect or fill natural waterways could potentially worsen drainage problems.[68] The plan also exposed Lengiprogor's ignorance of left bank topography. Even with closed drainage, the region's topographical features could inhibit rectilinear development of the sort that Solofnenko proposed. Even the Expert Council of the Scientific-Technical Council (NTS NKKKh RSFSR) argued that Lengiprogor should preserve the area's existing streams and reservoirs.[69] Nonetheless, despite environmental objections, unfinished research, and the challenge of implementing any plan, the iconographic aesthetic prevailed, and the Russian Commissariat of the Municipal Economy approved the proposed melioration system in January 1937.[70]

Although fully conforming to the state's political aesthetic, the plan was met with local resistance. Echoing the wisdom of former city council chair, Klavdiia A. Zimina, city engineers objected to the plan's lack of realism. In seeking a grandiose architectural plan, they complained, Solofnenko's planning team ignored the city's economic and technological limitations, not to mention its shortage of personnel. Although a Party member, engineer Gleb V. Greiber of the city planning department complained, "Moscow is Moscow, but Gorky is Gorky." As he warned: "This is not a project, but one beautiful picture which will hang nicely and which will characterize a particular era in their research, but which will by and large remain, in practical terms, unrealized."[71] In his review of the plan, in 1937, Ivanitskii would largely say the same. In February

1939, experts in both Gorky and Moscow would again question the viability of the plan.[72]

Such opponents would prove correct, as the plan stumbled over its own excessive ambition. Plans to build a twenty-five kilometre architectural ensemble along both banks of the Oka River came to naught – not only because of the expense, but because successful bridge-building would require the melioration of the right bank slope. As Ivanitskii later noted, the Lengiprogor planning team failed to carefully study the soils that would one day sustain the five bridges over the Oka River.[73] Street widening also failed. Officials did build a row of housing behind the frontal buildings along Pokrovka Street, as preparation for the never-to-occur removal of the buildings along one side of the street, but succeeded only in increasing the density of construction in that area.[74] Thus, the iconographic plan was and would remain, as Greiber said, "Nothing but a pretty picture."

Some of the resistance to Lengiprogor's new policies appeared in purely aesthetic form, as architects continued to incorporate constructivist elements in their work, thus refusing the imperatives of monumentality and ornamentation.[75] In the provincial design bureau, Kraiproekt, architects would stubbornly defend the merits of modernist functionalism as opposed to monumentalism, pursuing the former in their industrial design. This did not prevent many older constructivist buildings from being refaced, in order that such edifices might sport a more suitably "classical" and "historic" façade.[76] But, modernist creativity nonetheless continued to be the subject of aesthetic experimentation. (See figure 4.4.)

Yet, the plan was not fundamentally rooted in local concern, or even concern for physical functionality. It stumbled on its ignorance of everyday economic, scientific, and financial indices, because it was designed to project a communal aesthetic. Its image of the socialist future mattered as much as, if not more than, its realizability. As Svetlana Boym might say, the plan offered "didactic transparency." Through it, one did not come to a better understanding of the physical city, but rather to a sense of the Party leadership's vision for the future.[77] This was not visionary planning, rooted in scientific perception, but iconographic design meant to portray the sacralized space of the future.

Conclusion: Iconographic Planning as Stage Set

Although merely "a pretty picture," the new plan played an important

4.4. Radial building in residential block no. 8 of Avtozavod (N.S. Poliudov and N.A. Krasil'nikov, 1935–1937). Olga Orel'skaia, *Arkhtektura epokhi sovetskogo avangarda v Nizhnem Novgorode* (Nizhnii Novgorod: Promgrafika, 2005), 115.

role in projecting the power of the Stalin-dominated state into the provinces. By homogenizing the state's urban aesthetic, it offered symbolic unity, subordinating the provinces (realms of "derivative architecture") to Moscow. The spaces of the iconographic were designed to offer hope, community, and a sense of pride in the Soviet state – ironically, at the expense of more tangible, material benefits. Yet, insofar as people generally fail to be critical consumers of political ideas, perhaps such technical shortcomings did not matter. The plan served its political purpose.[78]

Indeed, despite its attempt to assert regulatory and scientific authority, even the Scientific-Technical Council did not resist.

For many planners, the technical flaws of the radical variant produced cognitive dissonance, a deep-rooted discomfort with their new plan, especially given that any misjudgment on their part might result in purge or arrest. The plan had done violence to their professional sense of what was realistic, possible, and desirable in a city plan. Despite pressure to conform and silence fears, planners' scientific training and mandate compelled them to recognize the flaws in iconographic planning. Engineers in particular remained stubbornly critical of the radical plan's impractical aspects. As they emphasized, Lengiprogor's general city plan was neither a viable development strategy nor a "blueprint" for solving social problems. Instead, it was a cultural and political device developed in and for Moscow, not Gorky.

Yet, planners could exploit the very "stagecraft" that rendered this plan impractical. Its iconography permitted them to grasp at the hem of Stalin's robes, so that they – like their city – might be clothed in Stalin's mantle. Insofar as the city became a stage for Stalin's power, it could also serve as a platform for their *own* enactment of power. Although tentative, often challenged, and muddled by the Stalin cult, planners' own scenario of power nonetheless advanced their authority, even as it ceded scientific credibility. As the next chapter suggests, the results of this stagecraft were mixed.

Chapter Five

Stalinism as Stagecraft:
The Architecture of Performance

Democracy is a method, a scientific technique of evolving the will of the people.
Mary P. Follett, *The New State*[1]

Society is generally more interested in standing on the side lines and watching itself go by in a whole series of different uniforms than it is in practical objectives.
Thurman Arnold, *The Symbols of Government*[2]

Under Solofnenko's watch, Lengiprogor participated in a grand the-atrical act that deliberately thrust itself through the fourth wall – into that theatrical realm where actors forcibly incorporate off-stage space into their act, drawing the audience and the imaginary into the show. Highly ritualized, Solofnenko's performance brought to life the vari-ous collective representations that mediated between Soviet state and society, including popular voice, Stalin's love, and the expert's master skill. Designed to make the complex, often dark and hidden world of state operations more understandable, identifiable, and comfortable, Solofnenko's act fostered prescribed, democratic interaction between planners and people. His aim, in this, was to offer a multivalent and yet "welcome" image of power, one that might gloss over complex expert-worker and state-people clashes in belief, experience, and identity.[3]

In scripting his act, Solofnenko benefited from Stalin's self-identifica-tion as the Architect of Communism, a title clearly donned to capture all the multifaceted ways in which Stalin shaped – or claimed to have shaped – Soviet society. Western commentators have often stressed Sta-lin's putative dogmatism, paper pushing, and thuggishness, but Stalin obviously wished for a more illustrious image, one that might present him as creative and productive, able to outfit Soviet society with both modern efficiency and luxurious beauty.[4] Arrogating himself to an almost divinized position, he proclaimed himself the sole spokesperson for the higher, "objective" reality affiliated with Lenin and Marx.[5] Thus asserting his status as Soviet society's progenitor, Stalin assumed the power to define the very foundations of the Soviet system, his grand edifice.[6]

Having ceded much of their scientific authority, planners could no longer claim to be the primary authors of Soviet city plans. Authorship went to the Party and to Stalin, leaving planners with a highly limited career choice: either tow the state's line or cease to work as architects.[7] To garner power and security under these circumstances, planners had to serve as agents of popular will, both in and of itself and as supposedly embodied by Stalin. Shrewdly turning this duty into opportunity, architects in the City of Gorky exploited Stalin's self-representation as architect in order to clothe themselves in Stalin's authority. They performed their state-mandated role as emissaries in such a way as to augment their freedom and power of movement on the collective stage.

Through the Fourth Wall: Agonistic Frames

From the very moment that Nikolai Alekseevich Solofnenko took charge of planning the City of Gorky, he launched a powerful smoke-and-mirrors circus act. Ordered by the Russian Commissariat of the Municipal Economy to frame his reports in such a way as to win the city council's support for planning activities, Solofnenko deftly effected a public relations coup.[8] Pulling melioration plans and architectural sketches out of his bag of tricks, Solofnenko thrilled the city council, whose members eagerly devoured his many sketches and melioration plans as visual (albeit false) evidence of progress. Solofnenko also co-opted audience members as props and stage-hands, making their participation in city planning a central and dominant element in his act.

Solofnenko's new technique was placed on display at the city council's discussion of the Moscow city plan in the autumn of 1935. Following discussion, Solofnenko elicited collective, ritualized vows in support of city planning. Because his audience stood to gain from such an act – in fact, some proposed to forward the transcript of their vow-taking to the Central Committee and the Russian Council of People's Commissars together with a plea for money – they boldly promised their diligent assistance. One by one, they swore to familiarize themselves with Lengiprogor's work, in order that they might propagate planners' vision in the city's many workplaces, particularly on the shop floor.[9]

Not content to manufacture consensus among the powerful, Solofnenko also sought to co-opt common citizens. Stepping beyond the corridors of power, Solofnenko cultivated cross-class commitment to the
making of the new Soviet city. Thus, the first exhibit of Lengiprogor's
work in 1935 opened with a fanfare of press coverage, as well as with
speeches from such local luminaries as Lazar Kaganovich's brother
Iulii, the head of the provincial government.[10] With the assistance of the
provincial branch of the Union of Soviet Architects, Solofnenko also
arranged for three collective farmers to attend as symbolic witnesses of
the future of all citizens. They, with their urban counterparts, received
an invitation to subject Lengiprogor's work to their careful scrutiny,
demanding changes as might befit their own needs.[11]

In themselves, such attempts to broadcast architectural achievements
to the urban public were hardly novel. In 1934, the Party faction of the
Union of Soviet Architects pressed its members to teach the virtues of
Soviet design to the common people. Moscow's architectural community
had already begun to place comment books on display with its plans and
sketches, as a way to encourage popular feedback.[12] In 1934, the Gorky
city council held an open forum on the city plan in the factory district
of Kanavino, in order that officials might discuss the city's development
with factory workers. Local architects often placed their drawings and
sketches in downtown shop windows. They also contributed to the Soviet
Academy of Architecture's documentary on Soviet architecture.[13]

But Nikolai Alekseevich Solofnenko sought more than exhibits or
the mere transmission of technical information about Soviet urban
planning. Through his presentation, Solofnenko aimed to bind audience and actor together in the shared performance of belief. This was
no bread-and-circus performance, meant to placate and entertain.[14]
Through such events, Solofnenko instituted ritualized mechanisms for
managing the tensions in Soviet society.[15] By presenting scientific work as
the manifestation of both Stalinist care and popular desire, Solofnenko's
theatrics elided the conflict between the top-down thrust of planning science and the bottom-up thrust of Soviet claims to democratic rule. They
also crafted a new transcript of power, one that emphasized planners'
closeness to the people and planners' importance as agents of beneficent modernization.[16]

To compel expert participation in this ritual performance, Solofnenko
fabricated a tale of local experts' resistance to planning and public out-
reach. At the February 1936 Provincial Conference of Soviet Architects,
he joined Vasilii F. Boronin, vice president of the city council, in publicly

berating architects for their purported laziness and apathy. Solofnenko censured local architects for their failure to fully acquaint themselves with Lengiprogor's planning materials prior to the conference, and then Boronin accused "architectural society" of being excessively "inward-focused" (*zamknuty*), with insufficient ties to the working class and too little concern for supervising the realization of their projects on the construction site.[17]

Such agonistic rhetoric irritated many delegates, for Solofnenko's accusations misrepresented several important facts. Solofnenko had attacked architects for not reviewing the city plan, and yet Lengiprogor's materials had arrived too late for such a review. The visuals were received just days before the conference, and the textual materials did not appear until the opening day. To compensate for Lengiprogor's tardiness, the local union of architects had assigned to specialists acquainted with Lengiprogor's work the task of summarizing it for conference delegates. These still-uninformed colleagues, some of whom travelled from distant cities such as Cheboksary, were probably unaware that the city plan would be the topic of the day; after all, the keynote speaker was scheduled to discuss the general state of Soviet architecture, not the plan for the provincial capital.[18]

Boronin's accusations stirred even greater outrage. In response to his claim that architects failed to monitor the construction process, architect Anatolii F. Zhukov angrily retorted that local leaders ought to have the "civic manliness" (*grazhdanskoe muzhestvo*) to acknowledge their own poor management and not blame architects for the state's ills (*ne valit's bol'noi golovy na zdorovuiu*). Offering a strong show of support, delegates applauded.[19] Clearly, everyone knew that they had been framed, unjustly convicted of a crime they had never committed.

But Solofnenko and Boronin had no intention of holding a fair trial; their indictment aimed not to capture reality in a static frame, but rather to outline a narrative of action. Despite their prosecutorial tone, the entire conference had been staged in such a way as to cast architects as the Soviet nobility, the new sovereign's ambassadors of style, culture, and beneficent rule. Even as he criticized architects' supposed apathy, Boronin outlined a script according to which planners might lay claim to a form of nobility, provided that they accepted the role assigned to them by the state.[20] How architects theorized art, society, or their work lay beyond his realm of concern, if not beyond his ken. From architects, he sought the collective performance of social concern and commitment, the enactment of socialism as an active force in society. If architects played this role well, he promised, they would gain all the privileges of Soviet "society" (*obshchestvennost'*), a body of politically aware and engaged social activists working under the loose direction of the state apparatus.[21]

To set the stage for this performance, Solofnenko and Boronin arranged for their "new nobility" to meet in the Heraldry Room (*Gerbovyi zal*) of the former city duma building. The hall overlooked Soviet Square, which was the main square in the upper city, located outside the eastern gates of the kremlin, the site of the province's administrative buildings. All of the city's historic streets converged at this point, which was and remained the city's centre of political, economic, and social power. Using this carefully selected platform, Boronin instructed architects to "*zarabotat' gerbom*" (to work with honour) – a play on the phrase "*zarabotat' gorbom*," meaning "to work to exhaustion." Only, in substituting "gerbom" ("with heraldry," or "with honour") for "gorbom" ("to exhaustion"), Boronin promised honour in return for sacrifice – at the same time making a clear allusion to the illustrious facilities in which the conference was held.[22]

Even as Boronin's word play charged architects to tackle the difficulties of their time with energy and enthusiasm, it also explicitly identified their entry into the "intellectual stratum" of society (as enshrined in the 1936 Constitution) as the beginning of obligation, not simply as the end of class warfare against "bourgeois experts."[23] Boronin's allusion to noble honour inferred that planners had a prestigious role to play in the Soviet Union. Not unlike Catherine the Great's nobles and ennobled architects, they would serve as agents of the Enlightenment in the interior. Even more, they would *embody* the enlightened power and splendour of the ruler.[24]

Boronin's substitution of "gerbom" for "gorbom" went still further, suggesting that duty generated nobility – not simply in the sense that diligence was praiseworthy, but in the sense that the task of "working on oneself," or "becoming Soviet," belonged to the realm of public ritual. A few years before, architects themselves had designed housing combines in such a way as to force the individual into the collective, which was viewed as the site through which to effect self-transformation. Private sleeping cells, which offered distance from society as well as space for self-reflection (or self-vision), had largely been deemed barriers to moral improvement, not a means of it.[25] Making the same assumption, Boronin implicitly appealed for architects to combat the ills of self and society through their *collective* performance of duty, reason, and democratic consultation.[26]

Delegates surely could not have misinterpreted his meaning, for the pomp and ritual that marked this event lacked precedent in Gorky's city planning history. Under Ivanitskii, public exhibitions and discussions of planning had been rather mundane affairs. When placing his star-city plan on exhibit in 1932, Ivanitskii had made no serious effort to elicit popular interest.[27] Except for one article criticizing the relatively closed nature of the exhibit, local newspapers had made no mention of the event.[28] By contrast, the Provincial Conference of Architects in 1936 was clearly designed to drive planners from their offices and into the streets, alleys, and outlying areas of the city, not so much to test the validity of how they *envisioned* the city (as Ivanitskii had done), but rather in order that they might *perform* power, democracy, and concern for common inhabitants.

Despite Zhukov's outraged objection to Boronin's slander, delegates ultimately performed the expected ritual, vowing to carefully study and critique Lengiprogor's work, as well as to bring information about Lengiprogor's plans to factory workers. Putting this promise into action a month later, the provincial union of architects sent its members to local factories and organized a mass press campaign. By mid-March, architects and engineers had made sixteen reports to large audiences of approximately one hundred factory workers, including all the major production sites in the city in their "missionary circuit." They also published an unusually high number of articles about architecture and city planning in the local press.[29]

Lengiprogor's To-the-People Campaign: Ritualized Democracy

When Solofnenko spoke at the 1936 Provincial Conference of Architects, he targeted a much broader audience than the architects in attendance. Seeking to make urban planning a collective endeavour, he appealed for broad societal involvement. His opening address, the extensive press coverage, and his large public display of hundreds of sketches and large maps (2 x 1½ metres) were carefully orchestrated to attract the entire urban public as well as architects elsewhere in the Soviet Union.[30] Solofnenko's speech invited the everyday inhabitant to view the exhibit and vote for one of the two featured designs for Soviet Square, which could be viewed through the windows of the building that hosted the exhibit.[31] He also welcomed general feedback, emphasizing that suggestion boxes would be made available.[32]

Helping to engage the entire population, the local Party organization marched 350 Komsomol youths from Gorky's Stalin District to the exhibit.[33] The press, without which no such public campaign could be orchestrated, joined in, with the newspaper *Gor'kovskii rabochii* launching two new regular columns: "The Future of Our City" and "Let's Discuss the City Plan."[34] The first column offered inspirational descriptions of the future city, whereas the latter delivered scientific and technical information about the plan, printing specialists' debates over the plan's more controversial elements.

Through such extensive coverage, the public could follow all the twists and turns of the planning process. Solofnenko's opening exhibit, for instance, featured the pragmatic and radical variants of the general city plan (on which no decision had yet been made), as well as draft designs for various municipal buildings and facilities, all described in great detail.[35] Had they read carefully, residents not only would have learned about Lengiprogor's plans to construct a lengthy ensemble along the Oka River, but they also would have discovered the breadth of opposition to this plan from local engineers. Had they wished, they could have participated, vicariously, in debates over tearing down the eastern kremlin wall in order to make Lengiprogor's riverside ensemble visible from Soviet Square.[36] They might have followed a similar debate over the placement of the city's Gorky and Minin monuments.[37] To those with literacy as well as the time and desire to peruse the newspapers, the press debate offered insight into specialists' struggles to define the city's future, while making their direct or vicarious involvement in the planning process possible.

Eager to foster popular interest, the press covered all planning-related issues, even those certain to arouse popular anger and opposition. Inviting readers to comment, specialists discussed residential housing, particularly the need for such practical and aesthetic improvements as added storage space, balconies, improved modern conveniences, finished interiors, bright and stuccoed exteriors, larger windows, larger rooms, and more.[38] Risking more controversy, planners also published their proposal to tear down a large swath of recently built low-rise housing in Sormovo. City council members and planners, led by Solofnenko, bravely took this portion of their exhibit directly to Sormovo, comment books in hand. There, they arranged a public meeting with workers to explain the logic behind their controversial choice.[39] Even the touchy matter of incomplete melioration plans received thorough coverage.[40]

Newspapers also featured letters and articles that represented the voice of the everyday urban inhabitant. One writer questioned the wisdom of building five bridges over the Oka River, proposing that at least one of them be replaced by a ferry.[41] Another lobbied for cable radio, arguing that radio antennas would deface the city.[42] Even though both authors may have been "insiders," possibly figures of some stature in Party or state institutions, their tone was simple, even populist.

Such letters raised the question of the city's tram elevator, whose possible fate elicited wide concern. Until 1928, the elevator had provided residents with mechanized transportation up the steep slope from the river to Soviet Square, the high point of the city. Citing falling rates of public use, the Trust for Mechanical Transportation had ceased to run the elevator, much to the chagrin of its remaining users.[43] Taking advantage of Lengiprogor's public discussion of the plan, these residents lobbied to have the elevator restored, or at least for the construction of an escalator in its place.[44] When Lengiprogor then promised to restore the elevator, the team conveniently appeared to be heeding popular opinion.[45] Of course, the letter requesting that the elevator be restored might have been placed in the newspaper by Lengiprogor itself, setting the stage for Lengiprogor's concession to public opinion. But contrived or not, Lengiprogor clearly wanted to communicate responsiveness.

The campaign made citizen feedback a controlled but genuine principle of design long before public consultation became standard practice in the West. Even Soviet scholars are likely to associate such consultation with the Brezhnev era, not the Stalinist period.[46] Yet, in the City of Gorky in the 1930s, planners repeatedly welcomed public commentary, assuring the public that its advice was heard and valued, making a direct impact on the plan. Sustaining this image, in 1938, Chief City Architect A.G. Dzhorogov – who was responsible for reviewing and implementing Lengiprogor' work – publicly solicited letters and comments from everyday residents, stressing that these would be valued by the city planning department.[47] Similarly, in drafting plans for a Pioneer Palace (a clubhouse for children ages 9 to 14), the architect in charge opted to invite the building's future consumers, the city's children, to express their wishes. The published responses were then printed, turning the Pioneer Palace into the symbolic embodiment of collective dream, a means of co-opting and directing the realm of childhood fantasy.[48]

Such published debate and discussion opened the message of Soviet propaganda in a structural sense. According to most reports, in the 1930s, Soviet media pummelled the Soviet population with endless messages, using everything from Party meetings and newspapers to the radio speakers located on main city squares.[49] Such media represented what Marshall McLuhan would have called "hot media," for it showered a closed, finished message on listeners. By contrast, Lengiprogor's exhibit was what McLuhan would label "cool media," for it bore a message that remained open and unfinished. Everyday city inhabitants were invited to fill in the missing portions of plans and designs for themselves.[50] At least in structure, then, Lengiprogor's media campaign had a dialogic component.[51]

Although such calls for public feedback legitimized popular voice, popular viewpoints had limited impact on the city plan. Lengiprogor's iconographic plan served the needs of state. Consultation did not alter this fact, but rather served as a mechanism for educating the public and shaping popular perception of the Soviet city.[52] As a veteran member of the city planning department said, "The people need to be taught what to desire."[53] Scripting popular acceptance of their work, planners often ended their consultation sessions with the ritual of vow taking, whereby citizens in attendance publicly committed themselves to supporting Lengiprogor. Lengiprogor even elicited such vows from workers in Sormovo, to whom – as noted earlier – planners presented a controversial plan to tear down a large swath of Sormovo's low-rise housing.[54] As with the preliminary discussions of the 1936 Stalin Constitution, the comments and vows of ordinary citizens served as welcome symbols of Soviet democracy, but did not alter the nature of the state's plans or documents.[55] Their involvement consisted of ritualized participation – real, but controlled.[56]

To elide the contradiction between the top-down nature of planners' work and the bottom-up power symbolized by planners' consultation with the general public, planners draped themselves in the robes of Stalin's authority. Assisting Stalin in his efforts to cultivate popular identification with the state and with himself, as its personification, Lengiprogor's team celebrated the cityscape as a manifestation of Stalinist care (*Stalinskaia zabota*). Thus, although Stalin himself was not directly involved in planning the city, both Lengiprogor's plan and city buildings came to play a central role in the Soviet "economy of the gift," whereby all Soviet citizens were indebted to the great leader for his supposed generosity, wisdom, and virtue, as represented by the new plan and by the city's new edifices.[57] Exploiting this concept, architects described their city as a medium of "Stalinist care."[58] In the words of the city's chief architect, "the Stalinist principle of love for the human being ... [marked the foundation of] ... truly human (*chelovecheskaia*) architecture."[59] By acting as Stalin-like father figures who cared about Soviet workers, architects could suggest that fatherly wisdom, not academic arrogance, inspired their decision to reject many of the wishes that ordinary citizens voiced.

The Terror of the People

As elsewhere in the Soviet Union, however, the campaign for greater democracy and openness served as the backdrop to – and sometimes the source of – terror.[60] Even as Lengiprogor orchestrated a public discussion of its work, Party purges, police sweeps, gatherings dedicated to self-criticism and denunciation, and the ritualized mass condemnation of putative enemies dominated political, professional, and social life. Thousands of innocent citizens were arrested, summarily tried, and either executed or sent to camps and prisons.[61] Most architects escaped purge, but not all. Mikhail A. Okhitovich, a prominent Soviet architect, suffered arrest in 1935, followed by incarceration until his death in 1937.

Architects in the City of Gorky keenly felt threatened. Well aware of his colleagues' fears, Gleb V. Greiber (an engineer, Party member, and outspoken critic of Lengiprogor) reiterated Boronin's earlier promise of security for service. He assured his planning colleagues in Gorky that the Soviet state would not punish specialists for their earlier political and aesthetic errors if they served the state faithfully.[62] Such words did not drive away all fear, of course. Local architects expressed particular frustration with the state's contradictory demand that they be "close to the people" and yet also assert their authority as architects over the cityscape, something that antagonized construction crews, for instance. Planners' job was fraught with danger, for their work involved the imposition of rules, regulations, and restrictions. Many argued that they could not be both democratic and authoritative at the same time.

Although designed to manage popular sentiment, Lengiprogor's consultation campaign in many ways threatened to augment experts' risk of being assaulted from below.[63] That the consultation campaign doubled as a mechanism for the intra-elite exchange of ideas furthered this risk. On one hand, broad public discussion ensured that architects did not "stew in their own juice," as architect Iosif A. Kashnikov noted.[64] On the other hand, by combining criticism (i.e., critique from below) with self-criticism (i.e., disputation within the elite), the consultation campaign brought questions of "ideological validity" and "social awareness" into what otherwise might have been purely scientific disputes, waged in the manner of Ivanitskii's showdown with the Scientific-Technical Council in 1932. This enabled citizens' complaints to become fodder in the arsenal of professional battles for power and prestige. Any citizen could deploy the language of Stalinist love or democratic voice for purposes unforeseen by professionals. As with the mock show trials of the 1920s, although the form of Lengiprogor's theatre of consultation was fixed, its final outcome was not. Intra-elite discussion, particularly within the context of mass consultation, could at any time derail Lengiprogor's plans.[65]

To their credit, architectural and planning professionals in Gorky did not permit the ritual of criticism and self-criticism, which defined their consultation campaign, to spin out of control. Although they suffered the interpersonal squabbles typical of most workplaces, the public presentation of their authority remained intact. They behaved as a body of experts unified by authority and knowledge, no matter what their professional disagreements might be. Thus, when critiquing Lengiprogor's plans in the press, experts carefully maintained a coolly scientific tone, no matter what the personal commitments or frustrations fuelling their commentary. Although they spoke frankly about the plan's weaknesses, particularly behind closed doors, they did not conflate decisions to which they objected with "wrecking" (*vreditel'stvo*).[66] Showing a similar interest in harmony, not conflict, the younger generation of architects did not treat the consultation campaign, which played out against the backdrop of purge and terror, as an opportune moment in which to denounce their superiors, thus advancing their own careers.

Even more impressive is the fact that provincial architects and Lengiprogor's planners did not act as cowed, passive figures, but rather wielded state demands, including the promise of honour and privilege, to their own advantage. In the fret-filled purge year of 1937, the provincial union boldly petitioned for more professional facilities, including a House of Architects, a library, and a conference hall, as well as a number of dachas for the purpose of rest and relaxation.[67] Acting with still greater boldness, when the state ordered them to discuss ways in which to foster architectural Stakhanovism, they twisted the discussion around, so that it became a forum for airing their grievances over wages and working conditions.[68] Observing such claims to entitlement, not to mention some architects' penchant for lavish designs, a visiting German architect, Hans Blumenfeld, dubbed the entire group "a nest of the nobility," utterly removed from the concerns of the working class.[69]

Similar attitudes were on display in the Union of Soviet Architects in Moscow, although architects in that city did not escape the violence so typical of the Great Purges. Even as Mikhail Okhitovich suffered denunciation, purge, and execution, many of his peers fought back. Troubled by the ferocity of the 1935 attack on Okhitovich, a vocal contingent of union members condemned the growing spiral of denunciation and purge. Many demanded that heated rhetoric be toned down, lest unfair accusations embroil other union members. Meanwhile, still others continued to uphold much-maligned constructivist ideas of design, laughing at those who denounced such ideas as counterrevolutionary. Genuine terror did not preclude acts of bravery.[70]

In such boldness, one can find early hints of what Vera Dunham dubbed the postwar "big deal," a compact between professionals and the state, whereby professionals offered faithful service in return for material privilege and security. The roots of this deal can also be traced to Boronin's speech at the Conference of Provincial Architects, where he promised noble privilege in return for loyal service.[71] As noted elsewhere, by the late 1930s, the media's treatment of engineers and planners had improved; they were no longer reviled as "bourgeois specialists."[72] In all of this, planners' proactive stance in the 1930s merits particular attention, for planners and architects turned an era of rituals and promises – Boronin's speech, the consultation campaign, and the conflation of architecture with "Stalinist care" – into a set of demands. Although most scholars attribute such demands for greater professional and personal freedom after the Second World War to the experience of war itself, its real roots lie here – in this mixture of threats, promises, and professional assertiveness.[73]

The Dangers of Ritualized Democracy: The Kokushkin Affair

Despite architects' bold assertion of their rights, they were not released from the confines of state service or Stalinist ritual, for their authority no longer rested on scientific objectivity and independence. Instead, their authority came to rest on demonstrative compliance with state dictates, including their performance of the delicate and sensitive ritual of consultation, with all its attendant risks. Although, for the most part, local architects appear to have fared well, escaping purges from within their own ranks, their consultation campaign nonetheless empowered at least one protestor, who took Lengiprogor's ritualized "people power" quite seriously.

This challenge to Lengiprogor hailed from the director of construction at the Park of Culture and Rest in Sormovo. Donning the mantle of popular will, Director Ia. Kokushkin submitted a letter of protest to the Sormovo district paper, *Krasnyi Sormovich*. In it, he lampooned Lengiprogor for its failure to consult with local society, the very thing that Lengiprogor had just made a "splashy" show of doing. To add insult to injury, Director Kokushkin charged planners with "formalism," an accusation that he reserved for state figures who applied policies indiscriminately, without proper consideration for the intricacies of a specific time and place.[74] In Kokushkin's view, in presenting the urban landscape as both Stalin's gift and as the people's right, Lenigiprogor had divested itself of the right to wield scientific authority without actively hearkening to local viewpoints. And so, Kokushkin's free voice escaped the confines of ritual, both fulfilling and confusing Solofnenko's carefully crafted transcript of power.

Kokushkin's outrage was sparked by the top-down thrust of Lengiprogor's planning work, which displayed total ignorance of the geography and culture of Sormovo. Loathe to use the city's notoriously unreliable transportation system, especially for a lengthy trip to an outlying region, Lengiprogor's members tended to plan Sormovo from afar. In its draft plan of 1936, Lengiprogor erroneously described Sormovo as a geographically flat and culturally sleepy (*spokoinyi*) region with a small number of low-rise homes situated on large, spacious lots – quite an error, given that the highly industrialized District of Sormovo had some of the densest and most overcrowded housing in the city.[75] When the city planning department noted the error, Lengiprogor members angrily retorted that they had been misled by reports that the landscape of Sormovo would not pose a challenge for planners.[76] They did not mend their ways, however.

In the radical variant of the general city plan, Lengiprogor's planning team proposed to impose a rectilinear transportation network on the Sormovo District, although a more fluid structure would have better suited its topography and existing infrastructure. Viewing linearity as a "civilized" and "developed" aesthetic, something apparently required for this working class region, Lengiprogor aimed to lay wide boulevards directly from Sormovo to nearby city districts, lining all major roads – in "compact plan style" – with multi-storey housing that would mask the boggy, undeveloped patches that divided Sormovo from the rest of the city. The new roads would come at the expense of existing "irregular" roadways, which were to be decommissioned, along with the housing and infrastructure that ran alongside.[77]

Although he knew nothing of Lengiprogor's faulty data about Sormovo, Kokushkin had no doubt that Lengiprogor's proposal to realign district roads would wreak havoc on local development. Being personally acquainted with local officials, he knew that the plan would bring all new construction in this underserviced but burgeoning region to a halt, as local officials declined to fund new housing along existing roads, simply because these were destined for obsolescence. Had Lengiprogor prioritized the construction of new roads, Kokushkin might have been calmed, but the general city plan was to be realized within a twenty-five year time frame. No new roads for Sormovo were proposed in the immediate future. For the people of Sormovo, that would admittedly be quite some time in which to await new roads and homes.[78]

Kokushkin's outburst represented the resistance of the local to abstract concepts of social identity developed elsewhere. Devoted to his working-class district, he had spent most of his adult career seeking a better life for the people of Sormovo. He had fought for a House of Culture and lobbied for the expansion of the Park of Culture and Rest. Now, he was combatting Lengiprogor's designs.[79] In this, Kokushkin was guided by a place-shaped sense of moral imperative. Determined to defend Sormovo against arbitrary policies formulated elsewhere, Kokushkin exploited the mechanism of consultation, upstaging Solofnenko in his own performance. In this new scenario, Kokushkin, not Solofnenko, stepped forth as the agent of popular will.

Recognizing the danger posed by Kokushkin's news article, Solofnenko immediately published a refutation in the main city newspaper, *Gor'kovskii rabochii*. Carefully welcoming Kokushkin's activism, Solofnenko shrewdly portrayed Kokushkin as a misguided enthusiast. Underscoring Lengiprogor's "diligent" research and putative "concern" for local need, he nonetheless asserted the necessity of making the region more regular and legible (*stroinaia i iasnaia*). Arguing that the plan would preserve "valuable" buildings (however "valuable" might be defined), he warned that Kokushkin's alarmism threatened to confuse (*zavodit' v zabluzhdenie*) local workers. Given the twenty-five year time frame in which the general city plan was to be executed, he assured readers, temporary repairs to existing homes and infrastructure would continue, as would the construction of low-rise, "temporary" homes.

His forceful response notwithstanding, Solofnenko's charade of popular support for his work had been exposed. Bereft of Stalin's mantle of "care," Solofnenko proudly placed himself on the high ground of "unassailable" scientific authority. In warning that Kokushkin threatened to mislead Sormovo's workers, he also drew attention to Kokushkin's lack of scientific expertise, asserting the superiority of scientific over local knowledge. Grasping for higher validation of some sort, Solofnenko also reported that the Russian Commissariat of the Municipal Economy had already approved Lengiprogor's plan for the region, meaning that Kokushkin's appeal was not only time-barred, but was somehow subversive, opposing state-sanctioned policy.[80]

Kokushkin was not so easily put off. With encouragement from power-ful figures in the local and national planning community, he pursued his cause.[81] Several specialists in the city planning department covertly supported Kokushkin's mini-campaign – not in the press, but in the backrooms of city planning offices. These individuals – including Gleb V. Greiber and Nikolai V. Malakhov – were long-standing critics of Len-giprogor's radical plan, not to mention enduring adherents of Ivanitskii's pragmatism. They embraced Kokushkin's stubborn protest as a public relations wedge, something with which they might pry open the door to a realistic, common sense approach to urban design. Second and third reviews of Lengiprogor's proposals resulted.[82] As one of these reviewers, Ivanitskii also backed Kokushkin. In his unpublished 1937 review of Len-giprogor's work, Ivanitskii argued that Kokushkin's objections merited serious reconsideration of Lengiprogor's plan.[83]

Such opportunism on the part of Ivanitskii and his supporters, no less than Solofnenko's harsh retort, testifies to fact that campaigns of the sort orchestrated by Lengiprogor rendered bottom-up power legitimate, not just legitimizing. Although Kokushkin's protest did not change the outcome of the city plan, it did provoke serious discussion. Neither Kokushkin nor his supporters suffered personal, professional, or mate-rial penalty for their involvement in this affair, for their actions were con-sidered to be acceptable, given the politics of the era. At the same time, however, the episode by no means stripped Solofnenko of authority or security. Although the ritual of consultation slipped out of his control, the decision of the Russian Commissariat of the Municipal Economy nicely resolved the dispute, averting negative consequences.

The Terror of Completion: Hidden Transcripts

Despite Kokushkin's challenge, Lengiprogor appeared to make confi-dent, unbroken strides towards the completion of the general city plan. As already noted, on 21 March 1936, the Russian Commissariat of the Municipal Economy approved the radical, iconographic variant of the draft city plan, making it the official foundation for the coming general city plan.[84] That summer, the Russian Council of People's Commissars placed its stamp of approval on the same plan, despite its excessively ambi-tious Oka-centred aesthetic and its radical plan for left bank roads and topography.[85] Less than a year later, in April 1937, Lengiprogor finished its first complete draft, which it submitted to expert and local review. By August 1937, the submitted plan won the approval of the Expert Council of the Russian Commissariat of the Municipal Economy.[86] Determined to preserve its reserve lands, which Lengiprogor proposed to turn into a waterfront park, the Gorky Automobile Factory protested. But, for the moment, even this clause in the general city plan held fast.[87]

Further progress was delayed by terror and purge. In June 1938, former city council president Radion S. Semenov was arrested as an enemy of the people and sentenced to execution, effected a month later. Although he had been transferred to the Stalingrad Provincial Executive Committee a year prior, the news sobered and alarmed the city council, which resolved to review the city plan, searching for evidence of Semenov's "wrecking."[88] Worried about the involvement of now- or soon-to-be-purged officials in the planning process, council members revisited questions that the 1936 approval of the radical variant had supposedly resolved, such as the potential for left bank flooding and the social and economic cost of redirecting left bank streets. In the fret-filled years of 1937–1938, the picture sketched by Lengiprogor's radical/iconographic plan no longer seemed pretty, but dark and threatening, a potential justification for their denunciation and purge, despite the plan's iconographic status. As one Party official noted with alarm, Gorky was a city of small crude homes (*izbushki*), a place without the resources needed to realize Lengiprogor's plan.[89]

Facing peril, local government bodies found themselves performing a high-wire balancing act, whereby they held an unapproved and potentially problematic city plan in one hand and Moscow's repeated demands for its approval in the other. Uncertain as to how Stalin might interpret the "socialist script," whose meaning and thrust now seemed unclear, local politicians launched the next act of local socialism by borrowing a tactic from the Scientific-Technical Council. Not unlike the Council in 1932, they declared that the plan merited yet another round of study. And so, although the plan passed muster with the Expert Council of the Russian Commissariat of the Municipal Economy in August 1937, city officials engaged in what Soviet authorities called *ochkovtiratel'stvo* – a term usually translated as "quackery," although here a less conventional and more literal translation, "eyeglass wiping," applies. Afraid to either approve or disapprove of the general city plan, local city officials opted to stand aside, rub their eyeglasses, and insist that they needed further time to examine "the issue," whatever it might be, yet one more time.[90]

Frustrated by such inaction, central officials repeatedly demanded that "eyeglass wiping" cease. In November 1937, the Main Architecture and Planning Administration (GlavAPU) of the Russian Federation ordered local authorities to approve Lengiprogor's plan. Next, the Central Committee of the Communist Party ordered the Russian Commissariat of the Municipal Economy to "facilitate" the city's review.[91] But although local leaders promised to finish their review in May 1938, they further stalled until February 1939.[92] Perhaps it mattered little, for the recipient organization (the College of the Russian Commissariat of the Municipal Economy) then delayed approval by another year, so that Lengiprogor's plan did not reach the Russian Council of People's Commissars until 7 October 1940.[93]

At this point, Lengiprogor's earlier shows of productivity, particularly its surfeit of visuals, returned to haunt officials.[94] Local experts had objected to the time squandered on such illustrative materials, but Lengiprogor had ignored such complaints, catering to the city council's explicit demand for sketches.[95] As a result, Lengiprogor produced a large surfeit of planning materials. Now, as the city council stonewalled, demanding repeat reviews and reports, the overall volume of planning materials increased. Every document ever written had to be reviewed, and the number of documents continued to grow. Reluctant to ship a truck load of materials, including excess visuals, to the capital for review, in 1937 city officials asked officials from the Russian Commissariat of the Municipal Economy to verify the materials on site, in Gorky.[96] This cumbersome excess offered only one potential benefit – namely, to ensure that the search for "wrecking" would take many, many months, permitting further delay.

Pictures, performances, and eyeglass wiping – all sought to carve out a modicum of security for the elite, often at the expense of the sort of political and administrative efficiencies that ought to have been the source of administrative power. Out of fear, city officials reneged on their earlier commitment to efficiencies of time, as imposed on Ivanitskii. Although state agents and therefore extensions of Stalin's power, they subverted the rituals of power from within – a classic tactic of the weak.[97] They engaged in the very "double dealing," or subversion, that the purges were supposed to uproot.[98] They, like planners, opted to perform concern for the people's needs, as embodied in the plan. But their act was driven, for the most part, by fears for their own security.

Conclusion: Breaking the Fourth Wall

Although the "pretty picture" qualities of the iconographic plan made it impractical, injecting fear into the hearts of the city's elite, the most experienced of the city's planners confidently advocated approval by explaining that plans were always made and unmade, changed by events beyond anyone's control. As one highly annoyed member of the Gorky city planning department said in 1938, at the height of endless fear-inspired reviews, "Comrades, this is the seventeenth time I am hearing about the general plan ... Now, we need to confirm her or not confirm her ... Life will introduce its own alterations."[99] Solofnenko, too, argued for approval, suggesting that any necessary alterations could be made later, as detailed plans were drawn up. Both men recognized that the city plan was something malleable and unstable, produced and affirmed for the pleasure of others, but realized through and at locals' discretion.

Indeed, the power to effect any plan, approved or not, would derive in no small part from the rituals enacted on an iconographic stage. Despite the gap between the iconographic image and the realities of planning, iconographic planning established the city as an extension of the sacralized space of Moscow, intricately identified with Stalin's charisma. Planning, too, served as an extension of Stalinist power – not only insofar as all new construction was attributed to Stalin's wise rule, but also insofar as architects wrapped themselves in Stalin's populist mantle, presenting themselves and their work as manifestations of his "care."

As ritual, this set performance created and yet demanded interaction with the audience, breaching the fourth wall of the city stage. Inseparable from claims to democracy or Stalinist care, planners' performance *was* the space of ideal socialism, a future of monumental progress and people power. This imaginary expanse inspired Kokushkin's activism and, perhaps, even Ivanitskii's hope that Kokushkin would succeed. It certainly lay at the heart of vows and rituals in which the urban public became a central figure in city planning, representing an imagined and co-opted democratic voice. When this voice threatened planners' security, it was readily silenced, as Solofnenko's response to Kokushkin so aptly proved. Pushing aside the drama of consultation, Solofnenko temporarily placed the buffer of scientific authority between himself and his accuser, closing the fourth wall as a way to maintain his control over the stage.

That Solofnenko could survive purge, even Kokushkin's assault, testifies to his savvy ability to manage Stalinist ritual. By forcing planners onto the stage, the iconographic not only rendered professionals vulnerable to popular criticism and assault, but also gave them room in which to manoeuvre, so that their scientific knowledge might be occasional shelter, but never a trap. Seeking to bolster his authority, Solofnenko readily crafted a performance that mixed competing languages of legitimacy, including those of scientific authority, Stalinist care, and people power.[100] Enacting these, he deftly deployed ritualized consultation as a way to incorporate and yet control popular desire. Although Kokushkin's fury eluded such control, Solofnenko's urban plan nonetheless withstood the attack. His performance, both scientific and political (and arguably more political than scientific), garnered power.

Chapter Six

A City That Builds Itself:
The Limits of Technocracy

The streets are our brushes. The squares our palettes.

Vladimir Mayakovsky, "Prikaz po armii iskusstva"[1]

Architects must take responsibility for the upbringing of the troubled children that they bring into being, because those to whom they entrust their "children" tend to cripple and deform them.

Construction control officer, City of Gorky, 1938[2]

As Nikolai Alekseevich Solofnenko took refuge in the shadows cast by the bright light of Stalin's loving care, he nonetheless fully recognized the mythologies perpetuated by both plan and consultation. Like engineer Greiber, Solofnenko knew that his radical plan was nothing more than a "pretty picture," or monumental dream. Contracting a Faustian pact with Stalinist leaders, he had relinquished his right, as a scientist, to define the city's aesthetic and form. Although he retained prestige and authority as an expert, he derived his security and status from his role as emissary of the myths of Stalin's care, democratic voice, and the Socialist Realist city of the future.

Although many members of the city planning department resented Lengiprogor's plan, which would be impossible to achieve and for whose realization they, not Lengiprogor, would answer, they nonetheless had a vested interest in the plan's approval. In their opinion, even an iconographic plan would be invaluable once made official, for it would bear the imprimatur of the highest agencies in the Soviet state. Too often, local city planners lamented, local industry and construction trusts dismissed existing zoning by-laws, which were devised to make short-term growth conform to the city's incomplete and tentative plan, as mere "hypotheses."[3] To planners' chagrin, this permitted "spontaneous" (*samotekom*) growth, as the city threatened to "build itself" (*zakonchit' svoiu stroiku*) without any supervisory restraint from planners.[4]

Visions of an approved plan played a central role in planners' distinctly modernist fantasy of total visual legibility, objectivity, and authority. As a techno-social mechanism, a "high-quality plan" backed by the Soviet state promised to serve as a self-regulating guide to local development.[5] Such a plan would put an end to constant battles for authority over the cityscape, thought planners. By modifying its fine details, they hoped to remake the city without having to directly engage the volatile and often chaotic world of urban construction. An approved plan, they surmised, would bring construction of a faulty, illegal, or irregular nature to a permanent end.

In embracing the plan as the solution to all the ills of urban development, these city planners conveniently denied nagging problems that would have made any plan, no matter at what level it was affirmed, impossible to enforce. A great deal of responsibility for construction and housing had been handed to individuals and industries whose activities eluded close state supervision.[6] Poorly trained architects, underskilled foremen, and a Party apparatus that showed scant regard for the state regulatory system also undermined the efforts of the city planning department.[7] Even after Soviet administration improved in the late 1940s, local industry continued to ignore the regulations of the city planning department.[8]

Historical Mythologies: Institutions and Inoperability

In seeking to make sense of disarray in urban construction, planners tended to emphasize the putative "backwardness" of Soviet city planning, as defined by the lack of planning agencies and experts, not to mention a plan itself. Although this narrative has shaped much subsequent scholarship on the matter, this explanation was ironic, for Soviet modernization produced the very dysfunction – or backwardness – that planners proposed to overcome through the further application of state power.[9] Shortages emerged in the course of rapid growth, often thanks to purges and policies that hindered or reduced the former educated class. Although the Soviet state admittedly did suffer from a paucity of maps, data, researchers, and effective institutions of oversight, backwardness as an explanation conveniently proposed to solve all the dysfunctions

of the Soviet system through a further application of state-led development, with all its attendant challenges.

The very concept of backwardness posed part of the problem – not
because institutional development was not required (it was), but because
it overlooked countervailing forces in Soviet society. The term "backwardness" implied an absence that could be filled, ideally by the Soviet
state with planners at its side. As a concept, backwardness played a role in
denying the fragmented and highly personal nature of state operations.
Much of the disorder that planners viewed as "backwardness" resulted
from the state's modus operandi. The further application of state power
would solve nothing.[10] Planners did not wish to acknowledge such truths,
however, for their own power and legitimacy depended on belief in the
Soviet state's ability to step forward as the agent of modernization.

Such rhetoric about "backwardness" unfortunately distracted from the
striking number of agencies and individuals that had the official power
to regulate urban development. By 1934, the City of Gorky had its own
city planning department, known as the Architecture and Planning
Administration (APU), as well as a chief city architect.[11] The APU not
only inspected and critiqued the work of Lengiprogor, but also monitored all urban construction, ensuring that it conformed to the outlines
of Lengiprogor's draft plans, to which municipal decree granted legal
force. Because the reception of land, funds, and construction materials required a permit from the city council's planning department, the
city council had the legal and administrative power to curb construction
that did not conform to the city plan, even before the plan was made
official.[12] Even institutions directly subordinate to ministries in Moscow
rather than to local agencies had to comply. Architects, too, received
orders to sustain municipal authority by refusing contracts to produce
projects for non-compliant associations.[13] The legal codes and institutions required to assert power over urban growth existed.

What these institutions lacked was the power to implement and
enforce these laws. Economic shortfalls, a lack of administrative technologies such as maps, in-fighting and weak organization, and general
disregard for by-laws and planning regulations undermined their work.
Such problems would persist for decades, long after the infrastructure
for urban planning was well established. No plan and no institution
could operate effectively without the cooperation of the entire Soviet
governing apparatus.

The most persistent and pressing problem that city planners confronted was the shortage of funds, without which their legal authority

came to naught. APU financing depended on the good will of a cash-strapped city council, whose members catered to the needs of powerful and wealthy local industries, often at the expense of their own planning department.[14] Reluctant to expend scarce resources on regulatory bodies, in 1936 the city council imposed a self-financing regime on the APU. Compelling the APU to charge fees to its clients ideally would have extracted funding from industry, an APU client that tended not to pay planning-related taxes. But, charging fees merely antagonized the agencies that relied on APU services, while failing to generate sufficient revenue.[15] Unrelenting, in 1937 the city council threatened to augment APU duties by assigning to it the task of detailed planning (i.e., the final stage of planning, following the approval of a general city plan). Luckily, Lengiprogor insisted on its right to this contract, as agreed when it negotiated its initial planning contract in 1935. In response to this turn of events, however, the city council further reduced the APU budget.[16]

The APU's attempt at self-financing floundered in part because of the seasonal nature of its work. Each spring, the planning department faced a deluge of requests for lot designations, projects, and permits. According to Soviet law (i.e., a joint decree of the Central Committee and the Council of People's Commissars), construction trusts were supposed to submit their list of approved projects to city planning agencies like the APU at least one year prior to construction. Yet, most trusts persisted in submitting last-minute requests, and political pressure compelled the APU to fulfil all of these.[17] Long days and sleepless nights followed, as planning department staff rushed to complete orders for building projects.[18] Unfortunately, such work distracted the APU from meeting its other responsibilities, such as supervising bodies to whom some aspect of planning work had been contracted, including Ivanitskii's Mosgiprogor and Solofnenko's Lengiprogor.[19]

Always overworked, the APU regularly sought to delegate a large portion of its duties to subsidiary bodies. In 1935, authorities created Gorproekt, which assumed the APU's responsibility for drafting projects for residential construction.[20] They also established the Expert Architectural Council (EAS), which scrutinized all projects for possible technical and aesthetic flaws.[21] In addition, in 1935, authorities temporarily delegated responsibility for lot designations to district (*raion*) governments. This latter effort failed, as district authorities were deficient in funds and staff. Only Sormovo successfully dispatched its flood of applications, likely by neglecting to carefully oversee the entire process – something that may explain Lengiprogor's later concern about an unusually high concentration of "unplanned" development in that region.[22]

Such problems were exacerbated by a lack of essential tools and equipment, which augmented the workload of the city's limited personnel. In Gorky, no maps suitable for accurately assessing or documenting lot designations existed – something typical of all Soviet cities, but nonetheless intolerable.[23] Relying on outdated maps to the scale of one *verst per diem*, surveyors produced lot designations that were often rough and imprecise.[24] Buildings lay where city maps indicated there should be empty space, and empty space lay where buildings should have stood.[25] Even in 1938, after Lengiprogor completed the general city plan, the city planning department lacked up-to-date geodesic, topographical, climate, and detailed city maps.[26] The few in their possession were not only outdated, but difficult to access, being stored in Nativity Church, a too-small facility located far from planning offices.[27] No wonder that neither the city council nor Lengiprogor wanted responsibility for lot designations![28]

Forced to collaborate in determining what lots could be set aside for construction each year, the planning department and Lengiprogor would send entire teams of experts to evaluate and designate each potential building site. Lacking suitable maps, team members quickly drew ad hoc maps and descriptions.[29] If they were fortunate, they and the builders understood one another's description of the lot, so that the building was erected on the appropriate location. If they were unlucky, as was often the case, the building was positioned incorrectly.[30] Of course, without proper surveys and maps, who could blame builders for transgressing the boundaries of the lot?

These technical problems were exacerbated by the inadequate number of well-trained, experienced staff in the city's design institutions, Kraiproekt and Gorproekt. Both agencies had recruited a number of recent graduates from Soviet technical schools, where they had received a narrow, practical education, nothing like the broad aesthetic and theoretical training of the 1920s. Soviet schools suffered from an excess of underprepared entrants, to whom they offered a too limited set of skills.[31] Of the 114 staff members of Kraiproekt, only seventeen had architectural education, and only three of these had both architectural education and significant experience. In Gorproekt, there were twelve professional architects, but only three had the training and experience required to oversee the production of an architectural project.[32]

Recognizing the need for training, which junior architects demanded, both organizations arranged for exhibits of staff members' designs, work-place competitions, collective criticism, and excursions to professional institutions in Moscow, as well as courses in drawing, painting, construction, geometry, and foreign languages. None of this transformed junior, poorly trained team members into highly capable professionals. Junior staff members required greater oversight and on-site training, which unfortunately their superiors had too little time to offer.[33]

Poor supervision of junior staff resulted in oft-faulty design projects. Because new Soviet graduates needed supervision, Gorproekt established three design studios, each with a single architect in charge. This presiding architect answered for the quality of the studio's work, earning the title of "project author," although subordinates within the studio completed final drawings and cost projections. The system was designed to ensure that senior architects reviewed the work of junior staffers, but it proved slow. Senior architects frequently overlooked errors in their subordinates' work, partly because they desperately tried to avoid visiting Gorproekt's overcrowded, noisy offices.[34] There, ninety staff members squeezed into a mere 300 square metres of space, leaving insufficient room for desks on which to lay out designs. The premises were humid, and the noise of the office (typewriters, calculator, abacus, and the chatter of clients) distracted from work. Gorproekt's senior members were later forbidden to work at home, but there is no evidence that this improved the quality of oversight.[35]

Kraiproekt likewise failed to provide adequate oversight and training to junior staff. Having established an assembly line for the production of architectural designs, this bureau assigned responsibility for a small element in each project to individual staff members. This system allowed junior draftsmen to become heroes of Stakhanovite productivity in their narrow sphere of work (e.g., in sketching), but it limited their knowledge of design as a whole, frustrating their ambition for greater knowledge and experience. They were, for all practical purposes, engaged in piecework, as carried out in an overcrowded and noisy space. This arrangement also made it difficult to trace the source of errors in a project, because dozens of signatures would cover the completed product, as each member of the team claimed "authorship" for one small portion of design.[36]

Meanwhile, compensation levels for architects remained all too low. In 1935 to 1936, pay rates would drop statewide by an average of 20 per cent. In 1936, many junior architects would prove unable to find any work at all. Those sent to the provinces often lacked lodgings, long after arriving at their destination. This upset junior architects, who responded by supporting their superiors, whose more powerful voices were more likely to win improved training, working conditions, and compensation for *all* local architects.[37]

All of these problems were in many ways by-products of Soviet modernization. Local planning bodies lacked skilled workers, funds, and maps largely because of the Soviet drive to build first and plan later. Poorly trained staffers were suffering the long-term impact of Soviet affirmative action policies for workers. They had been given a rapid, technically focused education in order that they might join the workforce promptly. As a result, they could fulfil only minor tasks in workplaces too harried to provide further training. Meanwhile, everyone involved in city planning suffered from deplorable working conditions, high stress, and low pay. Although such difficulties could be attributed to the need for skills, maps, and more planning institutions – all problems associated with "backwardness" – the challenges that planners faced cannot be reduced to the mere absence of development, for the very structure and nature of Soviet modernization further interfered with planners' regulatory work.

From Planning Politics to Red Tape

Although planners served as agents of Soviet power, the Soviet state tended to undermine planners' technologies of rule. Economic dysfunction, irrational pricing norms, and the weak enforcement of building codes – all of which could be attributed to some agency of the Soviet government – made effective construction control impossible to achieve. Attempts to effect oversight merely generated a surfeit of bureaucratic red tape, which was exacerbated by in-fighting within the planning community. The resulting bureaucratic morass spawned Party support for construction that flouted the planning department's procedures and regulations. Even the city council ignored planning codes.[38] More institutions and a finished city plan would never have solved these problems.

From the perspective of construction trusts, the red tape that bound their hands and delayed their projects almost always came from the Expert Architectural Council (EAS), more commonly referred to as "the Expert Council."[39] All construction projects in the city required this council's stamp of approval at three different stages of project development: first, after completing the proposal; second, after drafting technical designs; and third, after finishing cost projections.[40] To the chagrin of construction trusts and foremen, the Expert Council rarely met, and it tended to demand costly and time-consuming alterations to proposed projects. Alteration requests were issued so frequently that many felt that the Council's demands were arbitrary, serving no purpose beyond a display of watchfulness.[41]

The Expert Council's rulings admittedly did tend to be arbitrary, but this had nothing to do with the pursuit of vigilance, genuine or otherwise. Wracked by conflict between two of the city's project bodies, Gorproekt and Kraiproekt, the Expert Council's definition of quality design varied wildly, depending on which agency's representatives enjoyed numerical superiority on the Expert Council at the time. Kraiproekt, which produced industrial projects, tended to favour sleek, functionalist design. Being responsible for civic architecture, Gorproekt encouraged its architects to produce ornament-rich, monumental projects. This Gorproekt-Kraiproekt conflict was a microcosm of the Union-wide tension between architects, who dominated the world of planning in the 1930s, and engineers, who would come to dominate both planning and design in the post-Stalin period.[42] Engineers tended to be neo-constructivists, eager to defend modernist-style projects, whereas architects tended to defend expensive, ornament-rich construction.[43]

The indeterminacy of Socialist Realism as an aesthetic doctrine contributed to this tension. Although instructed to avoid both eclecticism (i.e., excessive historical quotation) and formalism (i.e., excessive modernist asymmetry and simplicity), architects and engineers lacked a clear indication as to what Soviet architecture ought to be. Arguing that the aesthetic and visual impact of the cityscape ought to take priority, Gorproekt's architects tended to dismiss Kraiproekt's work as "formalist." Architect Zhukov went so far as to argue that the architects serving on the Expert Council should be granted the power to veto any project with alleged aesthetic flaws.[44] Dominated by engineers of a neo-constructivist orientation, Kraiproekt's designers joined Alexander A. Vesnin (an eminent member of the avant-garde) in equating the promotion of beauty in architecture with reactionary politics. Engineer Gleb V. Greiber, the bureau's most ardent advocate, argued that proper engineering, not an excessively expensive aesthetic, should be the measure of a successful project.[45]

Such internal politicking did not bode well, as one agency frequently overturned the rulings of the other. Such gaming ensured that even standardized designs failed to win rapid approval from the Expert Council. Produced elsewhere and modified to meet city needs, standardized designs – at least in theory – required neither expert architects nor expert review. But standardized designs were not so simple to use: they required modification to suit the city's unique scale, soil, and climate. Such alterations raised highly involved technical and aesthetic questions, which would be discussed by members of the Expert Council. As one local architect (A.N. Tiupikov) warned, "Grief comes to those who come to the Expert Council with a modified version of a standard design."[46]

From the perspective of the city planning department, the Council's main flaw lay not in its production of red tape, but in its failure to prevent flawed construction projects from proceeding. Too few meetings and too many projects to review ensured a surfeit of errors. Meetings were held at the director's will, however regularly or irregularly that might be. When the Council met, therefore, it faced a daunting stack of projects to examine. To facilitate review, the director appointed an expert to comment on each project. These reviewers often lacked the technical knowledge required to properly critique the technical aspects of a design, and they often received inaccurate information.[47] Without the time and expertise required to carefully review submissions, let alone verify the information submitted, the Expert Council often approved faulty proposals.[48]

Because design agencies such as the Expert Council were prone to error, delay, in-fighting, and charging high fees, Soviet construction trusts typically accused them of "bureaucratism" and "formalism," after which they proceeded with construction, with or without the approval of the Expert Council.[49] Although illegal, working without official permits and designs was necessitated by the fact that successful construction had to begin in the early spring, with the hiring of labour and the purchasing of materials. Since approved designs were rarely available before mid-summer, Party officials actually encouraged builders to flout APU authority, even assisting in illegal recruitment and procurement activities.[50] Because of such Party support for unauthorized construction, state institutions refused to enforce planning regulations, too.[51] Thus, although law forbade the Central Bank from dispensing funds for unapproved designs, the Central Bank almost unfailingly funded such illegal construction projects. The city council tended to do the same.[52]

As a result of such activity, complained local planners, unauthorized construction spread like wild mushrooms after a rain.[53] In a documented case in Sverdlovsk District, hotels, schools, and residential buildings were built without technical documentation, cost projections, or sketches.[54] In Sormovo, in 1933, a housing commune under construction lacked plans for the front columns and roof. In Kanavino, child care facilities lacked plans for electricity and plumbing. Fighting unapproved building, the city planning department warned construction trusts that such unauthorized construction projects often contained serious defects.[55] But, their voice was hardly audible above the hammer-and-nail din of "progress."

The Politics of Scarcity

With regard to unauthorized construction, ineffective planning institutions bore only a portion of the guilt. Everywhere in the Soviet Union, Soviet institutions were asked to deliver housing and services as soon as possible, and with as few resources as possible. Shortages threatened to stall many projects, driving construction trusts and foremen to demonstrate innovativeness and "time-mindedness" by substituting cheap, readily available goods for costly or unattainable materials.[56] As the state's list of deficit (i.e., off-limit) materials grew, substitutions such as replacing wooden for steel roofs became unavoidable.[57]

Such supply shortages were worsened by the lack of transportation, particularly transportation for construction materials. Although the Province of Gorky enjoyed vast resources of wood, lime, and bricks, it did not have the means to prepare and deliver these materials to the sites where they were needed. For instance, the construction trust Soiuzstroi lacked the equipment with which to move heavy blocks from the cement factory to the construction site. Similarly, the supply organization Gorstroisnabsbyt could not obtain the railway cars required to move its goods. Even when the city council and provincial government intervened to make cars available, the trust had to wait for the spring thaw, so that goods unloaded from train cars could be shipped by boat.[58]

Local supplies of construction materials also proved inadequate, both in quality and in quantity. Many factories were hopelessly outdated, turning out brick and stone of irregular size and form, while local lumber was improperly sawn and dried, resulting in twisted, irregularly sized, and otherwise defective boards.[59] New city zoning laws exacerbated matters by banning industry from the city centre and other newly designated residential zones, resulting in the closure of several factories producing construction materials. As for Gorstroisnabsbyt, the local construction supply trust, it not only failed to meet local demand, but also proved unable to accurately track supplies or forecast future needs.[60]

Although the city council and local construction organizations repeatedly committed themselves to establishing new factories for the production of construction materials, they did not follow through on their

promises – in part, because the materials with which to build the factories were in short supply.[61] In July 1936, the city council presidium asked
Lengiprogor to reorganize the construction industry and promote the
creation of new construction facilities, but the ensuing years witnessed
only further complaints about the lack of factories producing bricks.
The issue was again raised in 1938, as part of discussions about implementing the general city plan, but no actual plans to build or upgrade
construction supply factories were made.[62]

Such deficits drove up the cost of materials, as Soviet institutions competed for scarce construction materials in a shadow market spawned by
the inefficiencies of the Soviet economic system.[63] Although technically a
centrally managed system, the Soviet economy often fell victim to political choices that defied strictly economic logic. The economy's resultant
irrationalities generated a host of informal market mechanisms, cobbled
together as a way to compensate for overall economic mismanagement.
Such mechanisms, including *blat* (connections), the *tolkach* (unoffi-
cial facilitator of exchange), and *shturmovshchina* (rushing to complete
work), further interfered with effective central control, as did overlapping administrative assignments and irrational pricing mechanisms.[64]

The resultant gap between normative state prices and the real, black
market price of goods wreaked havoc on planning bodies. According
to local estimates, shadow market prices in 1931 exceeded normative
prices by 20 per cent. When Soviet authorities tried to reduce the cost
of construction materials by lowering normative prices, they merely
succeeded in increasing the gap between normative and true market
prices.[65] Suppliers and middlemen sought to make up the difference
by raising unregulated costs, such as the price of transportation. As a
result, the actual cost of a given item remained indeterminate, despite
the existence of normative prices. The price of alabaster could vary from
55 rubles 4 kopeks to 58 rubles 29 kopeks, while the cost of red bricks
could range from 104 rubles to 228 rubles, even when both quotes came
from agencies working in the same district simultaneously and all prices
were supposed to be regulated.[66]

As shortages caused the cost of materials to skyrocket, architects
clashed with their clients. In producing their projects, architects consistently used normative prices, which kept the estimated costs of their
projects down. Had the use of artificial, normative prices (as opposed to
real market prices) lowered the projected cost of a design, their clients
might not have complained, for the Expert Council's fees were directly
linked to the overall price of the design. However, architects often failed

to negotiate prices with their clients prior to commencing work. Critics argued that this was done intentionally, to permit Gorproekt in particular to produce more costly and elaborate projects.[67] The cost of their project designs therefore remained high, even though such projects vastly underestimated the real cost of a building. This infuriated their critics, for builders who ran over budget ran the risk of arrest.[68] Construction agencies therefore lobbied architects to base their calculations on real market values. Local architects responded by accusing such agencies of inflating prices in order to pad their accounts.[69]

Desperate to resolve this impasse, the City of Gorky Office of Municipal Services (*gorkomkhoz*) proposed the formation of a provincial planning commission that might arbitrate between builders, suppliers, and architects by fixing prices. As they noted, not only were market prices unstable, but even normative prices could be uncertain. Too often, as the state debated price reforms, normative prices remained undetermined, leaving everyone involved in construction in limbo. While architects awaited the figures on which to base their cost estimates, their clients simply began construction without approved designs.[70]

Builders ultimately won this battle over budgeting by working on the sly to remove ornamentation and other costly features from architects' designs. To save money, they might use substandard materials in their buildings, resulting in weak foundations, roofs, and walls. City officials reprimanded foremen for such deviations, but most foremen simply ignored such reprimands. As one foreman retorted, "You are not the foreman, so why do you stick your nose into things? This is of no concern for you!"[71] As for the small 100-ruble fines imposed for infractions, these had little impact, especially where illegal changes lowered costs or helped meet deadlines.[72]

With fines proving powerless, many architects returned to the mantra of "backwardness," or "backward" foremen. To combat unapproved design modifications, they proposed to offer free training to foremen, who admittedly found technical projects difficult to decipher. Being unfamiliar with contemporary materials, Soviet foremen generally failed to understand the risk incurred when they swapped one building product with another. As architects knew, construction trusts did not have the freedom to fire underqualified foremen, for foremen with any degree of experience and education were far too scarce. A centuries-old problem, the shortage of qualified construction foremen would last to the 1950s.[73] Until this changed, architects could only hope that education would improve the work of foremen, if not also their relationship to architects.

Against System: Resilient Citizens and Resistant Industry

Construction trusts could flout the demands of city planners because they generally had the backing of industrial bodies, whose political and economic power far outshone that of the city council. Soviet industry controlled resources, both money and materials. Determined to meet Moscow's production targets, industry readily disregarded laws, regulations, bureaucratic controls, and financial plans, focusing solely on quantitative output. The city council was unable to prevent this, for its fines were minimal and industry could access resources with or without council approval. Frankly, the city council depended on industrial good will. Although Soviet commissariats allocated specific quantities of goods to municipal construction, they typically shipped these goods to the localities via industry. Because these shipments included both municipal and industrial supplies, the total sum of which often failed to meet the quota allocated for industry alone, resource-hungry and law-flouting factories frequently laid claim to entire shipments. Later, they might use their access to scarce goods as a bargaining chip, offering supplies to the city council in return for building permits or the rezoning of land.[74]

Local industry also undermined city council authority by encouraging workers to ignore decrees forbidding the illegal construction and occupation of homes. With the collusion of their employers, individual homebuilders dismissed regulations that banished temporary, sub-standard housing to the city outskirts, instead building houses along major arterial roads, close to the city's core. Because all land was state owned and the Soviet state guaranteed housing to workers, such homes generally became unplanned and yet enduring features of the urban landscape.[75] The city Party organization and the city council tried to prevent such construction by placing more responsibility for inspection and control in the hands of district (*raion*) councils, but district officials lacked the legal authority (and often the heart) to tear down illegal working-class housing. Besides, such councils could not cope with the sheer number of petitions for individual housing permits, space for which was provided in the new plan.[76] The Soviet state's desire to foster citizens' initiative in building housing offered still another incentive to turn a blind eye to illegal edifices.[77]

Residents not only engaged in illegal construction, but also blocked legal construction projects. Appealing via courts or employers, they overturned decisions calling for the destruction of their homes or simply refused to vacate the premises.[78] Such citizens' initiative postponed the construction of the city's new, three-corpus District House of Special-ists.[79] The construction of a road to the Oka Bridge was likewise delayed by citizens who filed a court challenge to the city council's plans to tear down their homes, which stood in the path of the proposed roadway.[80] Such events captured the fact that Soviet private property existed de facto, albeit not de jure. Although in theory the state exercised total control over all land and housing, in fact individual claims to personal property (*lichnaia sobstvennost'*) could pose a serious obstacle to city plan-ners' designs.[81]

The city council also proved unable to prevent citizens from moving into unfinished or uninspected buildings, although no building author-ity was supposed to admit residents without approval from a team of building inspectors (*priemochnaia komissiia*). In citizens' defence, many finished but uninspected buildings were perfectly inhabitable, although the yards and interiors might be unfinished. The city council nonethe-less sought to prevent such citizen action, because construction trusts generally abandoned their projects immediately after residents moved in, leaving messy grounds behind them. They were also known to aban-don buildings that still lacked heat and running water. Once citizens moved in, the city council lost its leverage to demand the completion of the project, something that ultimately benefited neither the building's inhabitants nor the city council.[82]

Such "resistance" to the city council and its planners was so wide-spread and pervasive that "resistance" may not be the correct term to use. "Resistance" implies principled opposition to authority. These resistances, however, were not anti-state events, but rather embedded in Soviet systems and modes of operation. Resistances of this sort pit one institution or program against the next in the name of socialism.[83] In the case of housing, resistance to city planners constituted a recognition of human need, as well as a demand that the state fulfil its promise to shel-ter its citizens. Arbitrary arrest might have been a common feature of the 1930s, but eviction at the hands of a city planning department was not. When citizens resisted local planning regulations, they realized socialism for themselves. And so, the practice continued.

"Na Lesa!" or Construction-Site Battles

All of these problems had social, economic, and political roots. Scar-city, political pressures, and the desire for both resources and influence brought about endless conflict over everything from aesthetics and the evaluation of designs to access to materials and control over the construction process. These tensions were exacerbated by the Soviet tendency to pin responsibility for systemic problems on individuals, who were forced to act outside of regular controls in order to obtain goods, services, supplies, and more. The resultant chaos further weakened the management systems upon which planners' techno-social agencies relied.

Just as the city council had once threatened to blame Ivanitskii for all the shortfalls of local city planning, so political officials threatened to blame architects for the proliferation of ugly, deficient, and unfinished construction all across the city. Formulating a new slogan, "Architect, to the scaffolds!" ("*Na lesa!*"), they demanded that architects do more to assert their authority over the construction process, particularly by verifying that builders understood and faithfully adhered to their designs.[84] Resisting this challenge, which conflated organizational dysfunction with professional malfeasance, local architects responded much as Ivanitskii had: they refused to accept responsibility. Indeed, architect Anatolii F. Zhukov's outburst at the Provincial Conference of Architects, as documented in the previous chapter, directly objected to this new framing of events. As he had shouted, political leaders ought to have the "civic manliness" (*grazhdanskoe muzhestvo*) to take the blame for their own errors.[85]

Architects everywhere in the Soviet Union found supervising construction to be a daunting and often futile task. In a speech to the Union of Soviet Architects, Moisei Ginzburg complained about architects' inability to "direct their own work." Although sometimes misinterpreted as a lament over the lack of artistic freedom, Ginzburg's comment should be viewed as an appeal for the Soviet state to bolster architects' authority on the construction site. Architects lacked the funding and legal protection required to exercise control over the realization of their design projects. Any attempt to assert their authority merely fractured their already problematic relationship with Soviet building agencies.[86]

Complaints voiced in the press and at architectural gatherings clearly illustrate the breadth of this problem. Gorproekt's three senior architects often supervised four, five, and more construction projects at one time, in addition to drafting projects and supervising junior staff members. Overseeing such widely scattered construction was extremely difficult, especially given unreliable or non-existent transportation to outlying districts. To worsen matters, there was no reimbursement for construction-site supervision in Gorproekt. Kraiproekt architects did receive some compensation, but even these architects lacked time to visit sites, except late in the evening.[87] Such troubles were hardly unique to Gorky, either.

In the face of such difficulties, architects everywhere preferred to remain in the design bureau or at home.[88]

To complicate matters, visits to the construction site irritated construction trusts, which sought to limit such supervisory visits to no more than one every five days, even when construction was moving ahead rapidly. In the opinion of foremen and construction trusts, architects too often demanded that construction be halted or that changes be made, issuing fines and reprimands as they did so. Usually, these actions did nothing more than slow construction until the construction trust paid its fines and proceeded with its work, hoping that the author of the architectural project would not return.[89] If the architect made repeated visits to the construction site, further disrupting work, he risked antagonizing his client. With such tensions and difficulties, architects tended to visit the construction site only when explicitly invited by the foreman.[90]

A contemporary anecdote illustrates these problems. Reportedly, when the architect A.N. Tiupikov castigated builders for applying the wrong colour of paint to a building, he was arrested for "wrecking," on the claim that his preferred paint colour was a deficit item, a valuable in such short supply within the Soviet Union that it could be used for only the most important projects.[91] True or not, the archival record indicates that Tiupikov sustained a strong aversion to on-site supervision. He proposed that architects seek to resolve issues by producing simpler, more legible designs that would make treks to the construction site unnecessary.[92]

Because the Soviet state nonetheless demanded that architects supervise construction, architects chose to co-opt the *Na lesa!* slogan, taking the opportunity to appeal for greater legal and administrative authority on the construction site. Rather than reject political interference of the sort represented by the slogan, they sought to redirect it, using it to augment their control over urban development. They demanded better financial compensation and more effectively enforced laws, as well as education programs to eliminate the problem of "backward" foremen. They also took the opportunity to describe the world from their perspective, as figures whose rational charts, calculations, and design were repeatedly thwarted by economic shortages and socio-political decisions that challenged planners' elaborately conceived systems of regulatory power.[93]

Conclusion: Plan as Panacea

Despite this wide range of problems, architects continued to cling to the

6.1. "A Cozy Nest" – A newspaper cartoon in which a bourgeois crow "wrecker" feeds three chicks: disarray, thick-headedness, and irresponsibility. The cartoonist plays on the homonym "*lesa*," which means both "scaffolds" and "woods." *Nizhegorodskaia kommuna* 38 (8 Feb. 1931): 3.

idea that an officially approved plan would assure total control over construction. To them, it represented science's visual prowess, something that might regulate the cityscape if only Moscow would grant its official stamp of approval. Architects thus voiced the desire for "high-quality plans" – something that was not, as is sometimes suggested, a testament to their embrace of a "totalizing" Socialist Realist aesthetic. To the contrary, this was their plea for plans that might act as effective agents of their decisions.[94]

In a world of contested power and insufficient resources, no plan of any quality would have solved architects' problems. Even direct intervention from Moscow would not have helped, for state policies often underlay planners' troubles. The pervasiveness of low-quality materials, uncertain systems of supply, arbitrary production deadlines and schedules, and pressure to build even when supplies and skilled labour were absent – all of these problems could be traced to Soviet modernization practices. Denied technocratic powers, experts had to improvise, as did other actors on the urban stage.

As both state and plan failed to shore up planners' regulatory power, planners invoked yet one more strategy in their playbook, a strategy that sought to elicit popular support and compliance by appealing to people's "culturedness" (*kul'turnost'*). In discussing construction-site disputes, many architects proposed that they influence foremen by presenting respect for the architect's design as a "cultured" act.[95] If backwardness represented the absences that planners sought to fill, then culturedness represented the sort of city – and the types of citizens – that they deemed desirable. Culturedness represented a plenitude of knowledge, order, and respect for science. In the absence of effective technical and administrative systems of power, planners turned to the ranks of the "cultured" in their city.

Chapter Seven

Performing Socialism: Connecting Space to Self

They cultivate their gardens with great care, so that they have vines, fruits, herbs, and flowers in them; and all is so well ordered, and so finely kept, that I never saw gardens anywhere that were both so fruitful and so beautiful as theirs. And this humour of ordering their gardens so well is not only kept up by the pleasure they find in it, but also by an emulation between the inhabitants of the several streets, who vie with each other; and there is indeed nothing belonging to the whole town that is both more useful and more pleasant.

Thomas More, *Utopia* (1516)[1]

For all of its fantastic elements, idle talk about the need for an all-powerful city plan conveniently focused planners' attention on absences to be filled – that is, on the lack of administrative power, up-to-date maps, mechanisms for enforcement, and political support from Moscow. In theory, all such issues could be solved through the greater application of the state's administrative and scientific power, of which planners were agents. Yet, the Soviet state relied on citizens and industries to show initiative in building, developing, and supporting domestic and industrial programs. Such activities generally eluded the oversight and control of urban planners. To shape this quasi-independent world of human endeavour, planners resorted to combatting perhaps the most elusive absence of all: the lack of popular appreciation for their expert guidance, a problem that many planners associated with a lack of culture. With this, the battle for *kul'turnost'* (culturedness) began.

Mediated through campaigns for *blagoustroistvo* (urban improvement), planners' battle for *kul'turnost'* grappled with the self-contradictory principle of spontaneous mobilization, the guiding principle behind such orchestrated mass events. Recognizing the street as a site for self-expression, both planners and city officials sought to foster citizens' identification with the Soviet urban landscape, defined as a site of order, beauty, cleanliness, and grace.[2] However, to Party members, campaigns for blagoustroistvo were an end in themselves, a way of publicly demonstrating the collective commitment to cultured living. By contrast, planners wished to deploy culturedness as a weapon against "the city that built itself." Planners hoped that the drama of culturedness, as expressed through these campaigns, would foster respect for the regulations and demands of the city planning department. Unfortunately, the institutions that initiated these campaigns – the city council and the Russian Commissariat of the Municipal Economy (NKKKh RSFSR) – sought genuine spontaneity, which pushed these campaigns for blagoustroistvo in directions inimical to planners' goals.[3]

Blagoustroistvo: The Challenge of Mobilization

The year 1934 was not only the year of the Kirov murder and the "Congress of Victory," which celebrated the purported economic success of the First Five-Year Plan, but also the year of blagoustroistvo, marked by mass attempts to bring cleanliness and beauty to the Soviet city. In that year, as Socialist Realism became the official aesthetic doctrine of the Soviet Union, the Gorky city council established the Architecture and Planning Administration (APU), a city planning department. This agency was responsible for monitoring the work of Mosgiprogor and Lengiprogor (agencies hired to produce a general city plan) as well as for overseeing urban development. As part of this endeavour, the APU found itself participating in a series of Moscow-initiated mass campaigns for clean streets, homes, and yards.

The task of urban development would have been impossible for this inexperienced, understaffed, and underfunded agency to realize on its own. Blagoustroistvo required everything from lush parks and elegant buildings to effective snow and garbage removal, not to mention suitably maintained buildings and well-appointed homes. It encompassed care for properties under state control, as well as for lots and buildings that, in practice, were the responsibility of their inhabitants. All the ingredients of urban well-being, including roads, street lights, sanitary systems, and greenery, had to be provided in order that the city might be *blagoustroennyi* (literally "well structured"). In the words of chief city architect Vladimir F. Grechukho, their city had to become a veritable city beautiful (*gorod-krasavits*).[4]

Without funds for building and planning, let alone for blagoustroistvo, the city council could not afford to tend city gardens, remove waste, repair individual apartments, or tidy public parks. Thus, in addition to expecting citizens to tend their own places of abode, the city planning department demanded broad citizen participation in such blagoustroistvo endeavours as garbage removal, home winterization, and tree planting. Dependent on mass assistance, city leaders devised a plan to extract five to six days of free labour from every urban resident, as a "labour tax" (*trudovoi zaem*). To make such payment more palatable, they organized mass campaigns that deployed a mix of social pressure, administrative fiat, and the lure of monetary prizes.[5]

As the city council transferred the managerial and fiscal burdens of blagoustroistvo to the population, mass campaigns for urban beautification swept across the entire city. In the next two years, the city council mobilized hundreds of thousands of citizens, sometimes entire city districts, behind blagoustroistvo-related programs, from tree planting and home repair to the assembly of street lights.[6] In 1935, in Sormovo alone, authorities mustered over thirty-four thousand individuals for garbage clean-up and garden tending, work valued at just under forty thousand labour days. With the help of fifty-two cars and almost three hundred horses, Sormovo residents carted away twenty-five hundred loads of garbage, cleaning over four thousand metres of ditch. They also dug 890 holes, into which they planted 221 trees (apparently, the hole-diggers were overly enthusiastic), and turned potting soil into future flowerbeds.[7]

To bolster these efforts, authorities built on the precedent set by the industrial *massovki* of the mid-1920s, when the state's belt-tightening campaign for industry resulted in the widespread use of socialist competition to raise productivity. In 1934, the Supreme Council of the Municipal Economy (VSKKh pri TsIK SSSR) set the stage by challenging city councils to win a Union-wide competition for the best city council performance in home maintenance, repair, and winterization. Taking its cue from its superiors, the city council likewise invited its subsidiary departments and their employees to compete for status as the most effective state workers in the spheres of housing, street committees, yard keeping, and editing wall newspapers. These various sections and street committees then organized their own citizens' competitions in home repair, garbage removal, and tree planting.[8]

Unlike the industrial massovki of the 1920s, these new mobilizations were not presented as re-enactments of the Revolution and Civil War.[9] Despite the militaristic overtones of this new "war on disorder," these campaigns were scripted somewhat differently – not as an assault on a class enemy, but as a means through which to effect and express self-transformation. Popular involvement was greeted as a signal that the population had become more assertive, cultured, and educated.[10] Both provincial Party secretary Iulii M. Kaganovich and the city council president of the time, Radion S. Semenov, presented blagoustroistvo as a response to workers' social ambition, with popular involvement signalling the force of popular demand for a more ordered city.[11]

Newspapers played a central role in organizing and scripting these events. Even as they spread the message that urban dirt and decay were unacceptable, they documented the putative transformation of Soviet workers, as signalled through their participation in urban improvement initiatives. Working to facilitate this human "transfiguration," newspapers announced campaigns, monitored their progress, and cajoled officials, citizens, and organizers into realizing the state's goals. As in Lengiprogor's consultation campaign, newspapers simultaneously served as a medium for the exchange of information among the elite. Urban planners and local officials alike published their critiques of these campaigns, and the newspapers dutifully reported and analysed events that were complete flops.[12]

The script of the campaign, as outlined in newspapers and reiterated by experts and officials, presented the cityscape as a stage on which to enact communal pride and achievement. By participating in blagoustroistvo campaigns, they suggested, individuals merged with the collective. Unlike the housing combines of the Cultural Revolution, which sought to achieve communalization through the physical design of the combine, these campaigns attempted to forge collectivism through ritual and drama. According to this script, individuals' participation in a campaign was, in and of itself, a sign of moral transformation. Although citizens might have participated out of peer pressure or pure self-interest (campaigns were mediums for the transmission of supplies and expert assistance), their engagement was interpreted as an act of will and enthusiasm, a moment of "collectivism achieved."[13]

Eager to encourage and exploit such campaigns, the city council reorganized its fiscal and administrative operations to accommodate these "voluntary" events. In 1935, it opened hardware stores and nurseries, enabling inhabitants to purchase their own blagoustroistvo supplies. In 1936, the city council transferred its home-repair budget to competition organizers, particularly to prize committees.[14] That same year, officials broke the city's three large districts into five smaller districts, assigning responsibility for blagoustroistvo to district leaders and Party organizations, bodies that might better monitor the street committees on which citizens' success in home repair, *ozelenenie* (planting greenery), and garbage and snow removal depended.[15]

Enacting Culturedness: Blagoustroistvo as Street Theatre

In addition to forging collectivism, campaign organizers hoped to foster culturedness (*kul'turnost'*). To support this, newspapers cast individual participation in these campaigns as a symbol and means of integration into a *cultured* collective. According to this reading, the streetscape served as more than the mere object of mass action. It became the extension of the collective, an object only as cultured as the citizens themselves.[16]

The emergence of culturedness as a Soviet value system in the 1930s has rightly been linked to the rise of a new generation of professionals and managers. Promoted through affirmative action programs, as well as through the purge of their erstwhile superiors, these new men and women lacked the rich learning and culture of their predecessors. By embracing social distinctions once identified as "bourgeois," including cleanliness and tasteful home décor, they sought to acquire the *kul'tura*, or sense of refinement, that they lacked by heritage. They presented this acquisition not as the perquisite of a new ruling class (such an admission would have been viewed as counterrevolutionary), but rather as a down payment on the promise of material comfort and social mobility for all Soviet citizens.[17]

Soviet culturedness encompassed the knowledge of what Soviet citizens ought to know (e.g., world literature and music) and a sense of what goods ought to be obtained (e.g., curtains and certain styles of clothing), as well as decency in manner and deportment.[18] A matter of "good taste," culturedness expressed itself in the houseplants, picture frames, and furnishings of the well-appointed apartment, as well as in one's choice of leisure activity.[19] It was manifested in the desire to consume cultured items, as well as in the self-control essential to showing selectivity in the quality and quantity of one's purchases. Being an act of will, efficiency, and savvy, kul'turnost' was the spatialized performance of the disciplined self.[20]

As an externalized expression of self, Soviet kul'turnost' could readily be extended to public space as the object and site of cultured action. Train curtains, clean store shelves, polite service, and sophisticated systems of retail trade were all deemed "cultured," as were tidy city streets.[21]

Seeking to foster this more expansive sense of culturedness, local leaders directed the cultured person's love for neatness, plants, furnishings, and comfort to the city as a whole, treating the city as a stage where culturedness might be performed, realized, and internalized, all at the authorities' behest. The streetscape thus served as the external expression of the self, both individual and collective. Even outlying districts, far from the "capital section" where the homes of the former elite stood, were to be clean, ordered, and cultured. No longer would lovely streets, effective transportation, and public parks be limited to the city centre alone.

Although the identification of kul'turnost' with the city beautiful (*gorod-krasavits*) presented civility as a desirable attribute of all members of urban society, not just the elite, Soviet culturedness nonetheless asserted hierarchy. To be cultured was to be a "cut above," for culturedness, as a matter of material and intellectual acquisition, was not (yet) attainable by all.[22] In the Soviet literature of this period, experts like A.P. Ivanitskii and G.V. Greiber, not the common worker, served as emblems of modern intellect and behaviour, as figures of culture par excellence.[23] These men enjoyed advanced education and better pay than the average worker, together with the right to claim extra living space to meet their needs as "creative" individuals. As for common workers, insofar as the state controlled the distribution of the goods required to rise to cultured status, their pursuit of the attributes of culturedness required behavioural discipline and subservience. They literally had to "line up" for cultured goods.[24]

Seeking to exploit this aspect of culturedness, local planners scripted their own scenario of power, one in which both city and citizen exuded the sort of culturedness desired by urban planners. As with Lengiprogor's ritualized consultation, the script of this drama aimed to sculpt and direct popular will. Local planners therefore co-opted citizens' complaints, turning their demands for better living conditions into state-approved lists of blagoustroistvo activities, which were then realized at workers' expense. Many an everyday life conference was distorted in this way, as workers' complaints were redirected to suit state goals.[25] Workers found themselves compelled to engage in activities whose public meaning was controlled by the authorities, who masked exploitation under the guise of collective self-realization. At least, blagoustroistvo initiatives directly targeted social needs, something that Lengiprogor's own rituals generally failed to do. As opposed to Lengiprogor's aesthetics of distraction, the city planning department offered concrete tasks to fulfil.[26]

Blagoustroistvo as Chistka (Purge)

By encouraging blagoustroistvo, Soviet authorities sought to achieve a pure society from which dirt and disorder had been removed – not just on the streets, but in citizens' souls. In this, blagoustroistvo campaigns fit into the broader Soviet attempt to cultivate the incorruptible society, physically and morally ordered. Purges from the Party eliminated not only those who were inept or of incorrect class backgrounds, but also those who were deemed guilty of drunkenness, sexual debauchery, swindling, or moral degeneracy. Ethical behaviour and home life were patrolled as closely as administrative efficacy.[27]

Campaigns for blagoustroistvo were therefore linked to *chistka* (purge) in every sense of the word. At its most literal level, chistka referred to the removal of snow or garbage, tasks that posed perpetual challenges for the city administration. However, chistka could also entail moral cleansing, such as the purge of "merchant nastiness," which local newspapers conflated with any and all administrative and cultural practices deemed to be outdated or politically incorrect.[28] In this latter sense, the chistka was closely linked to Party purges (*chistki*), which in 1934 to 1935 involved the dismissal of Party members deemed unworthy for reasons of ineptitude, moral laxity, or "incorrect" class origins. Perhaps fittingly, many of those removed from the Party were condemned for failing to provide effective blagoustroistvo, particularly waste and snow removal.[29]

This linkage of the moral with the biological found expression in the very term applied to those who were purged from society. The much-maligned Soviet "wreckers" (*vrediteli*) featured in the Shakhty trials and purges were not Luddites or hooligans placing a stick in the spokes of the Soviet economic wheel, as the English term "wrecker" suggests. A more accurate translation of "wrecker" (*vreditel'*) would be "pest," a vile insect threatening to consume the state's carefully cultivated social garden.[30] Such pests were viewed as threats to the (organic) collective in both material and moral terms, a threat to the "pure" society for which the "gardening state" of the Soviet Union strove.[31]

While this linkage of moral and biological purity had its Western equivalent, the Soviet conceptualization was distinctly its own. In the West, sanitary infrastructure had been introduced as a way to protect upper-class lives and living spaces from lower-class contagion. Western urban reformers viewed sanitary systems as agents of discipline, selfhood, and social integration.[32] By contrast, the Soviet leadership did not fear lower-class contagion, but rather a much more elusive and insidious enemy – namely, individuals who appeared to be socially integrated, but were actually alienated from the Soviet collective. The state's defence against such a threat did not consist of such social technologies as the public sewer, but rather of a script – a theatre of self-transformation, featuring the new Soviet man and woman as achieved through collective campaigns to combat dirt and disorder.

Nonetheless, Soviet campaigns for blagoustroistvo were also driven by the fear of physical contagion, traceable to poor sanitation. Most buildings in the Soviet Union lacked running water and sewer connections, and many homes did not have outhouses or cesspits. Human waste was dumped, with garden waste, into pits and ravines. Despite such filth and the lack of running water, public bathhouses remained insufficient. Dirt and disease were therefore a persistent menace.[33] By conflating physical purge with moral purge, Soviet leaders conveniently placed responsibility for battling the threat of disease on citizens. In the language of the campaign, throwing excrement in the courtyard was "uncultured." The lack of state-provided waste facilities offered no excuse for residents' contamination of city streets.

Biological metaphors of society had long shaped how urban planners conceptualized the city, but the biological metaphors deployed by planners lacked the moral connotations inherent to Party terminology. Planners referred to city greenery as "lungs" and to roads as "arteries."[34] In metaphorical and literal terms, their city's well-being relied on the healthy circulation of fluids (water and human waste), nourishment (traffic, goods, and commerce), and air (parks and walkways), as well as on space for growth (economic, human, and cultural).[35] Placing such organic metaphors in an ideological frame, planners described "merchant Nizhnii" as a "dying (odriakhlevshii) organism" weakened by the "harmful narcotic of profit," something destined to be replaced by a newborn babe, "socialist Gorky."[36] Such figures of speech echoed the nineteenth-century concept of the city as a greenhouse, a notion that made an indelible impact on early city planning endeavours.[37]

As defined by planners, blagoustroistvo denoted a socio-technological infrastructure that would do away with the need to police human attitudes and behaviour. In this approach to blagoustroistvo, the lungs required to freshen the city were not human lungs, breathing heavily in the exertion of the mass campaign, but rather well-established swaths of green. If experts had their way, the circulatory system of the city would have consisted of pipes and power lines, not human beings and horses assigned to haul fuel or excrement. Unfortunately, in the Soviet Union of the 1930s, this technocratic vision remained impossible to realize. Planners, with the Party and state, had to rely on mass initiative.

The application of biological metaphors to urban life scripted a prominent role in blagoustroistvo initiatives to society women (*obshchestvennitsy*). In a world where the divide between public and private remained liminal, care for the self and the home served as a mark of social advance, worthiness, and state-mindedness. Soviet kul'turnost' thus infused domestic affairs with state import. As masters of the hearth, not to mention figures responsible for nurturing the next generation, women served as powerful agents and symbols of the new collective. They were therefore responsible for the cultivation of a more lovely and well-ordered city, a Soviet home and family writ large. As symbols of fertility and family, their public role reinforced the state's pro-natalist message, even as it extended the duty of motherhood to the entire cityscape. As one news headline begged, mimicking the voice of a child, "Water the trees, mother!"[38]

First mobilized by Sergei Ordzhonikidze, the commissar of heavy industry, these wives of Party and state elites served as models of "good taste," the vanguard of culturedness in the realms of dress, home life, hygiene, and cultural entertainment.[39] As society women, they mobilized to improve health, hygiene, and child care. In addition to organizing citywide *subbotniki*, in which citizens "offered" to help remove garbage or plant trees, they sponsored the creation of city playgrounds and ensured that local stores stocked items essential for home renovations, such as paint, wallpaper, and curtains.[40] As Party ideologues proclaimed, "Housewives are a mighty force!"[41]

The rise of society women marked a turning point for all Soviet women. Earlier attempts to integrate women into the collective had involved the concerted attempt to destroy home life, deemed the site and source of women's oppression. By contrast, these campaigns embraced motherhood and domesticity as desirable traits. Rather than abolish the domestic realm, authorities endeavoured to order it, embracing the very neatness, furnishings, and flowers that the Party's cultural theorists had previously considered to be the very emblem of philistine *poshlost'* (the crude or banal). What had been regarded as bourgeois kitsch, both prior to the Revolution and throughout the 1920s, was now embraced as a means of providing the order, cleanliness, and psychological support essential to (male) productivity outside the home.[42]

Due to the state's embrace of domesticity, the "public intimacy" of the

Soviet family reached into the "intimate public" of the Soviet home, in all its overcrowding and lack of privacy. Acting as agents of surveillance, society women organized random inspections of working-class women's apartments to determine what repairs ought to be done and to enforce standards of cleanliness.[43] The city council and district officials likewise conducted unannounced examinations of all individuals and institutions involved in competitions for home repair and maintenance. For surveillance purposes, they enlisted the assistance of yardkeepers, whose victory in blagoustroistvo competitions depended not only on their tending the space in and around buildings, but also on their close monitoring of the comings and goings of all residents and visitors. Wall newspapers and comrade courts also exercised supervisory power, ensuring residents' faithful observance of the new Soviet norms of cleanliness and order.[44]

Such invasiveness enabled the Party to engage working-class women, a notoriously disengaged and disenfranchised group. Thanks to domestic burdens and lesser education, working women had traditionally lacked the time for Party education and involvement.[45] The Revolution of 1917 naturally affected these women's day-to-day affairs, but it did not necessarily engage them in study circles and other ideological work. While such campaigns subjected these women's domestic lives to public surveillance, they also provided a means through which these working women might merge with the collective, specifically as mothers and homemakers. Even common cleaning ladies were deemed "commanders of cleanliness," or women in the front lines of the war on dirt.[46]

Although women often took centre stage, their husbands and sons did not escape the attention of campaign organizers. The state wished to bring culturedness to the factory in the form of order, cleanliness, discipline, and respect for equipment. Seeking to foster workers' diligent cultivation of these traits, newspapers proclaimed, "A shock worker of production is a shock worker of blagoustroistvo," adding that it would be a "striking contradiction" (krichashchee protivorechie) for a Soviet worker to tolerate dirt and disorder anywhere.[47] A Soviet worker was, by Soviet definition, civilized and therefore an enemy of filth in the factory, on the street, and in the home.[48]

To reinforce this message, campaigners promoted a "bring flowers to the factory" movement, placing live plants and flowers on the shop floor.[49] Here, said factory managers and party propagandists, the flowers were to "chase away the dirt and rust that blossomed [there]."[50] Bolstering this effort to turn the city into "a nursery (rassadnik) of culture and cleanliness," Party organizers placed a large bouquet of flowers on display at a gathering dedicated to blagoustroistvo, as if its very beauty might drive away disorder, both moral and physical.[51] At times, such programs overreached themselves, as directors brought potted plants into food-processing facilities, where they posed a sanitary hazard. But, the campaign – with its message – continued.[52]

The Challenge of Directed Enthusiasm

Blagoustroistvo campaigns operated according to a circular logic, whereby authorities and planners sought to mobilize the very sentiments that these campaigns were supposed to foster, including identification with the city, a desire for public order, and the thirst for cultured status. Radion S. Semenov, city council president from 1935 to 1937, suggested that planners had to "teach citizens to love their home town."[53] Yet, Soviet citizens naturally showed keen interest in better homes, services, and cultural facilities. When mobilization enabled them to achieve some of their goals, they participated eagerly. When citizens saw no benefit, mobilization proved difficult.[54] To ordinary participants, campaign organizers were facilitators who provided materials, not mobilizers of the human spirit. They co-opted citizens' interest in improved living conditions, but did not necessarily inspire it.[55]

Citizens' responses to these campaigns thus varied wildly. While some opted to become shock workers of blagoustroistvo, earning prizes and acclaim, others reportedly did their best to help neighbours winterize and repair homes, even without the incentive of a campaign prize.[56] Still others, rejecting the campaigns, stayed home, refusing forced or voluntary contributions to urban improvement initiatives. Thousands of workers refused to participate in the 1935 Sormovo garbage clean-up campaign. Even residents of the local House of the Militia, who might have been expected to enforce the organizers' wishes, stayed away.[57] In this case, their lack of enthusiasm might have derived from their privilege, or perhaps from a sense that their impunity would go unpunished.

To the extent that citizens did engage, they enabled authorities to achieve the seeming impossibility of free initiative confined within prescribed boundaries. In this, blagoustroistvo campaigns captured a paradox at the heart of Soviet society. As Alexei Yurchak explains, as agents of a truth behind and beyond history, Party members struggled to impose absolute truths on society without entirely squelching the human freedom that these truths were supposed to uphold and sustain.[58] Thus confronting a dilemma visible in conflicting interpretations of Lenin's

What Is to Be Done?, the Party struggled to discourage "ignorant" or "uninformed" spontaneity as opposed to "conscious" human initiative, or initiative inspired by what Soviet leaders viewed as authentic "class instinct."[59] Experts, too, sought to cultivate an audience that might accept their scientific plans for the city as their own.[60] As social engineers, they wished to inspire a particular type of performance, one that would conform to their own, carefully devised script.

Planners did not control the script of these campaigns, however. The focus of their co-organizers – the Party, the news media, campaign leaders, and city council members – tended to be the generation of spontaneity, often at the expense of constructive outcomes, such as trees that survived the planting process, pipelines that functioned, and streets that remained clean for more than an hour or two. Rather than combat disorder and chaos, as planners wished, many Party-sponsored or truly spontaneous events produced it. Planners in particular despised the activities of the Society of the Friends of Greenery, which they maligned for its members' habit of planting "*as they saw fit*," "*totally independent of expert oversight and district government*" (original emphasis).[61] Architects' preferred script featured the sort of behaviour modelled by a group of women whose "spontaneity" consisted of petitioning the Department of Blagoustroistvo for instructions on such minutiae as the colour in which to paint a fence.[62]

Had planners controlled access to supplies, perhaps they might have controlled the theatre of the campaign, for success generally depended on the organizers' access to materials, advice, and political support.[63] This was particularly true for initiatives that targeted low-status groups, like yardkeepers (*dvorniki*), who were one of the most underprivileged groups in the city. Many lived in squalor and went without pay for extended periods of time. Few did a stellar job of performing their landscaping and snow removal duties, because they generally lacked work clothes, shovels, brooms, gloves, watering cans, dustbins, and the like. Any attempt to mobilize this group without addressing this fundamental lack of equipment was doomed to fail.[64] To succeed in any campaign, yardkeepers depended on organizers' delivery of the clothes, tools, and pay that should have been provided long before.

Poor organization and inadequate supplies unfortunately resulted in many failed campaigns, and planners appear to have been unable to correct the situation. In a mass campaign to lay sewer lines in Avtozavod, organizers divided participants into two groups, which proceeded to lay pipes from opposite ends of the proposed line. Workers tackled their challenge with gusto, with the one group trying to beat the other in the race to the centre. Thanks to miscalculation or perhaps to the simple shortage of sewer pipes, the two groups failed to meet in the centre, leaving a gap of two hundred metres in the centre of the sewer line.[65] Tree-planting campaigns also tended to be infamous failures, as trees died from rough handling followed by total neglect.[66]

The flaws of these undertakings displayed themselves, yet again, in a major citywide campaign for garbage removal in 1934. Over ten thousand people participated, heaping large mounds of garbage in the streets for pick-up. Because shortages of horses, vehicles, and gasoline were endemic throughout the Soviet Union, organizers failed to procure the requisite garbage removal equipment. Although campaign organizers could often locate the requisite resources on a short-term or emergency basis, particularly for such bi-annual garbage clean-up campaigns, equipment supplies fell short. As a result, the collected heaps were soon dispersed by wind and rain. The mounds of garbage, once a symbol of collective enthusiasm, were now regarded as a nuisance, annoying centres of concentrated stench and filth. The campaign solved nothing. In fact, as Donald Filtzer reminds us, even successful campaigns achieved little, for they were nothing more than stopgap solutions to persistent and systemic problems.[67]

Despite such issues, organizers celebrated short-term quantitative results, ignoring the negligible long-term impact of any such campaign. Engaging in something of a Socialist Realist theatrical act, they celebrated the numbers of participants, relishing the campaigns' didactic display of a city beautiful crafted through popular mobilization. In their minds, the blagoustroistvo campaign mirrored Thomas More's utopian vision of carefree citizens motivated to tend gardens through friendly neighbourhood competition. The post-campaign heaps of garbage, like new mounds of snow or homes with faulty repairs, did not detract from their initial celebration of their cultured citizen-collective and its city beautiful.

Planners viewed these problems differently, however, for they sought concrete results, not just the symbolic celebration of Soviet kul'turnost'. Responding to this chaos in much the same way as they reacted to the "city that builds itself," they nurtured fantastic visions of fiat power. Many argued that they should provide a highly detailed maintenance plan for every last fence, building, sidewalk, tree, and flower in the city. Some proposed to attach a "care passport" to trees in the city, as a guide for citizens in their tending duties.[68] If only they could provide clear and detailed information related to the handling of each and every object that played a role in making the city orderly, green, and beautiful, they thought, then every last resident in the city would comply with their instructions. No shortage of paint, materials, or knowledge would prevent the experts from dictating fence colours, kiosk design, or the way in which plants were tended in public gardens.[69]

Such dreams testify to planners' lingering desire for technocratic means of urban governance. Elaborate designs for all elements of the cityscape, from the colour and design of kiosks to advertising signs and flower gardens, were to be self-explanatory. Of course, these did not substitute for infrastructure, which would have dispensed entirely of the need to seek or enforce popular compliance. Lacking this infrastructure, planners exploited the technology of type, deploying print communication as their new technology of social control. That such a technology required active compliance and enforcement appears to have escaped their reflection.

Unfortunately, many a petty leader opted to achieve blagoustroistvo by decree, a form of control likewise achieved, at least in part, through the technology of type. A petty official might order residents to place flowerpots in windowsills in order to avert rheumatism, which was blamed on high humidity. Municipal leaders might instruct all homeowners and institutional directors to pour asphalt pavement and paint their buildings in city-mandated colours.[70] In such cases, leaders managed lives rather than campaigns.

Perhaps sensing this problem, engineer D.V. Rudakov proposed a less fantastic way to beautify the city. Arguing that architects should offer less, not more, detail to campaign participants, he proposed initiatives suited to a mass public. Rather than a city of fancy gardens and exotic trees, Rudakov proposed a city lush with green grass. As he noted, digging drainage ditches and seeding grass were simple tasks that could be carried out under the auspices of "organized mass spontaneity."[71] This, he implied, would go much further towards meeting the city council president's demands for "authentic" as opposed to "ostentatious" or "showy" (*pokaznoe*) blagoustroistvo. It might even meet the state's demand for blagoustroistvo that was realized "even in the details."[72] To be achieved "even in the details," he argued, the details of blagoustroistvo had to be kept simple. Unfortunately, no one paid heed to this prudent advice.

Conclusion

In celebrating citizens' transformation into a "cultured collective," often through the act of planting a tree, these Soviet campaigns for blagous-troistvo hearkened to imperial tree-planting festivals, which were highly ritualized events that celebrated societal regeneration. In imperial celebrations, peasants' planting of young saplings represented the remaking of the nation, nature, and the common people – in effect, the rebirth of a community, as facilitated through the peasants' cultivation of living plants.[73] Similarly, in the Soviet case, a new collective self was to be effected through highly ritualized performance. That this often involved planting trees, which were symbols of renewal, was perfectly fitting.

Such performance was productive, but not definitive. The very ritual, symbol, and action that defined these campaigns were inherently polyvalent, open to a multitude of readings. Although the Party dictated one truth statement regarding the meaning and purpose of these events, the meaning ascribed by participants or crafted through the drama of performance did not necessarily conform to the Party's coding of the event. To put this in more theoretical terms, the constative (official) and performative (enacted) aspects of a campaign could remain dynamically connected, yet distinct.[74] Although participation sustained the Party's master narrative, neither participation nor embrace of the collective required an intellectualized embrace of the official script for such campaigns. As David Kertzer writes, "Solidarity is produced by people acting together, not by people thinking together."[75]

With regard to collective action, these campaigns captured the tension inherent to the Soviet citizen's role as both the object and agent of state initiative. Through state-led mobilization, local leaders sought to realize an idealized, abstract vision of popular will. In acting "as they saw fit," however, common citizens and campaign organizers flouted these reified images of the Soviet collective. Ironically, such subversive action was often facilitated by the Party, whose own populist tendencies inspired its embrace of human spontaneity at the expense of techno-social agencies of rule. In this, these campaigns suffered from the same paradoxes as ritualized consultation. Experts and authorities expected urban inhabitants to conform to a pre-ordained script, even as mass action escaped the script's confines. The fact that the denunciation-fed purges of the 1930s decimated the street committees on which many campaigns relied highlights the potentially destructive power of the very "mass spontaneity" that such events supposedly fostered.[76]

Despite their failures, however, such campaigns highlighted the dramatic role of the Stalinist cityscape. For all its monumentality, Stalinist architecture was not merely designed to deceive, distract, and awe, as some scholars suggest.[77] As a stage setting, it provided the backdrop for a citywide battle against disorder and dirt. Monumentality was not essential to this performance. Khrushchev's more functionalist aesthetic would serve the same purpose just decades later.[78] All that was required was a desire for a spatialized, public performance of collective selfhood, scripted as an act of renewal and regeneration. Monuments, situated on wide "airy" streets cleared of garbage and debris, were to be symbols of self, ritualized and effected through the drama of the campaign.

This battle for the street – and, by extension, for self – was highly ritualized, and yet never perfectly controlled by the authorities. As lived action, it left room for error and off-script behaviour, as well as for alternative interpretations of the entire affair. All of this marked socialism as something lived, as something with which one might identify, and perhaps also as something in which one could believe. But belief was not necessary, for the campaigns produced solidarity of action, which may or may not have equated to joint belief.

As before, the city planning department lamented its inability to dictate the course of urban development, as the Soviet city emerged out of socio-material and political forces with which department staff could interact, but which they did not control. As a drama of stage and audience, their city beautiful remained hopelessly off script – or at least, off the script as interpreted by urban planners. Although conforming to the vague outlines of the Soviet narrative of socialism and modern progress, this drama was always caught in a two-way translation between the visuality of text and the messiness of action – a tension that forever unsettled the best of planners' designs for the Soviet city.

Conclusion: Living Socialism in the Shadow of the Political

I love your firm design
And would gladly take this role
But now another drama plays
This time, let me go.
But, the act has already been scripted
And the end of the road cannot be averted.
I am alone. Everything drowns in Phariseeism.
Life is no walk in the park.

Boris Pasternak, "Hamlet," 1946

From planned cities to a socialist paradise, the entire Soviet system revolved around hope – always inspiring, always unfulfilled. It projected itself through a theatrical fourth wall, creating an imagined future that might be embraced, mocked, or enacted, thereby turning dream into being. As a space of hope and shared imagination, the Soviet cityscape became a site where the vestiges of the past confronted the light of the future, and the present seemed to slip away, as if non-existent. Here, on the set of the socialist city, Soviet authorities drafted plans for growth, urban planners schemed of ways in which to rationally order the city, and ordinary citizens found themselves collectively cajoled into banishing dirt and disorder from urban space. As ideas became actions and state projects became programs, socialism came to life – not so much in the form of realized initiatives as in the form of a socialist script that was performed.

In and of themselves, neither the plan nor city planners had the power to bring socialism into being, not as an object or fixed thing. They could not even offer a convincing vision of what socialism might be. Indeed, by the time the general city plan for Gorky was approved, local officials no longer believed in it. The all-too-visceral reality of political purge and the search for enemies made the iconographic plan, which lacked solid scientific foundations, seem surreal. Its grandiose boulevards, its putative image of "Stalinist care," and its broad ensembles conformed to a state-imposed political aesthetic, but could not silence the concerns that Director Kokushkin of the Park for Culture and Rest in Sormovo had voiced: the plan did not meet the everyday needs of existing individuals in present time and space. Its ambition was too broad, and its technological requirements were too great. Frankly, city officials lacked the administrative and financial tools required to achieve it.

Because of this, in early 1937, only the most experienced city planners were prepared to validate the iconographic plan. It was a mere picture, a deceptively simple image of an incredibly complex Stalinist state. In effect, it "de-realized" the very world for which it was designed, doing violence to local needs. Yet, for Nikolai Alekseevich Solofnenko, this mattered little. The plan served its political purpose, which was to obtain professional security by acknowledging and perpetuating Stalin's power. In any case, as the most experienced planners recognized, the plan was actually quite flexible. In projecting something to be, it was not a statement of fact, but a hypothesis of sorts. As Solofnenko stressed, planners could tailor its ambition to suit local needs and resources when they drafted detailed plans for particular roads, bridges, and the like. As one of Solofnenko's colleagues proclaimed, "Life will introduce its own changes."[1]

Local political leaders did not view this plan as a mere hypothesis, however. Not unlike many of the engineers who worked in the City of Gorky's city planning department, they sought a plan that might be both permanent and official, readily implemented once it earned the state's endorsement. They did not wish for something contingent, negotiable, and strategic, but rather a firm and politically acceptable road map to the future. As a result, after years of cheering Solofnenko onward, they delayed the approval of Lengiprogor's general city plan until 1939, too late to win approval from Soviet supervisory bodies before the beginning of the Great Patriotic War.[2] The iconographic plan thereafter fell into obsolescence, remaining – as Gleb V. Greiber predicted – "nothing but a pretty picture."

Perhaps the failure to win official status for the general city plan of 1937 was just as well, for the plan's foundations lay in the Russian imperial tradition of imaging power, not in socio-material needs. The unresolved problem of melioration ensured that, in practical terms, its physical foundations would actually collapse. In 1974 alone, a massive landslide swept away 170,000 cubic metres of soil along the right bank of the Oka River, the very soil on whose stability Lengiprogor's riverside ensembles would have depended.[3]

As an incomplete, flawed, poorly documented, and yet visionary document, the iconographic plan was a product of its time. Only a very few Soviet administrations finished and won approval for general city plans in the 1930s.[4] In all cities, planners worked without adequate technologies of power – without up-to-date maps, research, well-staffed and well-equipped planning offices, and data on their cities' hydrogeological foundations.[5] Many Soviet cities, like Gorky, were not only situated in boggy regions prone to floods, landslides, and malaria, but they would also be affected by the Great Volga Project. All faced the same dangerous world of Stalinist urban politics, the cowardice of scientific "eyeglass wiping," the bravado of meeting deadlines, and the all-out scramble for scarce funds. Each confronted the challenge of coupling scientific representation with Stalinist aesthetics. And like the plan for the City of Gorky, none of these plans would be fully realized, for life itself would force modifications.

Disjointed State, Conflicted Scripts

For planners in the Soviet Union, planning was the art of the possible, a craft that combined agency with complicity. At times, planners challenged state power from within, curbing the ambitions of industry and street-committee organizers or subverting state-mandated discussions of the Stakhanovite movement in such a way as to demand more privileges for themselves. At other times, they bolstered state power, as in their campaigns to market "Stalinist care." Because Soviet state power was diffuse and fragmented, each state agency and individual interpreted socialism in its own way – and sometimes in multiple ways. In such a competitive and fluid environment, planners could simultaneously resist one state agency or program while advancing another. Scientific professionalism blended with political strategizing as planners competed and collaborated with the powerhouses of their time.

To fully understand this dynamic, we need to remember that Soviet city planners operated in a complex social and political world that was discursively shaped, but never discursively defined. There was no simple, straightforward socialist agenda to resist or realize, but rather a host of competing forces striving towards an ill-defined goal named "socialism." All the key principles of Soviet life – socialism, progress, science, democracy, Leninism, and Marxism – remained fuzzy and fluid, open to conceptual manipulation by a host of societal groups as they battled for power and control. The master plot of socialism was polysemic, held together by recurring but evolving metaphors of socialist life, including such tropes as machines, gardens, spontaneity, and consciousness.[6] Even Socialist Realism, the state-imposed aesthetic of the Stalin period, mixed constructivist and monumentalist architectural elements throughout the 1930s, shifting only to a purer classicism in the postwar period. This representation of power, too, was open and negotiable.[7]

As agents of the Soviet master plot, planners were handed neither a set agenda nor a fixed definition of socialism. Rather, they were given a script – one that was not so much imposed as a part of a cultural ecosystem of power.[8] As actors on the stage of the Soviet city, they played a diverse array of roles in a variety of sites and situations, bringing ideas, words, and places associated with socialism to life. In this, they might act on- or off-script, under close direction or according to their own spontaneous inspiration. Everything in their performance concerned the site and nature of power, but this power not only continuously ordered society and politics, but was itself endlessly ordered and reordered, with no apparent constant beyond Stalin's dominance at the apex of the political system. Planners' own transcript of power was open to modification, as they sought to engage their audience, sustain belief, and co-opt new actors.

Planners' search for power was complicated by the fact that the Party's agencies of rule conflicted with their own. Consider their competing approaches to living space. For planners, living space was a quantitative measure defining the "sanitary minimum" of light, space, and air essential to public health. For Party activists, however, living space served as a measure of justice, a tool for depriving the former elite of "living space excess." Moreover, although common citizens ceded their power to calculate and distribute living space to Soviet experts and authorities, they nonetheless resisted any attempt to tear down homes in the name of an abstraction called the general city plan. Planners' instrument of technosocial control became, in the hands of common citizens, a measure of rights.[9]

Seeking to validate their control over the city, including living space, planners scripted their own scenario of power, featuring themselves as the bearers of progress, skill, and modernity.[10] They cast popular agency and resistance not as right or reason, but as absence – the absence of education, the absence of knowledge, and the absence of culturedness. They fought to identify subordination with civility.

Unfortunately for planners, the greatest absence was that of stable representation, or even the means of representation. Planners lacked maps, accurate population counts, apolitical calculations of productive capacity, and up-to-date information on housing. Soviet society, at this time, simply could not be represented *as it was* in any perfect, scientific sense. Surveyors' ad hoc assessment of building plots might be compared to the roughness with which the Soviet police calculated the number of enemies, arresting the innocent and manufacturing guilt as they did so. The very technologies through which the Soviet state apparatus perceived and acted on the Soviet population remained imprecise.

Definition, of course, was the prerogative of the state. Through it, the state sought to impose meaning on action, asserting itself as the omniscient narrator of the story of socialist development. However, life is not a narrative, but a drama. Stalin theoretically directed the drama of Soviet urban life, but even he could not be everywhere at all times. Nor could he control and define human motives, let alone dictate how the drama of socialist life might be received, for any act or ritual is open to a variety of interpretations.[11] Besides, the act that played on the political and public stage of the Soviet city did not preclude the existence of off-stage scripts, transcripts, and selves.[12] To understand such a drama, we need to permit a cacophony of voices, not grant definitive power to the state's authorial voice, or to our own.[13]

The stress on "cacophony" captures the confusion within the state's own transcript of power, as echoed in the paradoxes of planners' own authority. As demonstrated in this book, planners deployed their authority as scientists to validate the iconographic plan, which was rooted in the image rather than the substance of power. It represented Stalinist care, but not sound scientific study. Yet, Soviet planners used their authority as scientific experts to validate this plan, for this action helped secure their place in Soviet society as experts. Through this act, professionals mixed two competing visions of what Alexei Yurchak might define as "constative," or absolute, truth – that is, the Party line and planning science.[14] At times, as evidenced by the Kokushkin affair, the tensions inherent to this combination threatened their credibility. The rights and opinion of the Soviet people could challenge planners' authority as experts, for both Party policy and Lengiprogor's ritualized public consultation validated democratic voice. Nonetheless, to retain power in Stalinist society, planners such as Solofnenko necessarily laid claim to both democratic and scientific credentials.

What needs to be stressed, in all of this, is neither the power of representation – scientific, symbolic, or discursive – nor resistance to it, but rather how these representations scripted life on the Soviet stage, whether in the city, in the village, on the streets, or in the corridors of power. The enactment of the socialist script served as the medium through which ideas became an active force on the stage of the city, the very platform on which actors, through interaction with their audience, determined the meaning and success of the socialist show. The act, not the script itself, was what mattered.

Fourth Wall: Bringing the Concrete into the Conceptual

In the world of planning, there were multiple ways of perceiving the city, multiple ways of scripting the advance to socialism, and dozens of ways to resist or realize state power, both from within and from without. For the state was never a monolith, but absorbed the very society, materials, and traditions that it purported to govern, dragging all into a radically new drama: building, defending, imaging, and unceasingly reinventing socialism. This drama pulled planners out of the ivory tower, denying absolute power to the sort of scientific legibility of which planners claimed to be master. Even with the rise of a new generation of Stalinist planners, the populist and elitist impulses of the Party apparatus continued to upset and limit the technocratic aspirations of planning experts.

Because they worked with the city as something material, not simply imagined, planners had to translate their abstract aesthetic, scientific, and political ideas into practical policies for socio-physical spaces. In so doing, they stepped onto the stage of Soviet life, where they ad libbed, just slightly, to suit an audience, to interpret the text, and to put themselves forward as authoritative, sympathetic figures. Out of necessity, they mastered several different displays of power, each of which balanced scientific prerogative with state-mandated performance.

In breaking the fourth wall, planners strove to define and control the world in which the drama unfolded. They sought to control the "architecture of thought," as understood by Derrida. Just as a building defines its foundation, not vice versa (for a foundation is designed to support a building, whose design comes first), so grand meta-narratives craft their own foundational histories. In the same way, Soviet ritual and imagination cast working-class power, justice, science, and progress as the foundations of socialism.[15] Yet, as David Kertzer writes, "That people perceive the world through symbolic lenses does not mean that people or cultures are free to create any symbolic system imaginable or that all such constructs are equally tenable in the material world."[16] Real social, material, historical, and cultural foundations – everything from melioration problems to layered soteriological imagination – could expose the flaws in such ideological artistry, including that of the iconographic plan.

In all of this, architects' relationship to power tended to be conventional and opportunistic in the name of an ideal. Theirs was somewhat of a Faustian pact, whereby they ceded power as scientists, gaining power as purveyors of the Stalin cult, presenting their plan as the image of Stalin's care and popular desire. Here, they offered the image, but not the substance, of the purified society – a far cry from the "legibility" sought before. But the iconographic, unlike the scientific, offered the very mythic symbols with which citizens might identify, the flattened realities that dominate the representation of the state in all modern systems. It offered the illusion of the absolute and transcendent, pinning both to the all-powerful figure of Stalin. Through it, planners' security and authority came to depend on Stalin's arbitrary will and the capricious world of populist politics. This was particularly true of architects, who tended to lend greater support than engineers to the iconographic and monumental. Indeed, with Stalin's fall, their dominance in the world of urban planning would end, as engineers took the helm of the nation's planning institutions.[17]

Did these strategies save local city planners from the purges of the 1930s, at least? In her study of the statistical administration, Martine Mespoulet suggests that statisticians uncovered strategies that offered security, including total acceptance of the Party program and the silencing of one's own dissent. Similarly, Andrew Day suggests that architects' role as purveyors of Stalinism saved them.[18] Both arguments contain elements of truth, but surely the answers are more complex, for even the most loyal could be purged. In any case, in adopting these strategies, planners' search for power was directed horizontally, not just vertically. They sought power vis-à-vis other state agencies, not vis-à-vis Stalin himself. They enacted their roles not only out of fear, but out of ambition for greater authority over the cityscape.

Because their professional authority faced repeated challenge, planners tended to confuse the technologies of power with its substance – a weakness of all governments, who conflate legibilities of rule with the essence of power. They confused map with understanding, plan with process, and product with production. They clung to whatever transcendent perspective they might attain, whether scientific or iconographic, for they dreamed of a plan that might represent and realize fixed, stable power that lay beyond contestation. This was nowhere possible, not in a world of things, people, memories, and identities with the potential to challenge their power. A city is a complex mass of peoples, spaces, and ideas that are layered historically, geographically, and culturally. It has built-in resistances, even as it has in-built prejudices. One soterioscape shapes the next, even as historic infrastructure shapes future possibilities.

To tell the story of this past, we historians must rely on the Soviet state's machinery, its bureaucratic paperwork, the recorded transcripts of its agents, and the media's own interpretive frame. We unfortunately depend on these technologies of sight, although they did not represent the world so much as they bid for mastery over it. Through them, urban planners and other authorities "flattened" reality, seeking to mould it to their will. This failed, as images and programs proved inadequate to the task. But, this is not what mattered. What mattered was the drama of the attempt, in which lay all the hopes and frustrations of Soviet life. For every plan and chart was not just a vision, but a prop in a once-living drama. Following a loose, unfinished script, this performance defined socialism and the Soviet experience from the very start.

Notes

Introduction: Planners, Performance, and Power

1 I.G. Belenko et al., eds., *Gor'kovskii dizel'nyi: Ocherki istorii zavoda "Dviga-tel' Revoliutsii"* (Moscow: Mysl', 1985); B.D. Iurin et al., eds., *Gor'kovskii avtomobil'nyi: Ocherki istorii zavoda* (Moscow: VTsSPS Profizdat, 1964).

2 L.L. Trube, *Naselenie goroda Gor'kogo* (Gorky: Volgo-Viatskoe, 1982), 50. The population within the boundaries of Greater Nizhnii Novgorod – Sormovo, Nizhnii Novgorod, Kanavino, and nearby villages – jumped from 249,000 people in 1927 to 520,000 by 1936. For the 1927 data, see N. Karbovets, "Bol'shoi Nizhnii," *Nizhegorodskoe khoziaistvo* 4–5 (Jan.–Feb. 1928): 14.

3 For more information on the economic transformation of the city in these years, see V.P. Fadeev et al., eds., *Istoriia industrializatsii Nizhegorodskogo/ Gor'kovskogo kraia* (Gorky: Volga-Viatskoe, 1968), and A.V. Kozonim, *Istoriia "Krasnogo Sormovo"* (Moscow: Mysl', 1969).

4 On collectivization, see Lynne Viola, *Peasant Rebels under Stalin: Collectiviza-tion and the Culture of Peasant Resistance* (New York: Oxford University Press, 1998); Lynne Viola, *The Unknown Gulag: The Lost World of Stalin's Special Set-tlements* (New York: Oxford University Press, 2007). For an excellent study of peasant in-migration and its cultural impact in the Soviet period, see David Hoffman, *Peasant Metropolis: Social Identities in Moscow, 1929–1941* (Ithaca: Cornell University Press, 2000).

5 In his attitude to science and Soviet power, Ivanitskii displayed remarkable similarity to Peter Palchinsky, whose life is discussed in Loren Graham, *The Ghost of the Executed Engineer: Technology and the Fall of the Soviet Union* (Cam-bridge: Harvard University Press, 1993).

6 On professional support for state-led modernization, see Catherine Cooke, *Russian Avant-Garde: Theories of Art, Architecture, and the City* (London: Acad-

emy Editions, 1995), 189; K.N. Afanas'ev and V.E. Khazanova, eds., *Iz istorii sovetskoi arkhitektury, 1917–1925: Dokumenty i materialy* (Moscow: Akademiia Nauk SSSR, 1963), 13–25; Alexei Tarkhanov and Sergei Kavtaradze, *Architecture of the Stalin Era* (New York: Rizzoli, 1992), 189–90; Anatole Kopp, *Town and Revolution: Soviet Architecture and City Planning, 1917–1935*, translated by Thomas E. Burton (New York: George Braziller, 1970), 37.

7 For Ivanitskii's biography, see V.G. Davidovich and T.A. Chizhikova, *Aleksandr Ivanitskii* (Moscow: Stroiizdat, 1973).

8 Such centralization proved controversial in the medical profession, where localism dominated. See John F. Hutchinson, *Politics and Public Health in Revolutionary Russia* (Baltimore: Johns Hopkins University Press, 1990).

9 GARF, A-314, op. 1, d. 7494, l. 240ob.

10 See A.F. Khokhlov, *Universitet, rozhdennyi trizhdy: Istoriia sozdaniia i stanovleniia Nizhegorodskogo universiteta* (Nizhnii Novgorod: Nizhegorodskii universitet, 1998).

11 Catriona Kelly mentions the financial concerns that compelled many professionals to come to peace with Soviet power in "New Boundaries for the Common Good," in *Constructing Russian Culture in the Age of Revolution: 1881–1940*, ed. Catriona Kelly and David Shepherd (Oxford and New York: Oxford University Press, 1998), 243.

12 On the 25,000ers, see Lynne Viola, *The Best Sons of the Fatherland: Workers in the Vanguard of Soviet Collectivization* (Oxford and New York: Oxford University Press, 1987).

13 Cooke, *Russian Avant-Garde*, 13–19; Dmitrii Khmel'nitskii, *Arkhitektura Stalina: Psikhologiia i stil'* (Moscow: Progress-Traditsiia, 2007), 25–32; Selim O. Khan-Magomedov, *Pioneers of Soviet Architecture: The Search for New Solutions in the 1920s and 1930s*, translated by Alexander Lieven (London: Thames and Hudson, 1987 [1983]); Hugh Hudson, *Blueprints in Blood: The Stalinization of Soviet Architecture, 1917–1937* (Princeton: Princeton University Press, 1994), 16–17.

14 Kendall Bailes, *Technology and Society under Lenin and Stalin: Origins of the Soviet Technical Intelligentsia, 1917–1941* (Princeton: Princeton University Press, 1978), 47–59, 71, 131–43.

15 Party ideologues thus rejected Freudian psychology as "bourgeois," for instance. See Martin A. Miller, *Freud and the Bolsheviks: Psychoanalysis in Imperial Russia and the Soviet Union* (New Haven: Yale University Press, 1998). For more on the Party's attitude to science, see part three of Susan Gross Solomon, ed., *Doing Medicine Together: Germany and Russia between the Wars* (Toronto: University of Toronto Press, 2006).

16 On anti-intellectualism in the Party, see Richard Stites, *Revolutionary Dreams:*

Utopian Vision and Experimental Life in the Russian Revolution (New York: Oxford University Press, 1989), 72–6. Also see David Hoffman, *Stalinist Values: The Cultural Norms of Modernity, 1917–1941* (Ithaca: Cornell University Press, 2003), 39, and Michael David-Fox, *Revolution of the Mind: Higher Learning among the Bolsheviks, 1918–1929* (Ithaca: Cornell University Press, 1997), 116.

17 On the rise of this new generation, see Don K. Rowney, *Transition to Technocracy: The Structural Origins of the Soviet Administrative State* (Ithaca: Cornell University Press, 1989). On the socio-political turning point marked by this attack on the old regime's experts, see Sheila Fitzpatrick, *Education and Social Mobility in the Soviet Union, 1921–1934* (Cambridge: Harvard University Press, 1979), 113, and Mark R. Beissinger, *Scientific Management, Socialist Discipline, and Soviet Power* (Cambridge: Harvard University Press, 1988), 95.

18 Cooke, *Russian Avant-Garde*, 26–8; Hudson, *Blueprints in Blood*, 135.

19 Patrick Joyce, *The Rule of Freedom: Liberalism and the Modern City* (New York: Verso, 2003), 13. For more on cultural technologies of rule, see Francine Hirsch, *Empire of Nations: Ethnographic Knowledge and the Making of the Soviet Union* (Ithaca: Cornell University Press, 2005), 12–15.

20 The Soviet approach to reducing mortality and improving public health relied on education and emergency measures, not on the sorts of technological systems that Ivanitskii desired. For more, see Donald Filtzer, *The Hazards of Urban Life in Late Stalinist Russia: Health, Hygiene, and Living Standards, 1943–1953* (New York: Cambridge University Press, 2010).

21 Heather Hogan, *Forging Revolution: Metalworkers, Managers, and the State in St. Petersburg, 1890–1914* (Bloomington: Indiana University Press, 1993), 68, 90–1, 166.

22 Charles Maier, *In Search of Stability: Explorations in Historical Political Economy* (Cambridge: Cambridge University Press, 1987), 22–6, 32, 50. On the centralization of the Soviet economy, see David Shearer, "The Language and Politics of Socialist Rationalization," *Cahiers du monde russe et soviétique* 32/4 (1991): 581–608; Sheila Fitzpatrick, "Ordzhonikidze's Takeover of Vesenkha: A Case Study in Soviet Bureaucratic Politics," *Soviet Studies* 37/2 (1985): 153–72.

23 On Alexei Gastev, see Charles S. Maier, "Between Taylorism and Technocracy: European Ideologies and the Vision of Industrial Productivity in the 1920s," *Journal of Contemporary History* 5/2 (1970): 33–4; Kendall Bailes, "Alexei Gastev and the Soviet Controversy over Taylorism, 1918–1924," *Soviet Studies* 29/3 (1977): 373–94. On Stakhanovism, see Lewis Siegelbaum, *Stakhanovism and the Politics of Productivity in the USSR, 1935–1941* (Cambridge: Cambridge University Press, 1988).

24 On the literal and metaphorical aspects of the relationship between scientific knowledge and vision, see Chris Otter, *The Victorian Eye: A Political History of Light and Vision in Britain, 1800–1910* (Chicago: University of Chicago Press, 2008).

25 Cooke, *Russian Avant-Garde*, 110.

26 Peter Palchinsky, a Soviet mining engineer of Ivanitskii's generation, likewise found himself at odds with a society where scientific caution and human well-being were too often sacrificed. For more, see Graham, *Ghost of the Executed Engineer*, 41, 68–9, 90. Note that ethnographers faced a similar transition, being compelled in the late 1930s to rather arbitrarily alter their ethnographic data (as collected via censuses) to conform to Stalin's claims about the evolution of a "Soviet people." See Hirsch, *Empire of Nations*, 280–6.

27 On engineers who sought work in Moscow, see Bailes, *Technology and Society*, 268, 290.

28 For a discussion of such backwardness, defined in terms of the lack of experts and institutions, see Maurice Frank Parkins, *City Planning in Soviet Russia, with an Interpretative Bibliography* (Chicago: University of Chicago Press, 1953), 87. Note that Parkins' account is based on the Soviet scholarship of the time.

29 Bailes, *Technology and Society*, 268; Hudson, *Blueprints in Blood*, 143, 169, 176.

30 Karl Qualls, *From Ruins to Reconstruction: Urban Identity in Soviet Sevastopol after World War Two* (Ithaca: Cornell University Press, 2009), chapter 2.

31 On avant-garde complicity, see Boris Groys, *The Total Art of Stalinism: Avant-garde, Aesthetic Dictatorship, and Beyond*, translated by Charles Rougle (Princeton: Princeton University Press, 1992). On the "marionette" conformism of architects in the Stalin period, see Khmel'nitskii, *Arkhitektura Stalina*, 210.

32 Lynne Viola, ed., *Contending with Stalinism: Soviet Power and Popular Resistance in the 1930s* (Ithaca: Cornell University Press, 2002), 12.

33 Greg Castillo, "Stalinist Modern: Constructivism and the Soviet Company Town," *Architectures of Russian Identity: 1500 to the Present*, ed. James Cracraft and Daniel B. Rowland (Ithaca: Cornell University Press, 2003), 135–49.

34 The concept of *vnye* derives from Alexei Yurchak, *Everything Was Forever until It Was No More: The Last Soviet Generation* (Princeton: Princeton University Press, 2005), 131–3.

35 On the fluidity, or persistent "openness," of Socialist Realism as an aesthetic, see Thomas Lahusen, "Socialist Realism in Search of Its Shores: Some Historical Remarks on the 'Historically Open Aesthetic System of the Truthful Representation of Life,'" in *Socialist Realism without Shores*, ed. Thomas Lahusen and E.A. Dobrenko (Durham: Duke University Press, 1997), 661–86.

36 On generational and geographic tensions within the architectural profession, see Cooke, *Russian Avant-Garde*, 26–8, and Kendall Bailes, *Technology and Society*, 41, 63. On similar class and social tensions in the pre-revolutionary period, see Harley Balzer, "The Engineering Profession in Tsarist Russia," in *Russia's Missing Middle Class: The Professions in Russian History*, ed. Harley D. Balzer (Armonk and London: M.E. Sharpe, 1996), 72–3.

37 One used to find a similar lack of consideration for social context in scholarship concerning Soviet science. See Susan Solomon, "Reflections on Western Studies of Soviet Science," in *The Social Context of Soviet Science*, ed. Linda L. Lubrano and Susan Gross Solomon (Boulder: Westview, 1980), 1–30.

38 Boris Groys, "Self-Design and Aesthetic Responsibility," in *e-flux* (2009), accessed on 8 March 2009 at http://www.e-flux.co/journal/view/68.

39 For a discussion of such fissures, which Kotkin's work does not address in any complex theoretical sense, readers should consult Max Wigley's study of Derrida, *The Architecture of Deconstruction: Derrida's Haunt* (Cambridge: MIT Press, 1996). Although Kotkin does not refer to a "house" of socialism, I place Kotkin's ideas in such a frame because this metaphor is implicit to his work. On the "little tactics of the habitat," a game played within the literal and discursive space of Soviet socialism, see Stephen Kotkin, *Magnetic Mountain: Stalinism as a Civilization* (Berkeley: University of California Press, 1995), 149–56.

40 Consider the ambiguous meaning of class or the changing symbolism of the veil in Soviet Muslim society, as discussed in Sheila Fitzpatrick, "Ascribing Class: The Construction of Identity in Soviet Russia," *Journal of Modern History* 65/4 (1993): 745–70; Moshe Lewin, "Who Was the Soviet Kulak?" *Soviet Studies* 18/2 (1966): 189–212; and Douglas Northrop, *Veiled Empire: Gender and Power in Stalinist Central Asia* (Ithaca: Cornell University Press, 2003).

41 Consider the ever-shifting definitions of ethnicity, class, nation, and citizen in the Soviet borderlands, as discussed by Kate Brown, *A Biography of No Place: From Ethnic Borderland to Soviet Heartland* (Cambridge: Harvard University Press, 2005).

42 Words merely link object (world) to subject (person) in relationship, being defined by their interaction. To understand the source of this argument, see Mikhail Bakhtin, *Problems of Dostoevsky's Poetics*, translated by Caryl Emerson (Minneapolis: University of Minnesota Press, 1984). Also see Joyce, *Rule of Freedom*, 10–11.

43 Evgeny Dobrenko presents the image of socialism as the primary product of the Soviet Union's political economy in E.A. Dobrenko, *The Political Economy of Socialist Realism*, translated by Jesse Savage (New Haven: Yale University Press, 2007).

44 Walter Benjamin, "The Task of the Translator," in *Illuminations*, translated by Harry Zohn (New York: Schocken Books, 1986), 69–82.

45 Lynne Viola also refers to the "translation" of policy to suit local needs, in Viola, *Contending with Stalinism*, 12.

46 Henri Lefebvre, *The Production of Space*, translated by Donald Nicholson-Smith (Oxford: Blackwell, 1991), 32–3.

47 Henri Lefebvre, *The Urban Revolution*, translated by Robert Bononno (Minneapolis: University of Minnesota Press, 2003), 23–44. James Scott discusses a similar "blindness," as produced by state mechanisms for studying society, in *Seeing Like a State: How Certain Schemes to Improve the Human Condition Have Failed* (New Haven: Yale University Press, 1998).

48 Lefebvre, *The Production of Space*, 8, 32–3, 51–2.

49 On both towers of vision and the chaos of the world beneath them, see Michel de Certeau, *The Practice of Everyday Life* (Berkeley: University of California Press, 1984), 92–3.

50 The term "visionary planning" derives from S. Frederick Starr, "Visionary Town Planning during the Cultural Revolution," in *Cultural Revolution in Russia, 1928–1931*, ed. Sheila Fitzpatrick (Bloomington: Indiana University Press), 218.

51 Such a belief defines Taylorism as a management system (Maier, *In Search of Stability*, 23, 26).

52 On Moscow's iconic role, see Katerina Clark, "Socialist Realism and the Sacralizing of Space," in *The Landscape of Stalinism: The Art and Ideology of Soviet Space*, ed. E.A. Dobrenko and Eric Naiman (Seattle: University of Washington Press), 3–19; Dobrenko, *The Political Economy of Socialist Realism*, xiv–xvi, 45–6.

1 From Nizhnii to Gorky: Setting the Stage of Socialism

1 Lefebvre, *The Production of Space*, 34.

2 William Rosenberg, "Russian Labour and Bolshevik Power after October," *Slavic Review* 44/2 (1985): 213–38.

3 Cooke, *Russian Avant-Garde*, 19–20; James von Geldern, *Bolshevik Festivals, 1917–1920* (Berkeley: University of California Press, 1993); Catherine Cooke, V.P. Tolstoi, and I.M. Bibikova, eds., *Street Art of the Revolution: Festivals and Celebrations in Russia, 1918–1933* (London: Vendome, 1990).

4 Cooke, *Russian Avant-Garde*, 7–10, 22, 191.

5 David Hoffman attributes the persistence of Russian traditionalism in Soviet life to the imperatives of mass politics (*Stalinist Values*, 8–9). On the way in which religious belief shaped the popular reception of Bolshevism, see

Mark Steinberg, "Workers on the Cross: Religious Imagination in the Lives of Russian Workers," *Russian Review* 53/2 (1994): 213–39; Nina Tumarkin, *Lenin Lives: The Lenin Cult in Soviet Russia* (Cambridge: Harvard University Press, 1997).

6 Qualls, *From Ruins*, 5–8, 80–1, 131. Also see Karl Qualls, "Accommodation and Agitation in Sevastopol: Redefining Socialist Space in the Postwar 'City of Glory,'" in *Socialist Spaces: Sites of Everyday Life in the Eastern Bloc*, ed. David Crowley and Susan Reid (Oxford: Berg, 2002), 23–45.

7 John Czaplicka, Introduction, in *Composing Urban History and the Constitution of Civic Identities*, ed. John Czaplicka and Blair A. Ruble, with the assistance of Lauren Crabtree (Washington, DC: Woodrow Wilson Center Press, and Baltimore: Johns Hopkins University Press, 2003), 27.

8 Olga Sezneva, "Tenacious Place, Contingent Homeland: Making History and Community in the Repopulated City of Kaliningrad" (doctoral dissertation, New York University, 2005), 42–3; Olga Sezneva, "Dual History: The Politics of the Past in Kaliningrad, Former Königsberg," in Czaplicka et al., *Composing Urban History*, 58–85. Also consider the "rollback" of Soviet names and monuments in post-Soviet L'viv, as reported in Yaroslav Hrytsak and Victor Susak, "Constructing a National City: The Case of L'viv," in Czaplicka et al., *Composing Urban History*, 140–64.

9 On the power of inherited cultural codes, see David Kertzer, *Ritual, Politics, and Power* (New Haven: Yale University Press), 42. For a discussion of how locally defined social concerns, or "codes," shaped the response of the Nizhnii Novgorod population to the Bolsheviks, see Sarah Badcock, *Politics and the People in Revolutionary Russia: A Provincial History* (Cambridge: Cambridge University Press, 2007), chapter 4.

10 On the Soviet "cultural ecosystem," see Katerina Clark, *Petersburg: Crucible of Cultural Revolution* (Cambridge: Harvard University Press, 1995), ix–x. A similar idea is articulated in Katerina Clark, "Changing Historical Paradigms in Soviet Culture," in *Late Soviet Culture from Perestroika to Novostroika*, ed. Thomas Lahusen and Gene Kuperman (Durham: Duke University Press, 1993), 290.

11 My comments here are inspired, in part, by Viktor Buchli's emphasis on the need to pay attention to absence, discontinuity, and conflict in the historical record; see *An Archaeology of Socialism* (Oxford: Berg, 1999), 5.

12 I.A. Kir'ianov, *K voprosu o vremeni osnovaniia goroda Gor'kogo* (Gorky: Gosudarstvennoe knizhnoe izdatel'stvo, 1956), quoted in L.L. Trube and A.F. Shubin, *Gor'kovskaia oblast': priroda i naselenie* (Gorky: Volgo-Viatskoe, 1968), 117; N.F. Filatov, "Staryi gorodok XII veka v ust'e Oki – predshestvennik Nizhnego Novgoroda," *Nizhegorodskie issledovaniia po kraevedeniiu i arkheologii:*

Ezhegodnik (Nizhnii Novgorod: Nizhegorodskii gumanitarnyi tsentr, 1999), 104–8.

13 N.I. Khramtsovskii, *Kratkii ocherk istorii i opisanie Nizhnego Novgoroda* (Nizhnii Novgorod: Nizhegorodskaia iarmarka, 1998), 25.

14 Nizhnii Novgorod merchant Ivan Zadorin was one of these supporters of the Zealots of Piety. For more information, see Georg Bernhard Michels, *At War with the Church: Religious Dissent in Seventeenth-Century Russia* (Stanford: Stanford University Press, 1999), 60, 64.

15 Lewis Mumford, *The Culture of Cities* (New York: Harcourt, Brace, 1938), 61–2.

16 Such monastery-fortresses were widespread. Moscow was surrounded by a ring of these. See Alexander Opolovnikov and Elena Opolovnikova, *The Wooden Architecture of Russia: Houses, Fortifications, Churches*, ed. David Buxton (New York: Harry N. Abrams, 1989), 87.

17 Yarila Hill is mentioned in N.F. Filatov, *Nizhnii Novgorod: Arkhitektura XIV – nachala XX veka: Entsiklopediia Nizhegorodskogo kraia* (Nizhnii Novgorod: Nizhegorodskie novosti, 1994), 83–4.

18 This site was also the former location of the Monastery of the Exaltation of the Cross, which was moved to another region of the city in the early nineteenth century. See Filatov, *Nizhnii Novgorod: Arkhitektura XIV – nachala XX v.*, 39–41, and William G. Wagner, "Paradoxes of Piety: The Nizhegorod Convent of the Exaltation of the Cross, 1807–1935," in *Orthodox Russia: Belief and Practice under the Tsars*, ed. Valerie A. Kivelson and Robert H. Greene (University Park: Pennsylvania State University Press, 2003), 211–38.

19 On Zadorin's role in the construction of Nativity Church, see A.S. Gatsiskii, ed., *Nizhegorodskii letopisets, Nizhegorodskie byli* (Nizhnii Novgorod: Nizhegorodskaia iarmarka, 2001), 631. Also see Sergei Ivanovich Arkhangel'skii, ed., *Nizhnii Novgorod v XVII veke: Sbornik dokumentov. Iz materialov k istorii Nizhnego Novgoroda i ego okrugi* (Gorky: Gor'kovskoe knizhnoe izdatel'stvo, 1961), 96–7. On the construction of a new Nativity Church (to replace that financed by Zadorin), see Filatov, *Nizhnii Novgorod: Arkhitektura XIV – nachala XX v.*, 58, 95.

20 Lefebvre, *The Production of Space*, 34.

21 Lewis Mumford, *The City in History: Its Origins, Its Transformations, and Its Prospects* (New York: Harcourt, 1961).

22 For more on the assertion of imperial power through spatial symbols and rituals, see James Cracraft and Daniel Rowland, eds., *Architectures of Russian Identity: 1500 to the Present* (Ithaca: Cornell University Press, 2003).

23 James Cracraft, *The Petrine Revolution in Russian Architecture* (Chicago: University of Chicago Press, 1988).

24 Ernest Zitser argues that Peter the Great's parodies of Orthodox ritual and practice were designed to transfer sacrality to himself, not to deny the sacred altogether; see *The Transfigured Kingdom: Sacred Parody and Charismatic Authority at the Court of Peter the Great* (Ithaca: Cornell University Press, 2004).

25 Mumford, *The City in History*, 368–9, 378–9.

26 T.M. Sytina, "Russkoe arkhitekturnoe zakonodatel'stvo pervoi chetverti XVIII v.," *Arkhitekturnoe nasledstvo* 18 (1969), 70, referred to in N.F. Gulianit-skii, ed., *Moskva i slozhivshiesia russkie goroda XVIII – pervoi poloviny XIX vekov* (Moscow: Stroiizdat, 1998), 177.

27 As modern states imposed architectural and administrative uniformity on their terrain, local regions ceased to be spaces existing in their own right and became smaller parts of a much larger whole. Kenneth Olwig, *Land-scape, Nature, and the Body Politic from Britain's Renaissance to America's New World* (Madison: University of Wisconsin Press, 2002), xix.

28 Filatov, *Nizhnii Novgorod: Arkhitektura XIV – nachala XX v.*, 65–6. On the medieval city, see Mumford, *The City in History*, 302–7; Mumford, *The Culture of Cities*, 53–6.

29 N.F. Filatov, *Nizhegorodskoe zodchestvo XVII – nachala XX veka* (Gorky: Volga-Viatskoe, 1980), 66; E.I. Kirichenko and E.G. Shcheboleva, *Russkaia provint-siia. Kul'turnoe nasledie Rossii* (Moscow: Nash dom; L'Age d'Homme, 1997), 93.

30 S.L. Agafonov, *Kamennaia letopis' goroda* (Gorky: Volgo-Viatskoe, 1971), 20.

31 Chris Otter, *The Victorian Eye: A Political History of Light and Vision in Britain, 1800–1910* (Chicago: University of Chicago Press, 2008), 19.

32 On objectification, see Joyce, *The Rule of Freedom*, 13. Yuri Slezkine explores this change in the educated elite's perception of the world in "Natural-ists Versus Nations: Eighteenth-Century Russian Scholars Confront Ethnic Diversity," in *Russia's Orient: Imperial Borderlands and Peoples, 1700–1917*, ed. Daniel R. Brower and Edward J. Lazzerini (Bloomington: Indiana University Press, 1997), 27–57.

33 On draping robes of imperial authority, see Daniel R. Brower, *The Russian City between Tradition and Modernity, 1850–1900* (Berkeley: University of Cali-fornia Press, 1990), 8–9.

34 William C. Brumfield, *A History of Russian Architecture* (Cambridge: Cam-bridge University Press, 1993), 4. On the capital section, see Kirichenko and Shcheboleva, *Russkaia provintsiia*, 49, 57–62.

35 Such capital sections flourished in the age of Catherine the Great, who was a master of self-articulation through architecture. On architecture as a way of manifesting and representing the power of Catherine the Great, see Andreas Schönle, "Garden of the Empire: Catherine's Appropriation of the

Crimea," *Slavic Review* 60/1 (2001): 1–23, and Dimitri Shvidkovsky, "Catherine the Great's Field of Dreams: Architecture and Landscape in the Russian Enlightenment," in Cracraft, *Architectures of Russian Identity*, 51–65.

36　Filatov, *Nizhegorodskoe zodchestvo*, 70–1; Filatov, *Nizhnii Novgorod: Arkhitektura XIV– nachala XX v.*, 15–16, 63–4. For information on Russian planning in this period, see Kirichenko and Shcheboleva, *Russkaia provintsiia*, 64, 93.

37　Khramtsovskii, *Kratkii ocherk istorii*, 176, 179. For more on planning in this period, also see Iu.N. Bubnov, *Arkhitektura Nizhnego Novgoroda serediny XIX – nachala XX veka* (Nizhnii Novgorod: Volga-Viatskoe, 1990), 7–10.

38　See Alfred J. Rieber, "The Rise of Engineers in Russia," *Cahiers du monde russe et soviétique* 31/4 (1990): 553.

39　On the bureaucrats who conducted this research, see W. Bruce Lincoln, *In the Vanguard of Reform: Russia's Enlightened Bureaucrats, 1825–1861* (Dekalb: Northern Illinois University Press, 1982).

40　Reiber, "The Rise of Engineers," 542, 550–2.

41　Cooke, *Russian Avant-Garde*, 6–10.

42　Filatov, *Nizhnii Novgorod: Arkhitektura XIV– nachala XX v.*, 14, 33, 64, 95; Filatov, *Nizhegorodskoe zodchestvo*, 83–4; T.I. Pelevina et al., eds., *Ulitsy goroda Gor'kogo: Spravochnik* (Gorky: Volgo-Viatskoe, 1972), 99. L.L. Trube, *Naselenie goroda Gor'kogo* (Gorky: Volgo-Viatskoe, 1982), 21.

43　Kirichenko and Shcheboleva, *Russkaia provintsiia*, 60.

44　Kristina Küntzel, *Von Nižnij zu Gorkij: Metamorphosen einer russischen Provinzstadt* (Stuttgart: Franz Steiner Verlag, 2001), 44.

45　Küntzel, *Von Nižnij zu Gorkij*, 67–8; B.S. Khorev, *Gor'kovskaia oblast': Ekonomiko-geograficheskie ocherki* (Gorky: Volgo-Viatskoe, 1967), 141–2.

46　On the rise and fall of the trade fair, see Anne Lincoln Fitzpatrick, *The Great Russian Fair: Nizhnii Novgorod, 1840–90* (London: Macmillan, 1990). For more on the fair, see N.A. Bogoroditskaia, "Stranichki istorii Nizhegorodskoi iarmarki," *Voprosy Istorii [USSR]* 10 (1979): 179–83; A.P. Mel'nikov, *Ocherki bytovoi istorii Nizhegorodskoi iarmarki (1817–1917)*, 2nd ed. (Nizhnii Novgorod: Nizhegorodskii komp'iuternyi tsentr, 1993). On the fair's architecture, see S.M. Shumilkin, "Nizhegorodskaia iarmarka," *Arkhitekturnoe nasledstvo [USSR]* 29 (1981): 80–9.

47　S.L. Agafonov, *Gorod Gorky*, Arkhitektura gorodov SSSR (Moscow: Akademiia arkhitektury SSSR, 1949), 5.

48　Filatov, *Nizhnii Novgorod: Arkhitektura XIV– nachala XX v.*, 76, 80; Küntzel, *Von Nižnij zu Gorkij*, 56–7, 122. Iurii Adrianov and Valerii Shamshurin, *Staryi Nizhnii: Istoriko-literaturnye ocherki* (Nizhnii Novgorod: SMM, 1994), 69; S.M. Shumilkin, "Arkhitektura kupecheskikh postroek Nizhnego Novgoroda i iarmarki XIX – nachala XX v.," *Arkhitektura v istorii russkoi kul'tury*, ed. I.A. Bondarenko (Moscow: Kollektiv avtorov, 1996), 158–67.

49 Note that rule by technosocial system, as represented by such professionals, generally induced the transfer of power to local authorities (Otter, *Victorian Eye*, 259).

50 A.I. Vlasiuk, "Evoliutsiia stroitel'nogo zakonodatel'stva Rossii v 1830e–1910e gody," *Pamiatniki russkoi arkhitektury i monumental'nogo iskusstva*, ed. V.P. Vygolov (Moscow: Nauka, 1985); Olga Vladimirovna Orel'skaia, "Arkhitektura gorodov Gor'kovskoi aglomeratsii, 1920–1930-kh godov: Gorky, Balakhna, Dzerzhinsk" (unpublished dissertation, Moscow Institute of Architecture, 1986), 20.

51 Kirichenko and Shcheboleva, *Russkaia provintsiia*, 96; Filatov, *Nizhnii Novgorod: Arkhitektura XIV– nachala XX v.*, 76; V.V. Baulina, *Gde otdykhaiut Gor'kovchan'e, Gorod Gorky, 1221–1971* (Gorky: Volga-Viatskoe, 1971), 33–4.

52 Exhibitions and national festivals had been held in Nizhnii Novgorod before. Khramtsovskii, *Kratkii ocherk istorii*, 160–4.

53 Filatov, *Nizhnii Novgorod: Arkhitektura XIV– nachala XX v.*, 19, 26, 76; Iu.M. Kossoi, *Vash drug tramvai, 1896–1996: Vek Nizhegorodskogo tramvaia* (Nizhnii Novgorod: Elen'; Iabloko, 1996), 12–26.

54 Küntzel, *Von Nižnij zu Gorkij*, 121. See also Maxim Gorky's articles in *Odesskie novosti* on 11 June 1896.

55 Küntzel, *Von Nižnij zu Gorkij*, 118–23; Iu.N. Bubnov, *Vserossiiskaia promyshlennaia i khudozhestvennaia vystavka 1896 goda v Nizhnem Novgorode: K 100-letiiu so dnia otkrytiia* (Nizhnii Novgorod: "Dekom," 1996), 34; Filatov, *Nizhegorodskoe zodchestvo*, 107.

56 As Rydell notes, in *The World of Fairs*, almost all industrial exhibitions organized prior to the First World War served such a propaganda function. This changed after the war, when modern technology was propagated through consumption, not education; see *The World of Fairs: The Century-of-Progress Expositions* (Chicago: University of Chicago Press, 1993), 93.

57 Jacques Derrida, *Of Grammatology*, translated by Gayatri Chakravorty Spivak (Baltimore: Johns Hopkins University Press, 1976), 69, as analysed in Max Wigley, *The Architecture of Deconstruction*, 68–74.

58 Brower treats the 1896 Exhibition as a façade of modernization – i.e., as something that failed to hide the backwardness of Nizhnii Novgorod's annual trade fair, which was located immediately next to the exhibition site (Brower, *The Russian City between Tradition and Modernity*, 71–3).

59 Although Hamm does not explicitly distinguish between the need for modernization and the perception of that need, his article does focus explicitly on the growing public awareness of a modernization crisis. See Michael Hamm, "The Breakdown of Urban Modernization: A Prelude to the Revolutions of 1917," in *The City in Russian History*, ed. Michael F. Hamm (Lexington: University Press of Kentucky, 1976), 182–200. On the emergence of

what might loosely be called a "liberal" force of modernization that contributed to this sense of "modernization delayed," see Robert W. Thurston, *Liberal City, Conservative State: Moscow and Russia's Urban Crisis, 1906–1914* (New York: Oxford University Press, 1987). For more on a crisis, real or perceived, in urban development in this period, see Daniel R. Brower, "Urban Revolution in the Late Russian Empire," in *The City in Late Imperial Russia*, ed. Michael F. Hamm (Bloomington: Indiana University Press, 1983), 319–54.

60 For a highly readable overview of the emergence of this functional aesthetic in international circles, see Mauro F. Guillén, "Scientific Management's Lost Aesthetic: Architecture, Organization, and the Taylorized Beauty of the Mechanical," *Administrative Science Quarterly* 42/2 (1997): 682–715.

61 T.P. Vinogradov, "Sud'ba imperatorskogo pavil'ona," in *Gorod slavy i vernosti Rossii: materialy istoriko-kraevedcheskoi konferentsii, posviashchennoi 775-letiiu Nizhnego Novgoroda*, ed. Iu.G. Galai, N.A. Kuznetsova, and V.A. Shamshurin (Nizhnii Novgorod: Upravlenie kul'tury, 1996), 196–9.

62 On the use of the old grounds and facilities, see N.A. Bogoroditskaia, "Itogi ekonomicheskogo razvitiia," in *XVI Vserossiiskaia promyshlennaia i khudozhestvennaia vystavka 1896 goda v Nizhnem Novgorode: Ocherki istorii*, ed. N.A. Bogoroditskaia and N.F. Filatov (Nizhnii Novgorod: FISNIMO NNGU, 1996), 62; Baulina, *Gde odykhaiut*, 16–17.

63 Patricia Grimsted, *Archives of Russia* (Armonk: M.E. Sharpe, 2000), 827.

64 For a vivid and detailed description of entertainment on the pre-revolutionary streets of a vibrant provincial capital in these same years, see Patricia Herlihy, *Odessa: A History, 1794–1914* (Cambridge: Harvard University Press, 1986).

65 For a broader discussion of iconoclasm in the Russian Revolution, see Richard Stites, "Iconoclastic Currents in the Russian Revolution: Destroying and Preserving the Past," in *Bolshevik Culture: Experiment and Order in the Russian Revolution*, ed. Abbott Gleason, Peter Kenez, and Richard Stites (Bloomington: Indiana University Press, 1985), 1–24. Steven Maddox explores the symbolism of monuments and their destruction in his dissertation "Healing the Wounds: Commemorations, Myths, and the Restoration of Leningrad's Imperial Heritage, 1941–1950" (doctoral dissertation, University of Toronto, 2008).

66 Kertzer notes that unconscious forces can drive our lives, including our politics: "[people can] invent, revise, or reinvigorate ritual forms that have political effects without being conscious of what those effects will be" (*Ritual, Politics, and Power*, 41).

67 "Vpechatleniia o gorode," *Gor'kovskaia kommuna* 107 (11 May 1936): 4; L.F. Garanina, *Gorod Gorky: Putevoditel'* (Gorky: Volga-Viatskoe, 1964); Pelevina,

Ulitsy goroda Gor'kogo, 102; Iu.N. Bubnov and O.V. Orel'skaia, *Arkhitektura goroda Gor'kogo: Ocherki istorii, 1917–1985* (Gorky: Volga-Viatskoe, 1986), 36–7: Filatov, *Nizhnii Novgorod: Arkhitektura: XIV– nachala XX v.*, 91.

68 Pelevina, *Ulitsy goroda Gor'kogo*, 88–9.

69 L.M. Smirnova, *Nizhnii Novgorod do i posle: Istoriko-literaturnye ocherki* (Nizhnii Novgorod: Begemot, 1996), 103. For a broader history of the convent, see Wagner, "Paradoxes of Piety," 211–38.

70 The kremlin's Saviour Cathedral is not mentioned in the 1926 city guide – a likely sign that it was destroyed. See A.Ia. Sadovskii, "Pamiatniki Nizhe-gorodskoi stariny," in *Nizhegorodskii ezhegodnik: Administrativno-khoziaistvennyi spravochnik po Nizhnemu-Novgorodu i gubernii* (Nizhnii Novgorod: Komissiia po uluchsheniiu byta detei pri Nizhegorodskim GIK, 1926), 82. Also see Smirnova, *Nizhnii Novgorod do i posle*, 217; L.M. Smirnova and T.P. Zvantseva, *Tserkvi Nizhnego Novgoroda, unichtozhennye i utselevshie. Kratkii putevoditel' po staromu gorodu* (Nizhnii Novgorod: Nizhegorodskoe knizhnoe izdatel'stvo, 1991).

71 On similar renamings in postwar Sevastopol, see Qualls, *From Ruins*, 143.

72 John Murray, *Politics and Place Names: Changing Names in the Late Soviet Period* (Birmingham: University of Birmingham, 2000), 16.

73 Also see M. Kutuzov, "Istoriia i revoliutsiia v nazvaniia ulits," *Natisk* 7 (July 1937): 115–18.

74 P. Vysotskii, M. Polonskii, and K. Smirnov, eds., "Gorky-promyshlennyi tsentr, krupneishii gorod strany," *Gor'kovskaia kommuna* 245 (24 Oct. 1939): 2.

75 Initially, Soviet leaders renamed the street "Kooperativnaia." Only later did they change the name to Mayakovsky. Pelevina, *Ulitsy goroda Gor'kogo*, 94.

76 In 1938, the church served as a municipal museum (*kommunal'nyi muzei*). See I. Kashnikov, "Na obshchestvennyi prosmotr," *Gor'kovskii rabochii* 81 (9 April 1938): 2. Archival evidence suggests that the facility hosted permanent city planning exhibits (TsANO, R-6215, op. 1, d. 11, ll. 17ob–18).

77 S.L. Agafonov, "Nizhegorodskii kreml': Arkhitektura, istoriia, restavratsiia," *Arkhitektura SSSR* 1 (Gorky, 1971): 56–60; S.L. Agafonov, *Nizhegorodskii kreml': Arkhitektura, istoriia, restavratsiia* (Gorky: Volgo-Viatskoe, 1976), 40. For a complete architectural description of this building, which is now a historic monument, see Bubnov and Orel'skaia, *Arkhitektura goroda Gor'kogo*, 31–4.

78 To map this soterioscape, consult the "Architectural Guide to Nizhnii Novgorod," *Proekt Rossii* 4 (1997): 49–55, paying close attention to items 1, 5, 6, 9, and 33.

79 According to oral stories recorded by L.M. Smirnova, the monastery was turned into workshops for brick production, while a section of the monks'

residential quarters was made into a theatre (Smirnova, *Nizhnii Novgorod do i posle*, 86).

80 The formation of the municipal museum by 1938 was a hard won but short-lived victory. Earlier, many planning professionals had proposed that the Dmitriev Tower of the kremlin be put to this use (GOPANO, f. 30, op. 1, d. 952, l. 44). A petition for the formation of such a museum was submitted to the city council by the local Union of Soviet Architects in January 1937 (TsANO, R-6205, op.1, d. 7, l. 1). Although these requests were granted in 1938, the museum disappears from the historical record shortly thereafter.

81 John J. Czaplicka, "Conclusion: Urban History after a Return to Local Self-Determination – Local History and Civic Identity," in Czaplicka et al., *Composing Urban History*, 373.

82 I. Batanov, "Ulitsy stanut drugimi," *Gor'kovskii rabochii* 298 (27 Dec. 1936): 4; S.P. Uspenskii and L.V. Krylov, "O zastroike ulitsy Sverdlova," *Gor'kovskii rabochii* 27 (3 Feb. 1939): 4.

83 Murray, *Politics and Place Names*, 24, 29.

84 Lisa Kirschenbaum carefully avoids viewing common people's failure to use official names as resistance, arguing instead that personal associations and habits often mitigated against the use of new names. See Lisa Kirschenbaum, "Place, Memory, and the Politics of Identity: Historical Buildings and Street Names in Leningrad–St. Petersburg," in *Space, Place, and Power in Modern Russia: Essays in the New Spatial History*, ed. Mark Bassin, Christopher Ely, and Melissa Stockdale (Dekalb: Northern Illinois University Press, 2010), 244–5.

85 TsANO, R-2711, op.1, d. 1, ll. 1–2.

86 For example, thanks to the political upheaval of the Great Purges, in February 1937, Rykov Street became Metallurgy Street, Radek Street became Green Street, and Tomskii Street became Volochevskaia Street. (TsANO, R-2613, op. 1, d. 50, l. 32).

87 I take this concept of the "conceptual edifice" from Max Wigley, *The Architecture of Deconstruction: Derrida's Haunt* (Cambridge: MIT Press, 1996).

2 Visionary Planning: Confronting Socio-Material Agencies

1 Vladimir Kirillov, "My," *Literaturnyi al'manakh: Zhurnal Proletkul'ta* (1918): 10.

2 On the modern cityscape as a structure able to produce new modes of sociability, see Christopher Ely, "Street Space and Political Culture in St. Petersburg under Alexander II," in Bassin et al., *Space, Place, and Power in Modern Russia*, 167–94.

3 Kopp, *Town and Revolution*, 96; Cooke, *Russian Avant-Garde*, 112, 127; Kat-

erina Gerasimova, "The Soviet Communal Apartment," in *Beyond the Limits: The Concept of Space in Russian History and Culture*, ed. Jeremy Smith (Helsinki: SHS, 1999), 108–12.

4 Hudson, *Blueprints in Blood*, 62.

5 Richard Stites, "World Outlook and Inner Fears in Soviet Science Fiction," in *Science and the Soviet Social Order*, ed. Loren R. Graham (Cambridge: Harvard University Press, 1990), 301.

6 Maier, *In Search of Stability*, 23, 26, 50.

7 Cooke, *Russian Avant-Garde*, 112; Alexei Gastev, *Poeziia rabochego udara* (Petrograd: Proletkul't, 1918).

8 As cited in Lewis Siegelbaum, *Cars for Comrades: The Life of the Soviet Automobile* (Ithaca: Cornell University Press, 2008), 44.

9 For more, see Lynne Attwood and Catriona Kelly, "Programmes for Identity: The 'New Man' and the 'New Woman,'" in Kelly and Shepher, *Constructing Russian Culture in the Age of Revolution*, 256; Katerina Clark, "The Changing Image of Science and Technology in Soviet Literature," in Graham, *Science and the Soviet Social Order*, 266, 274–9.

10 S. Frederick Starr, "Visionary Town Planning during the Cultural Revolution," in Fitzpatrick, *Cultural Revolution in Russia*, 218.

11 Groys, "Self-Design and Aesthetic Responsibility."

12 S.M. Liubimov, "Vospominaniia i razdum'ia" (Nizhnii Novgorod: Muzei istorii OAO GAZa, n.d.), 1–2; Iurin and Shvorak, *Gor'kovskii avtomobil'nyi*, 17–19; Kurt S. Schultz, "Building the 'Soviet Detroit': The Construction of the Nizhnii Novgorod Automobile Factory, 1927–1932," *Slavic Review* 49/2 (1990): 203–4; "Gde stroit avtozavod," *Nizhegorodskaia kommuna* 98 (28 April 1929): 3; Orel'skaia, "Arkhitektura gorodov Gor'kovskoi aglomeratsii," 13–14, 54–5.

13 Richard Cartwright Austin, *Building Utopia: Erecting Russia's First Modern City, 1930* (Kent: Kent State University Press, 2004), 23; Kurt S. Schultz, "The American Factor in Soviet Industrialization: Fordism and the First Five-Year Plan, 1928–1932" (doctoral dissertation, Ohio State University, 1993).

14 Mira Wilkins and Frank E. Hill, *American Business Abroad: Ford on Six Continents* (Detroit: Wayne State University Press, 1964), 154–7; John B. Rae, *The American Automobile Industry* (Boston: Twayne, 1984), 63–76; I.I. Kiselev et al., eds., *Gor'kovskii avtomobil'nyi* (Moscow: Mysl', 1981), 40–2.

15 On such attempts to break peasant tradition, see Hoffman, *Peasant Metropolis*, 107–26, 158–89. Soviet journalists in this period also sought to curb rather than accommodate traditional cultural preferences. For more, see Matthew Lenoe, *Closer to the Masses: Stalinist Culture, Social Revolution, and Soviet Newspapers* (Cambridge: Harvard University Press, 2004).

16 Maier, "Between Taylorism and Technocracy," 30–4; Maier, *In Search of Stability*, 23–6, 50–6.

17 On such Fordist processes, see Kendall Bailes, "The American Connection: Ideology and the Transfer of American Technology to the Soviet Union, 1917–1941," *Comparative Studies in Society and History* 23/3 (1981): 421–48; Shearer, "The Language and Politics of Socialist Rationalization," 581–608.

18 Starr, "Visionary Town Planning," 212–16. For more on Miliutin's ideas, see his *Sotsgorod: The Problem of Building Socialist Cities*, translated by Anatole Senkevich (Cambridge: MIT Press, 1974).

19 See Ebenezer Howard, *Garden Cities of Tomorrow* (London: Swan Sonnenschein, 1902). For more on the garden city concept and its origins, see Parkins, *City Planning in Soviet Russia*, 23–4; Khan-Magomedov, *Pioneers of Soviet Architecture*, 284, 333. For a full treatment of the debates of this period, also see V.E. Khazanova, *Sovetskaia arkhitektura pervoi piatiletki: Problemy goroda budushchego* (Moscow: Nauka, 1980).

20 Established on 20 April 1929 by the Supreme Council of the Economy (VSNKh SSSR) to oversee factory construction, Avostroi operated out of Moscow until March 1930, at which point its operations moved to Nizhnii Novgorod, although a construction office remained in Moscow to deal with the Americans. See the *opisi* description for TsANO, f. 2431.

21 Hudson, *Blueprints in Blood*, 70–1; L.M. Sabsovich, *Goroda budushchego i organizatsiia sotsialisticheskogo byta* (Moscow: Tekhnicheskoe izdatel'stvo, 1929); Milka Bliznakov, "Soviet Housing during the Experimental Years, 1918–1933," in *Russian Housing in the Modern Age: Design and Social History*, ed. William Craft Brumfield and Blair A. Ruble (Washington, DC: Woodrow Wilson Center Press, and Cambridge: Cambridge University Press, 1993), 87, 116.

22 I. Nikanorov, "Avtostroi," *Revoliutsiia i kul'tura* 1 (15 Jan. 1930): 75–6.

23 Starr, "Visionary Town Planning," 211.

24 According to S. Frederick Starr, Moisei Ginzburg supported some sort of transitional housing already in the late 1920s, although the transitional combine was not outlined in detailed book form until he published *Zhilishche: Opyt piatiletnei raboty nad problemoi zhilishcha* (Moscow: Gosstroiizdat, 1934). See Starr, "Visionary Town Planning," 218. Hudson also suggests that most constructivists opposed such collectivist extremism (*Blueprints in Blood*, 59–60, 75).

25 Hudson, *Blueprints in Blood*, 74.

26 Kopp, *Town and Revolution*, 106; Starr, "Visionary Town Planning," 231. To see such a questionnaire, see "Anketa C.A. o Dome-Kommune," in Kopp, *Town and Revolution*, 92.

27 On the "specular" (liberal) subject's four dimensions, see Otter, *Victorian Eye*, 26–9, 47–9.

28 Julia Obertreis, "The Changing Image of the 'Individual' Apartment in the 1920s and 1930s: Individualism versus the Collective in Soviet Discourse on Housing," presented at the 34th National Convention of the AAASS, Pittsburg, Pennsylvania, 21 Nov. 2002.

29 On oligoptic as opposed to panoptic space, see Otter, *Victorian Eye*, 73–5, 134.

30 Anson Rabinbach, *The Human Motor: Energy, Fatigue, and the Origins of Modernity* (New York: Basic Books, 1990).

31 Mumford, *The Culture of Cities*, 301, 474.

32 TsANO, f. 2431, op. 2, d. 82, ll. 128–30.

33 Kopp, *Town and Revolution*, 143–5, 172; Starr, "Visionary Town Planning," 218–19.

34 Bubnov and Orel'skaia, *Arkhitektura goroda Gor'kogo*, 22.

35 N.A. Miliutin, "Osnovnye voprosy zhilishchno-bytovogo stroitel'stva SSSR," *Sovetskaia arkhitektura* 1 (1931): 2–4; Orel'skaia, "Arkhitektura gorodov," 67–8, 86, 97; Bubnov and Orel'skaia, *Arkhitektura goroda Gor'kogo*, 16, 23.

36 On these schools, see Khan-Magomedov, *Pioneers of Soviet Architecture*, 70, 193, 325–37, 535–600.

37 Blair A. Ruble, "Moscow's Revolutionary Architecture and Its Aftermath: A Critical Guide," in *Reshaping Russian Architecture: Western Technology, Utopian Dreams*, ed. William C. Brumfield (Washington, DC: Woodrow Wilson International Center for Scholars, and Cambridge: Cambridge University Press, 1990), 111–12, 137–8.

38 Cooke, *Russian Avant-Garde*, 164–6.

39 TsANO, f. 2431, op. 2, d. 82, ll. 53–9;d. 198, ll. 4–6.

40 For a complete description of all plans, see Orel'skaia, "Arkhitektura gorodov," 61; V.A. Lavrov, "Avtostroi – sotsialisticheskii gorod," *Stroitel'stvo Moskvy* 4 (1930): 20–3; Olga Orel'skaia, "Eksperiment prodolzhaetsia: iz istorii sovetskoi arkhitektury," *Zapiski kraevedov: Ocherki, vospominaniia, stat'i, dokumenty, khronika*, ed. N.I. Kuprianova and I.V. Sidorova (Gorky: Volga-Viatskoe, 1981), 39–48.

41 TsANO, f. 2431, op. 2, d. 58, ll. 97–8; d. 198, ll. 19–20.

42 As Hudson notes, leading OSA figures generally preferred voluntary communalism (*Blueprints in Blood*, 59–60).

43 For more images, see Cooke, *Russian Avant-Garde*, 33.

44 TsANO, f. 2431, op. 2, d. 58, ll. 57–9, 60–3; d. 82, ll. 39–45ob, 49–49ob.

45 Starr, "Visionary Town Planning," 224.

46 Bubnov and Orel'skaia, *Arkhitektura goroda Gor'kogo*, 15. For Kalmykov's

notes, see TsANO, f. 2431, op. 2, d. 82, ll. 36–7 and 84. Kalmykov's proposal likely served as his diploma project (he graduated from Vkhutein in 1930), but it hardly marks his most radical experimentation. In housing proposals for Central Asia, he adapted to variations in climate, terrain, economic activity, and local building materials. In a fantastic variant on G.T. Krutikov's "flying city," he designed a city that would orbit the globe at Earth's speed of rotation. For more, see Khan-Magomedov, *Pioneers of Soviet Architecture*, 257, 283. Note that Kalmykov's use of multiple styles actually embodied the sort of choice advocated by the OSA in these years (Hudson, *Blueprints in Blood*, 73).

47 Liubimov, "Vospominaniia i razdum'ia," 6.

48 Orel'skaia, "Arkhitektura gorodov," 61–3; Lavrov, "Avtostroi – sotsialisticheskii gorod," 21; TsANO, f. 2431, op. 2, d. 58, ll. 46–50.

49 TsANO, f. 2431, op. 2, d. 82, ll. 64, 131, 138ob–140ob, and 151–7; d. 198, ll. 25–25ob.

50 Three young classicist-trained architects – Georgy P. Gol'ts, Sergei N. Kozhin, and Ivan N. Sobolev – produced the MAO entry. For more about these architects, see Khan-Magomedov, *Pioneers of Soviet Architecture*, 22, 198–9, 229, 333, 347; Cooke, *Russian Avant-Garde*, 92.

51 TsANO, f. 2431, op. 2, d. 82, ll. 27–27ob, 64, 83–83ob, 151–7; Orel'skaia, "Arkhitektura gorodov," 61; Lavrov, "Avtostroi – sotsialisticheskii gorod," 20.

52 TsANO, f. 2431, op. 2, d. 198, l. 16; d. 82, ll. 138ob–142.

53 Ibid., d. 82, ll. 88ob–89, 104, and 132; d. 58, ll. 11–11ob; d. 198, l. 12ob; Orel'skaia, "Arkhitektura gorodov," 65; Bubnov and Orel'skaia, *Arkhitektura goroda Gor'kogo*, 15.

54 TsANO, f. 2431, op. 2, d. 58, ll. 9–10ob; d. 82, ll. 72–7.

55 Ibid., d. 198, l. 3; d. 82, ll. 78–80.

56 Cooke, *Russian Avant-Garde*, 9, 89.

57 Orel'skaia, "Arkhitektura gorodov," 61, 65. Bubnov and Orel'skaia, *Arkhitektura goroda Gor'kogo*, 15; Lavrov, "Avtostroi – sotsialisticheskii gorod," 20, 22.

58 Khan-Magomedov, *Pioneers of Soviet Architecture*, 124–6, 236–8, 260–83; Hudson, *Blueprints in Blood*, 63, 124–5, 147–8.

59 Interest in Soviet-Western collaboration tended to be mutual. For more on such interaction, see Anatole Kopp, "Foreign Architects in the Soviet Union during the First Five-Year Plans," in Brymfield, *Reshaping Russian Architecture*, 176–214.

60 Bailes, *Technology and Society*, 50; Maier, *In Search of Stability*, 44; Thomas Hughes, *American Genesis: A Century of Invention and Technological Enthusiasm, 1870–1970* (New York: Viking, 1989), 251; Austin, *Building Utopia*, 13–15, 18–19.

61 TsANO, f. 2431, d. 82, l. 79ob. Austin planned to send fifteen engineers to the site. Some would arrive in mid-April, while the rest would arrive in May.

62 In the absence of land property values (i.e., a real estate market), industry fought to occupy and control land in the city centre, because it cost them no more than land on the outskirts. R. Antony French, *Plans, Pragmatism, and People: The Legacy of Soviet Planning for Today's Cities* (Pittsburgh: University of Pittsburgh Press, 1995), 106.

63 TsANO, f. 2431, op. 2, d. 82, ll. 62–3, 79ob and 92ob–93; d. 198, ll. 65–6. For more on the early Austin submission, see TsANO, f. 2431, op. 2, d. 58, ll. 9–10ob. Also see Orel'skaia, "Arkhitektury gorodov," 66.

64 TsANO, f. 2431, op. 2, d. 82, l. 151.

65 Ibid., ll. 95ob–97ob and 128–30. As a result of this, some Soviet engineers would later claim that Russian experts, not Austin Company engineers, were the primary authors of the designs for both the factory and the socialist city. See Kiselev, *Gor'kovskii avtomobil'nyi*, 12.

66 TsANO, f. 2431, op. 2, d. 82, ll. 9–17, 128–30, and 151; Austin, *Building Utopia*, 46–9.

67 TsANO, f. 2431, op. 2, d. 58, ll. 1–10.

68 Austin, *Building Utopia*, 49, 166–8.

69 Lavrov, "Avtostroi – sotsialisticheskii gorod," 22; Orel'skaia, "Arkhitektura gorodov," 86; Bubnov and Orel'skaia, *Arkhitektura goroda Gor'kogo*, 22; Nikanorov, "Avtostroi," 76–7.

70 Austin, *Building Utopia*, 49–55, 167. Note that only Richard Cartwright Austin's book specifies that these units were communal apartments; elsewhere, they are simply called "family apartments." See, e.g., G.M. Sur'ianinov, "Kak eto bylo: letopis' organizatsii stroitel'stva, proektirovaniia ... i rekonstruktsii Gor'kovskogo avtomobil'nogo zavoda" (Nizhnii Novgorod: Muzei istorii OAO GAZa, 1971–1980), 289.

71 On the ways in which the communal apartment facilitated surveillance, see Svetlana Boym, *Common Places: Mythologies of Everyday Life in Russia* (Cambridge: Harvard University Press, 1994), 129.

72 TsANO, f. 2431, op. 2, d. 82, ll. 138ob–140ob and 147ob.

73 James C. Scott, *Seeing Like a State: How Certain Schemes to Improve the Human Condition Have Failed* (New Haven: Yale University Press, 1998).

74 Austin, *Building Utopia*, 167–8.

75 To better unify the administration of factory construction, in October 1930, the Supreme Council of the Economy subordinated Metallostroi to Avtostroi. This did not entirely solve the problem of overlapping administrations, for the All-Union Tractor and Automobile Association (VATO) was

also involved in construction. For more, see Kiselev, *Gor'kovskii avtomobilnyi*, 20–1.

76 Kiselev, *Gor'kovskii avtomobil'nyi*, 21–3; A.N. Muravlev, "Sotsgorod avtozavoda im. Molotova (k 10-ti letiiu so dnia osnovaniia)," *Biulleten' arkhitektury* (Gorky, 1940): 24.

77 Austin, *Building Utopia*, 49–50, 123, 166–8; Kiselev, *Gor'kovskii avtomobil'nyi*, 25, 40.

78 See "Sverdlovskaia partorganizatsiia v bor'be za sotsialisticheskuiu stroiku: K Sverdlovskoi raionnoi konferentsii VKP (b)," *Nizhegorodskaia kommuna* 106 (17 April 1931): 2; "O zadachakh perestroiki raboty sovetov," *Nizhegorodskaia kommuna* 52 (22 Feb. 1931): 1; V. Kuibyshev, "Velikii plan postroeniia sotsializma," *Nizhegorodskaia kommuna* 140 (23 May 1931): 1.

79 V.D. Fedorov, *Liudi novykh zavodov: Rabochie Nizhegorodskogo kraia v pervoi piatiletke* (Gorky: Volgo-Viatskoe, 1981), 30–50.

80 V.F. Arzhanova and I.M. Gur'ev, eds., *Ocherki istorii Gor'kovskoi organizatsii KPSS, 1918–1941* (Gorky: Volga-Viatskoe, 1966), 242–4; Kiselev, *Gor'kovskii avtomobil'nyi*, 27–33, 36–43; F.G. Evgrafov, "Kommunisty oblasti v bor'be za industrializatsiiu narodnogo khoziaistva," *Istoriia partiinoi organizatsii* (Gorky: Znanie, 1967), 24–5.

81 Kiselev, *Gor'kovskii avtomobil'nyi*, 36–43; A.N. Muravlev, "Sotsgorod avtozavoda im. Molotova (k 10-ti letiiu so dnia osnovaniia)," *Biulleten' arkhitektury* (Gorky, 1940): 24; G.M. Sur'ianinov, "Ne srazu sotsgorod stroilsia ...," from "Vospominaniia byvshego glavnogo inzhenera UKSa GAZa Sur'ianinova" (Nizhnii Novgorod: Muzei istorii OAO GAZa, n.d.), 3.

82 Liubimov, "Vospominaniia i razdum'ia," 4–5; Austin, *Building Utopia*, 95–131; Schultz, "Building the 'Soviet Detroit,'" 200–12.

83 Fedorov, *Liudi novykh zavodov*, 40–50; Kotkin, *Magnetic Mountain*, chapter 2; Donald Fitzer, *Soviet Workers and Stalinist Industrialization: The Formation of Modern Soviet Production Relations, 1928–1941* (Armonk: M.E. Sharpe, 1986).

84 Orel'skaia, "Arkhitektura gorodov," 86–7; Nikanorov, "Avtostroi," 76–7; Austin, *Building Utopia*, 55, 161–8.

85 I.M. Ashavskii, *Sotsgorod Nizhegorodskogo avtozavoda* (Nizhnii Novgorod: Nizhegorodskoe izdatel'stvo, 1932); Sur'ianinov, "Ne srazu sotsgorod stroilsia," 2; Orel'skaia, "Arkhitektura gorodov," 88; Muravlev, "Sotsgorod avtozavoda," 25.

86 Orel'skaia, "Arkhitektura gorodov," 68; Bubnov and Orel'skaia, *Arkhitektura goroda Gor'kogo*, 16–17; TsANO, f. 2561, op 1, d. 7, l. 5; Muravlev, "Sotsgorod avtozavoda," 24; Sur'ianinov, "Ne srazu sotsgorod stroilsia," 2; GARF, A-314, op. 1, d. 7497, l. 64.

87 Filtzer, *The Hazards of Urban Life*, 37.

88 Kotkin, *Magnetic Mountain*, 157–97.

89 Orel'skaia, "Eksperiment prodolzhaetsia," 39–48.

90 P.N. Fedoseev et al., eds., *KPSS SSSR v resoliutsiiakh i resheniiakh s"ezdov, kon-ferentsii, i plenumov TsK, 1898-1970*, 8th rev. ed., vol. 4, *1927–1931* (Moscow: Politicheskaia literatura, 1931), 116; Gerasimova, "The Soviet Communal Apartment," 113–15.

91 The term "agency of the material" comes from Joyce, *The Rule of Freedom*, 13.

92 TsANO, f. 2431, op. 2, d. 82, ll. 138ob–140ob.

93 G. Puzis, *Kommunal'noe i zhilishchnoe khoziaistvo SSSR za 15 let* (Moscow: Gosudarstvennoe sotsial'no-ekonomicheskoe izdatel'stvo, 1932), 74.

94 Liubimov, "Vospominaniia i razdum'ia," 2–3. Avtozavod included an "American suburb," a series of two-storey wooden structures with stucco façades. They were built in early 1930 (Bubnov and Orel'skaia, *Arkhitektura goroda Gor'kogo*, 16).

95 Bliznakov, "Soviet Housing during the Experimental Years," 87, 116; Mary McLeod, "'Architecture or Revolution': Taylorism, Technocracy, and Social Change," *Art Journal* 43/2 (1983): 139.

96 For information on the Russian city before Peter the Great, see chapter 1.

97 Vladimir Paperny attributes this shift from avant-garde to traditional architecture to a resurgent cultural desire for stability and hierarchy; see *Kul'tura dva* (Moscow: Novoe literaturnoe obozrenie, 1996).

98 Peter Hall, *Cities of Tomorrow: An Intellectual History of Urban Planning and Design in the Twentieth Century*, 3rd ed. (Oxford and Cambridge: Blackwell, 2002), 8–9.

99 For the classic interpretation of this reassertion of traditional values, see N.S. Timasheff, *The Great Retreat: The Growth and Decline of Communism in Russia* (New York: E.P. Dutton, 1946).

100 David Brandenberger, *National Bolshevism: Stalinist Mass Culture and the For-mation of Modern Russian National Identity, 1931–1956* (Cambridge: Harvard University Press, 2002). On the appropriation of nationalism and russocen-tric national policies, also see Terry Martin, *The Affirmative Action Empire: Nations and Nationalism in the Soviet Union, 1923–1939* (Ithaca: Cornell Uni-versity Press, 2001). Both authors view this shift towards more traditional means of rule as a pragmatic response to the challenge of governance.

101 Boris Groys, "The Art of Totality," in *The Landscape of Stalinism: The Art and Ideology of Soviet Space*, ed. E.A. Dobrenko and Eric Naiman (Seattle: Univer-sity of Washington Press, 2003), 96–124.

102 Cooke, *Russian Avant-Garde*, 106, 162, 193.

103 Elizabeth Klosty Beaujour, "Architectural Discourse and Early Soviet Litera-ture," *Journal of the History of Ideas* 44/3 (1983): 477–95.

104 Tarkhanov and Kavtaradze, *Architecture of the Stalin Era*, 13, 25.
105 Barbara Evans Clements, *Bolshevik Women* (New York: Cambridge University Press, 1997), 132–42; Hoffman, *Stalinist Values*, 109–10; Richard Stites, *The Women's Liberation Movement in Russia* (Princeton: Princeton University Press, 1978), chapters 7 and 8. Aleksandra Kollontai also ranked workers' rights over women's emancipation. Wendy Goldman, *Women, the State, and Revolution: Soviet Family Policy and Social Life, 1917–1936* (Cambridge and New York: Cambridge University Press, 1993), 1–49.
106 On this matter, see Wendy Goldman, *Women at the Gates: Gender and Industry in Stalin's Russia* (New York: Cambridge University Press, 2002).
107 See Leon Trotsky, *The Revolution Betrayed: What Is the Soviet Union and Where Is It Going?*, translated by Max Eastman (New York: Merit Publishers, 1965), 153.
108 Stephen Kotkin emphasizes that the enduring Soviet concept of "living space" asserted the state's right to intervene in home life, despite its rehabilitation of the family. See Stephen Kotkin, "Shelter and Subjectivity in the Stalin Period: A Case Study of Magnitogorsk," in Brumfield and Ruble, *Russian Housing in the Modern Age*, 171–210. Also see Hoffman, *Stalinist Values*, 107–9.
109 Anne Eakin Moss, "Stalin's Harem: The Spectator's Dilemma in Late 1930s Soviet Film," *Studies in Russian and Soviet Cinema* 3/2 (2009): 157–2.
110 Hudson, *Blueprints in Blood*, 73–4.
111 Khan-Magomedov, *Pioneers of Soviet Architecture*, 261, 264; M.G. Barkhin, *Metod raboty zodchego: Iz opyta raboty sovetskoi arkhitektury, 1917–1957 gg.* (Moscow: Stroiizdat, 1981), 70–2.

3 From Ivory Tower to City Street: Building a New Nizhnii Novgorod, 1928–1935

1 Karl Popper, *The Logic of Scientific Discovery* (London: Hutchinson, 1980), 314.
2 Cooke, *Russian Avant-Garde*, 110; Hogan, *Forging Revolution*, 65–6; Davidovich and Chizhikova, *Aleksandr Ivanitskii*, 17–18.
3 On the "absolute" of the city, see chapter 1 and the Glossary.
4 For population numbers, also see N. Karbovets, "Bol'shoi Nizhnii," *Nizhegorodskoe khoziaistvo* 4–5 (Jan.–Feb. 1928): 14; Agafonov, *Gorod Gorky*, 12–13.
5 For a study of the role of local industry in providing housing and social services to urban inhabitants, see William Taubman, *Governing Soviet Cities: Bureaucratic Politics and Urban Development in the USSR* (New York: Praeger, 1973).

6 For a statistical picture of this situation, see Filtzer, *Hazards of Urban Life*, 28–38, 76–7. Although Filtzer's statistics date to 1947, they apply to the city of the 1930s, too.

7 Orel'skaia, "Arkhitektura gorodov," 48; Nifontov, "Lengorodok," *Gor'kovskii rabochii* (4 Feb. 1976): 3.

8 Russian municipalities began to depend on revenue from such services in the 1870s; see French, *Plans, Pragmatism, and People*, 28–9. On these developments in the Nizhnii Novgorod region, see TsANO, R-5317, op. 1, d. 8, l. 69ob.

9 Khorev, *Gor'kovskaia oblast'*, 144.

10 On Gosplan's history, see chapter 2 of E.A. Rees, *Decision-Making in the Stalinist Command Economy, 1932–37* (London: Macmillan, and New York: St. Martin's Press, 1997).

11 Parkins, *City Planning in Soviet Russia*, 87; N.Kh. Poliakov, ed., *Spravochnik arkhitektora: gradostroitel'stvo*, vol. 2 (Moscow: Akademiia arkhitektura SSSR, 1946).

12 TsANO, R-5317, op. 1, d. 8, ll. 76–7.

13 When the Industrial Commission first formed, the Nizhnii Novgorod Mechanics and Machine-Building Institute (NMMI) did not yet exist and the Industrial Commission was still a part of this institute's forbearer – namely, the Faculty of Mechanics at Nizhnii Novgorod State University, which was dissolved in 1930. Neither the Industrial Commission nor the NMMI were returned to the university when it reopened in 1932–3. See Khokhlov, *Universitet, rozhdennyi trizhdy*, 343–56, 361–5.

14 GARF, A-314, op. 1, d. 7496, ll. 6–7; d. 7494, l. 240ob. As this anecdote suggests, the state's inventory of its buildings was poorly organized and often haphazard, a problem that lingered throughout the decade. For a 1938 discussion of this issue, see GARF, f. A-262, op. 1, d. 3650, ll. 4–97.

15 Davidovich and Chizhikova, *Aleksandr Ivanitskii*, 15–22, 65, 104; Bubnov and Orel'skaia, *Arkhitektura goroda Gor'kogo*, 17; Khan-Magomedov, *Pioneers of Soviet Architecture*, 276.

16 Hans Blumenfeld, *Life begins at 65: The Not Entirely Candid Autobiography of a Drifter* (Montreal: Harvest House, 1987), 30, 134–5.

17 GARF, A-314, op. 1, d. 7496, l. 6.

18 "K planirovke 'bol'shogo Nizhnego,'" *Nizhegorodskaia kommuna* 24 (28 Jan. 1928): 3; TsANO, R-5317, op. 1, d. 8, ll. 65–7. Both contracts were signed on 10 Feb. 1929.

19 On the schedule, see TsANO, R-5317, op. 1, d. 8, ll. 78–80. On annual plans, see GARF, A-314, op. 1, d. 7494, ll. 240–240ob.

20 Timothy Colton, *Moscow: Governing the Socialist Metropolis* (Cambridge: Harvard University Press, 1995), 6.

21 Charles Hachten offers a rich and complex discussion of the premium that the state placed on individual economic agency in "Property Relations and the Economic Organization of Soviet Russia, 1941–1948" (doctoral dissertation, University of Chicago, 2005).

22 On the challenges of defining resistance in the Soviet context, see James Harris, "Resisting the Plan in the Urals, 1928–1956," in Viola, *Contending with Stalinism*, 202, as well as James Harris, *The Great Urals: Regionalism and the Evolution of the Soviet System* (Ithaca: Cornell University Press, 1999), 4–6. Also see Elena Osokina, "Economic Disobedience under Stalin," in Viola, *Contending with Stalinism*, 178–200.

23 On the value of such local knowledge to state operations, see Scott, *Seeing Like a State*, 177–8.

24 See "K planirovke 'bol'shogo Nizhnego,'" *Nizhegorodskaia kommuna* 24 (28 Jan. 1928): 3; GARF, A-314, op. 1, d. 7497, ll. 24–6, 44–47ob, and 64; TsANO, R-5317, op. 1, d. 8, ll. 65–7.

25 GARF, R-7544, op. 1, d. 77, l. 3ob; GARF, A-314, op. 1, d. 7495, ll. 4–5 and 112–115ob; Molchanov and Agafonov, "Snizit' sebestoimost' stroitel'stva," *Gor'kovskii rabochii* 169 (26 July 1937): 2.

26 TsANO, R-5317, op. 1, d. 8, ll. 78–80.

27 Ibid., d. 7, ll. 5–9.

28 TsANO, R-2717, op. 1, d. 70, ll. 5–9.

29 On these negotiations, see TsANO, R-5317, op. 1, d. 8, ll. 78–80.

30 For precise data on the flows of the Oka and Volga rivers, see Khorev, *Gorkovskaia oblast'*, 31–3.

31 GARF, A-314, op. 1, d. 7497, l. 30. On this hydrogeological challenge, see L.N. Bernatskii, F.E. Vol'sov, and E.V. Milanovskii, *Opolzni srednego i nizhnego Povolzh'ia i mery bor'by s nimi* (Moscow and Leningrad: Glavnaia redaktsiia stroitel'noi literatury, 1935); N.M. Shomysov, *Geologicheskie ekskursii po Gor'kovskoi oblasti* (Gorky: Gor'kovskoe knizhnoe izdatel'stvo, 1954).

32 On attempts to resolve this problem, see GARF, R-7554, op. 1, d. 103, ll. 17 and 75; GARF, A-314, op. 1, d. 7497, ll. 59–60 and 64.

33 In 1935, e.g., planners were criticized for the fact that their economic and technical calculations were not based on new data from government and economic agencies (TsANO, R-2697, op. 1, d. 15, l. 1). Consider their exchanges with the Russian Commissariat of Transportation (NKPS) on the matter of earning NKPS approval for their road and railway plans. See TsANO, R-5317, op. 1, d. 8, ll. 10–12; R-2697, op. 1, d. 42, l. 31.

34 TsANO, R-5317, op. 1, d. 8, ll. 7–9, 37, and 76–7; GARF, A-314, op. 1, d. 7494, ll. 1, 21, 47, and d. 7496, ll. 7–9.

35 Although controversial in his assertion that the famine in Ukraine consti-

tuted genocide, Robert Conquest offers a powerful, emotive story of this catastrophe. See *Harvest of Sorrow: Soviet Collectivization and the Terror-Famine* (New York: Oxford University Press, 1987).

36 "Tsentr kraia dolzhen byt' blagoustroen," *Nizhegorodskaia kommuna* 56 (26 Nov. 1931): 3. For the Party discussion of these problems, see GOPANO, f. 30, op. 1, d. 121, l. 3.

37 A.N. Glubinova, G.I. Bravo-Zhivotovskaia, and B.M. Pudalov, eds., *Gosudarstvennyi arkhiv Nizhegorodskoi oblasti: Putevoditel'* (Nizhnii Novgorod: Komitet po delam arkhivov administratsii Nizhegorodskoi oblasti, 2000), 354.

38 TsANO, f. 78, op. 2, d. 230, l. 10; RGAE, f. 293, op. 3, d. 319, l. 45; A.A. Zhdanov, *O gorodskom khoziaistve Nizhnego Novgoroda* (Gorky: OGIZ, 1932), 5–6; GARF, A-314, op. 1, d. 7495, l. 4.

39 Mark Smith regards such decrees as merely empty rhetoric, which may be partly true. They nonetheless galvanized support for Ivanitskii's star-city plan; see *Property of Communists: The Urban Housing Program from Stalin to Khrushchev* (Dekalb: Northern Illinois University Press, 2010), 26.

40 GARF, A-314, op. 1, d. 7495, ll. 118 and 120; d. 7494, ll. 15–16 and 242–242ob.

41 Note that Alexander Ivanitskii did not identify the settlements in his plan as garden cities. I identify these as such because of the impact of garden city ideas on the factory town model. For more on Ivanitskii's plan, see TsANO, R-5317, op. 1, d. 9, ll. 29–29ob; d. 8, ll. 8–9. See also RGAE, f. 293, op. 4, d. 229, ll. 106–8.

42 GARF, A-314, op. 1, d. 7495, l. 34; d. 7494, ll. 86–7. Also see Davidovich and Chizhikova, *Aleksandr Ivanitskii*, 13.

43 GARF, A-314, op. 1, d. 7494, ll. 7–8.

44 Bubnov and Orel'skaia, *Arkhitektura goroda Gor'kogo*, 12, 18; Davidovich and Chizhikova, *Aleksandr Ivanitskii*, 73; RGALI, f. 2991, op. 1, d. 26, ll. 23–4.

45 Khan-Magomedov, *Pioneers of Soviet Architecture*, 277. V.N. Semenov, M.Ia. Ginzburg, and D.I. Bogorad also explored regional planning in the 1930s, although only M.Ia. Ginzburg's designs for the Crimea were realized. Orel'skaia, "Arkhitektura gorodov," 52–3.

46 Orel'skaia, "Arkhitektura gorodov," 51.

47 Davidovich and Chizhikova, *Aleksandr Ivanitskii*, 73–80; TsANO, R-5317, op. 1, d. 9, ll. 1–3, 19, and 29–29ob. For an excellent study of the discussion of Moscow's Green City in 1929–1930, see Harald Bodenschatz and Christiane Post, eds., *Städtebau im Schatten Stalins: Die internationale Suche nach der sozialistischen Stadt in der Sowjetunion, 1929–1935* (Berlin: Verlagshaus Braun, 2003), 78–85. Although Bodenschatz and Post lament the premature end to Green City planning, it is worth noting that Ivanitskii's Green City did come to fruition, albeit in slightly simplified form.

48 TsANO, R-2697, op. 1, d. 20, ll. 6–6ob.
49 Parkins, *City Planning in Soviet Russia*, 21.
50 French draws attention to this seeming blindness to socio-economic differences, in *Plans, Pragmatism, and People*, 131.
51 TsANO, R-2697, op. 1, d. 20, ll. 6–6ob.
52 RGALI, f. 2991, op. 1, d. 26, l. 21.
53 Bubnov and Orel'skaia, *Arkhitektura goroda Gor'kogo*, 18.
54 TsANO, R-5317, op. 1, d. 8, ll. 1, 10–12.
55 GARF, A-314, op. 1, d. 7494, ll. 81–2, 147, 158–60, and 162.
56 TsANO, R-5317, op. 1, d. 8, ll. 9 and 78. According to the regulations of 1928, the survey and city plan had to conform to the demands and instructions set forth in the NKVD RSFSR bulletin no. 21 of 4 July 1928. See GARF, A-314, op. 1, d. 7497, ll. 15 and 40; TsANO, R-2697, op. 1, d. 20, ll. 5–5ob.
57 GARF, A-314, op. 1, d. 7494, ll. 123–8. The Scientific-Technical Council heightened alarm by pointing out that the maximal flood levels (*pavodki*) of the the Moscow River were rising by 61 cm every twenty-five years, supposedly a portent of problems yet to come in Nizhnii Novgorod (GARF, A-314, op. 1, d. 7497, l. 32ob).
58 GARF, A-314, op. 1, d. 7494, ll. 97–9 and 119–21.
59 Ibid., ll. 30–30ob, 162–3, and 202–3.
60 GARF, A-314, op. 1, d. 7495, l. 34; d. 7497, ll. 17–18; d. 7494, ll. 72–3 and 80–1.
61 "Organizatsiia, sostav i podgotovka rabot po planirovaniiu Bol'shogo Nizhnego. Kratkoe soderzhanie doklada," *Trudy III Vsesoiuznyi vodoprovodnyi i sanitarno-tekhnicheskii s"ezd v Rostove-na-Donu* (1929), as referred to in Davidovich and Chizhikova, *Aleksandr Ivanitskii*, 65. Also see GARF, A-314, op. 1, d. 7497, ll. 17–18; d. 7494, ll. 178–80.
62 GARF, A-314, op. 1, d. 7494, ll. 76–9; d. 7497, l. 30ob. On the slight decrease in the number of infectious illnesses in the city, see "Epidemicheskie zabolevaniia v Bol'shom Nizhnem Novgorode," *Nizhegorodskaia kommuna* 281 (6 Dec. 1929): 4.
63 GARF, A-314, op. 1, d. 7494, ll. 74–5, 99, and 132. On existing and future green space, see GARF, A-314, op. 1, d. 7495, ll. 63–4; d. 7497, ll. 31–3.
64 The regulations to which they referred were the *Edinye normy stroitel'nogo proektirovaniia ser. X. NN. 1–2. Komitet po standartizatsii pri STO 14/III-32.* For arguments that Ivanitskii's plan did not meet these standards, see GARF, A-314, op. 1, d. 7494, l. 194.
65 GARF, A-314, op. 1, d. 7497, ll. 19–20.
66 On this July 1932 debate over temporary housing, see ibid., d. 7494, ll. 134–6.

67 Ibid., ll. 116–19 and 242; TsANO, R-5317, op. 1, d. 8, ll. 62–3.
68 GARF, A-314, op. 1, d. 7497, ll. 19 and 44; d. 7494, ll. 82, 88, and 141–2.
69 Ibid., d. 7494, ll. 158–60.
70 For studies that incorporate such analysis of "institutional pluralism," or institutionally shaped agendas, see Werner Hahn, *Postwar Soviet Politics: The Fall of Zhdanov and the Defeat of Moderation, 1946–53* (Ithaca: Cornell University Press, 1982), and Jerry Hough, *The Soviet Union and Social Science Theory* (Cambridge: Harvard University Press, 1979).
71 Catriona Kelly, "New Boundaries for the Common Good," in Kelly and Shepherd, *Constructing Russian Culture*, 255.
72 GARF, A-314, op. 1, d. 7494, ll. 115–16, 162–3, and 178–80.
73 Ibid., ll. 112 and 119–21; d. 7497, ll. 31ob–32ob; d. 7495, ll. 32–3.
74 The notion of "seeing like a state" derives from Scott, *Seeing Like a State*, 89.
75 TsANO, R-6205, op. 1, d. 13, ll. 2–3.
76 GARF, A-314, op.1, d. 7499, ll. 47–8, 55, and 72.
77 Ibid., ll. 31–4; d. 7494, l. 160.
78 On sanitary officials' concern, see ibid., d. 7499, ll. 31–4 and 57.
79 Ibid., ll. 47–55, 64, 72, and 205–12.
80 For the Council's approval of Gorstroiproekt's plans, see ibid., ll. 49–50, 64.
81 Alexei Kojevnikov, "Games of Stalinist Democracy: Ideological Discussions in Soviet Sciences, 1947–1952," in *Stalinism: New Directions*, ed. Sheila Fitzpatrick (New York: Routledge, 2000), 140–70.
82 GARF, A-314, op. 1, d. 7499, ll. 49–50, 64.
83 TsANO, R-2697, op. 1, d. 20, ll. 1–1ob.
84 RGAE, f. 293, op. 4, d. 229, ll. 106–8.
85 Trube, *Naselenie goroda Gor'kogo*, 24.

4 Stalinist Representation: Iconographic Vision, 1935–1938

1 Emphasis in the original text, which is taken from *Arkhitektura i Vkhutein* 1 (Jan. 1929): 8, cited in Khan-Magomedov, *Pioneers of Soviet Architecture*, 599.
2 Michael Walzer, "On the Role of Symbolism in Political Thought," *Political Science Quarterly* 82 (June 1967): 194.
3 For an analysis of how postwar professionals managed risk by asking political authorities to arbitrate their disputes, see Alexei Kojevnikov, "Games of Stalinist Democracy," 140–70.
4 Starr, "Visionary Town Planning," 238–9; Hudson, *Blueprints in Blood*, 143–5, 175.
5 GARF, A-314, op. 1, d. 7499, ll. 31–4.

6 Ibid., d. 7509, l. 25; d. 7499, l. 144. The documents recording the Scientific-Technical Council's approval can be found in TsANO, R-2697, op. 1, d. 20, l. 1.

7 TsANO, R-2697, op. 1, d. 20, ll. 1–1ob. On the lack of a melioration plan in 1936, see ibid., d. 36, ll. 49 and 55; d. 25, ll. 33–6 and 44–5; d. 45, ll. 6–6ob. On later concerns, see ibid., d. 36, l. 49ob; d. 57, l. 13ob.

8 On capital sections, see Kirichenko and Shcheboleva, *Russkaia provintsiia*, 9–49, as well as chapter 1 of this book.

9 Richard Antony French draws attention to the "imperial principle" in Soviet architecture, cited in French, *Plans, Pragmatism, and People*, 65.

10 Olwig, *Landscape, Nature, and the Body Politic*, xix.

11 On the application of this aesthetic to Gorky, see Orel'skaia, "Arkhitektura gorodov," 70.

12 French, *Plans, Pragmatism, and People*, 9, 63, 81–3; Blair A. Ruble, *Leningrad: Shaping a Soviet City* (Berkeley: University of California Press, 1990), 70–112; James H. Bater, *The Soviet City: Ideal and Reality* (Beverly Hills: Sage, 1980).

13 On the Moscow plan, see *General'nyi plan rekonstruktsii goroda Moskvy* (Moscow: Moskovskii rabochii, 1936); B.M. Frolic, "The New Moscow City Plan," in Hamm, *The City in Russian History*, 276–88; Colton, *Moscow: Governing the Socialist Metropolis*, 327–40; V. Nik., "Novaia Moskva," *Gor'kovskii rabochii* 52 (4 March 1935): 4.

14 Jeffrey Brooks, *Thank You, Comrade Stalin! Soviet Public Culture from Revolution to Cold War* (Princeton: Princeton University Press), 100.

15 Boym, *Common Places*, 112–13; Dobrenko, *The Political Economy of Socialism*, 10–19.

16 Sona Hoisington, "'Ever Higher': The Evolution of the Project for the House of Soviets," *Slavic Review* 62/1 (2003): 41–68.

17 TsANO, R-5317, op. 1, d. 124, ll. 104–104ob.

18 Poliakov, *Spravochnik arkhitektora*, 30.

19 TsANO, R-2698, op. 2, d. 2, ll. 53–6; GARF, A-314, op. 1, d. 7499, ll. 1–2.

20 GARF, A-314, op. 1, d. 7509, ll. 28–9. On the cathedral's destruction and later restoration, see M.S. Kudriavtsev, "Vozrozhdenie sobora Aleksandra Nevskogo," in *Rossiia i Nizhegorodskii krai: Aktual'nye problemy istorii* (Nizhnii Novgorod: Nizhegorodskii gumanitarnyi tsentr, 1998), 269–71.

21 GARF, A-314, op. 1, d. 7499, ll. 76–7.

22 Ibid., d. 7498, ll. 37–37ob.

23 "Pobol'she vnimaniia voprosam byta," *Nizhegorodskaia kommuna* 279 (1 Dec. 1928): 1; "Proletarskomu Kanavinu – sotsialisticheskoe blagoustroistvo," *Gor'kovskii rabochii* 30 (3 April 1934): 1; K. Neslavin, "'Melochi,'" *Gor'kovskii rabochii* 171 (28 July 1937): 2; "Dom soiuzov – vokzal s odnim peresadom,"

Nizhegorodskii rabochii 6 (12 June 1932): 2. Also see A.A. Zhdanov, *Otchet o rabote kraikoma* (Gorky: OGIZ, 1932), 45.

24 Lewis Siegelbaum, *Stakhanovism and the Politics of Productivity in the USSR, 1935–1941* (Cambridge: Cambridge University Press, 1990).

25 Postanovlenie TsIK SSSR i VSKKh pri TsIK SSSR, "Po dokladu Vsesoiuznogo soveta kommunal'nogo khoziaistva pri TsIK SSSR o vypolnenie plana zhilishchno-kommunal'nogo stroitel'stva za pervoe polugodie 1933 g.," *Sobranie uzakonenii i rasporiazhenii SSSR* 1/54 (9 Sept. 1933): 318, 600–1.

26 See, e.g., "Prikaz upol'nomochennogo po bor'be s navodneniem po gorodu Gor'komu," *Gor'kovskii rabochii* 57 (9 March 1935) 4; "Iacheiki – v avangard perestroiki raboty sovetov," *Nizhegorodskaia kommuna* 37 (7 Feb. 1931): 2; A. Larionov, "'Novoe Sormovo' nuzhdaetsia v pomoshchi," *Nizhegorodskaia kommuna* 38 (8 Feb. 1931): 3.

27 *Materialy k otchetu o rabote gorsoveta* (Gorky: Gorsovet, 1935), 45–6.

28 GARF, A-314, op. 1, d. 7498, ll. 31–3.

29 Ibid., l. 74.

30 *Materialy k otchetu*, 53.

31 GARF, A-314, op. 1, d. 7498, ll. 31–3 and 74.

32 Ibid., ll. 31–3.

33 Ibid., ll. 42–42ob.

34 TsANO, R-5317, op. 1, d. 8, l. 6.

35 GARF, A-314, op. 1, d. 7498, l. 35.

36 Parkins, *City Planning in Soviet Russia*, 50. For more on such planning bodies, see Andrew Day, "Building Socialism: The Politics of the Soviet Cityscape in the Stalin Era" (doctoral dissertation, Columbia University, 1998).

37 GARF, R-7544, op. 1, d. 92, l. 7; d. 174, ll. 15–17ob.

38 These were generally carried out by experts from the Russian Commissariat of the Municipal Economy's Bureau of Technical Consultation (BTK NKKKh RSFSR). See TsANO, R-2697, op. 1, d. 57, ll. 26–26ob.

39 TsANO, R-2697, op. 1, d. 8, ll. 42–3.

40 Ibid., d. 57, ll. 26–7.

41 GARF, A-314, op. 1, d. 7498, ll. 38ob–39, 42–42ob, and 74.

42 Ivanitskii reviewed the city plan in November 1937. Ibid., d. 7509, ll. 96–135.

43 Parkins, *City Planning in Soviet Russia*, 94–8.

44 GARF, A-314, op. 1, d. 7498, l. 38ob–41ob. Similar brigades were formed to plan other Soviet cities, including Baku, Stalinabad, Cheliabinsk, and Arkhangel'sk. See "Proektirovanie gorodov," *Gor'kovskii rabochii* 74 (1 April 1937): 2.

45 RGAE, f. 293, op. 4, d. 229, ll. 14–31.

46 On stipulations that they resubmit the zoning plan, adding greater scientific

and demographic detail, see TsANO, R-2697, op. 1, d. 57, ll. 20ob and 22–4; GARF, A-314, op. 1, d. 7499, ll. 104–21 and 144.

47 On the submissions, see GARF, A-314, op. 1, d. 7026, ll. 45–50; TsANO, R-2697, op. 1, d. 25, ll. 18–19. Before the Leningrad Scientific Research Institute took up the contract, the design trust "Kommunstroi" worked on melioration plans. GARF, A-314, op. 1, d. 7026, ll. 45–50.

48 GARF, A-314, op. 1, d. 7026, ll. 45–50. For a critique of the proposals, see TsANO, R. 2697, op. 1, d. 25, ll. 1–10ob.

49 For an outline of the stages of city planning, please review chapter 3.

50 TsANO, R-2697, op. 1, d. 57, ll. 23–4; TsANO, R-6205, op. 1, d. 4, ll. 16–17.

51 GARF, A-314, op. 1, d. 7503, ll. 20–1 and 30–1.

52 Evgeny Dobrenko, "Socialism as Will and Representation," translated by Jesse Savage and Gust Olsen, in *Kritika: Explorations in Russian and Eurasian History* 5/4 (2004): 704. Dobrenko's ideas here are taken from Alexander Panchenko, "'Potemkinskie derevni kak kul'turnyi mif," in A. Panchenko, *O russkoi istorii i kul'ture* (St. Petersburg: Azbuka, 2000), 426.

53 TsANO, R-2697, op. 1, d. 42, ll. 29–37.

54 Clark, "Socialist Realism and the Sacralizing of Space," 8–11. Without using the term "iconographic," Francis Parkins draws attention to the derivative and imitative nature of design in the Soviet Union of the 1930s, in *City Planning in Soviet Russia*, 30.

55 On Moscow as a model of urban design, see S.E. Chernyshev, "General'nyi plan rekonstruktsii Moskvy i planirovka gorodov," *Gor'kovskii rabochii* 131 (10 June 1937): 2.

56 TsANO, R-78, op. 2, d. 304, l. 5.

57 *Materialy k otchetu*, 53.

58 N.A. Solofnenko, "Gorod Gorky cherez 15–20 let," *Gor'kovskii rabochii* 255 (4 Nov. 1935): 3; N.A. Solofnenko, "Arkhitekturnyi obraz goroda," *Gor'kovskii krai* 1 (1936): 98.

59 TsANO, R-78, op. 2, d. 304, l. 21; N.A. Solofnenko, "Gorod Gorky cherez 15–20 let," *Gor'kovskii rabochii* 255 (4 Nov. 1935): 3.

60 Kazin, "Rekonstruktsiia ulitsy Sverdlova," *Gor'kovskii rabochii* 43 (22 Feb. 1936): 2. For an evocative description, see G. Fedorov, *Sotsialisticheskii gorod Gorky* (Gorky: OGIZ, 1939), 51–2. On the plan, see GARF, A-314, op. 1, d. 7501, l. 4; d. 7509, l. 21. For the orders of the provincial Party committee (in support of this plan), see TsANO, R-2697, op. 1, d. 60, ll. 9–10.

61 On *locus genii* and *genius loci*, see Volker M. Welter, "From *locus genii* to Heart of the City: Embracing the Spirit of the City," in *Modernism and the Spirit of the City*, ed. Iain Boyd Whyte (London: Routledge, 2003), 35–8. On the ways in which Russian thinkers invested the landscape with national meaning,

see Christopher Ely, *This Meager Nature: Landscape and National Identity in Imperial Russia* (DeKalb: Northern Illinois University Press, 2002). Also see Christopher Ely, "The Origins of Russian Scenery: Volga River Tourism and Russian Landscape Aesthetics," *Slavic Review* 62/4 (2003): 666–82.

62 GARF, A-314, op. 1, d. 7501, l. 4.

63 Ibid., d. 7509, ll. 28–9 and 39–40 (from Ivanitskii's critique in 1937). On the new provincial centre and its location, see N.A. Solofnenko, "Arkhitekturnyi obraz goroda," *Gor'kovskii krai* 1 (1936): 102; N.A. Solofnenko, "Siluet budushchego goroda," *Gor'kovskii rabochii* 29 (5 Feb. 1936): 2.

64 For a description of these plans, see A.F. Zhukov, "Kak rekonstruirovat' Sovetskuiu ploshchad'," *Gor'kovskii rabochii* 48 (28 Feb. 1936): 2; Nikolai Ushakov, "Kreml' i Sovetskaia ploshchad'," *Gor'kovskii rabochii* 40 (21 Feb. 1936): 2. For the decree approving the destruction of the kremlin wall, see "Ob osnovnykh polozheniiakh po sostavleniiu general'nogo plana rekonstruktsii goroda Gor'kogo," *Gor'kovskii rabochii* 164 (19 July 1936): 1.

65 Blair A. Ruble, "From Palace Square to Moscow Square: St. Petersburg's Century-Long Retreat from Public Space," in Brumfield, *Reshaping Russian Architecture*, 26–7. Note that Ruble does not comment on the problem central to Soviet concerns – namely, the fact that the old intimacy of small streets was shaped by exclusivity (i.e., the dominance of the nobility, as manifest in their special right to elite forms of dress, transportation, address, etc.).

66 GARF, A-314, op. 1, d. 7497, ll. 72–3; d. 7509, l. 100.

67 Ibid., d. 7497, l. 72; d. 7509, ll. 29–30. TsANO, R-2697, op. 1, d. 36, l. 64.

68 For information on earlier meliorative work, see Agafonov, "Nizhegorodskii kreml'," 56–60, and Agafonov, *Kamennaia letopis'*, 13.

69 GARF, A-314, op. 1, d. 7501, ll. 108 and 125ob–126.

70 Ibid., d. 7509, ll. 29–30.

71 TsANO, R-6205, op. 1, d. 4, ll. 16–17.

72 Ibid., d. 14, l. 3ob. TsANO, R-2697, op. 1, d. 36, l. 28; GARF, A-314, op. 1, d. 7509, l. 31.

73 GARF, A-314, op. 1, d. 7509, ll. 31 and 39.

74 Kazin, "Rekonstruktsiia ulitsy Sverdlova," *Gor'kovskii rabochii* 43 (22 Feb. 1936): 2.

75 For criticism of monumental design, as voiced by a local architect in 1940, see Muravlev, "Sotsgorod avtozavoda," 26. For similar criticism from members of the Union of Soviet Architects in the mid-1930s, see Hudson, *Blueprints in Blood*, 175. On lingering constructivism in local architecture, see Muravlev, "Sotsgorod avtozavoda," 25, 30; Sur'ianinov, "Ne srazu sotsgorod stroilsia," 2.

76 Garanina et al., eds., *Gorod Gorky: putevoditel'* (Gorky: Volgo-Viatskoe, 1964), 245.
77 Boym, *Common Places*, 91.
78 Antonia Gramsci, *Selections from the Prison Notebooks*, translated by Quintin Hoare and Geoffrey Smith (London: Lawrence and Wishart, 1971), 339, as noted in Kertzer, *Rituals, Politics, and Power*, 96–8.

5 Stalinism as Stagecraft: The Architecture of Performance

1 Mary P. Follett, *The New State: Group Organization – the Solution of Popular Government* (1918), 3rd ed. (London: Longmans, Green, and Co., 1934), 180.
2 Thurman Arnold, *The Symbols of Governance* (New Haven: Yale University Press, 1935), 17.
3 On the power of ritual to gloss over such tensions, see Kertzer, *Ritual, Politics, and Power*, 11, 28, 100.
4 For an example of propaganda on this theme, see the 1952 propaganda poster by N. Petrov and K. Ivanov. It features Stalin standing before one of Moscow's tall buildings with the words, "Praise to Stalin – Architect of Communism," in the foreground. To view this poster, see David Priestland, *The Red Flag: A History of Communism* (New York: Grove, 2009), image 15.
5 On Stalin as arbiter of discourse and meaning, see Yurchak, *Everything Was Forever*, 12–13.
6 On Stalin as "progenitor," see Groys, *The Total Art of Stalinism.*
7 This stark reality is noted in Greg Castillo, "Stalinist Modern: Constructivism and the Soviet Company Town," in Cracraft and Rowland, *Architectures of Russian Identity*, 135–49.
8 GARF, A-314, op. 1, d. 7498, ll. 41ob–43.
9 TsANO, R-2697, op. 1, d. 18, ll. 6–6ob, 22, and 40–40ob.
10 "U karty goroda Gor'kogo," *Gor'kovskii rabochii* 245 (23 Oct. 1935): 1; N.A. Solofnenko, "Gorod Gorky cherez 15–20 let," *Gor'kovskii rabochii* 255 (4 Nov. 1935): 3. Iulii Moiseevich Kaganovich (1892–1962) was the brother of Lazar Moiseevich Kaganovich (1893–1991). He began his career in the Province of Nizhnii Novgorod in 1922, working his way rapidly up the Party hierarchy to serve as head of the provincial government from 1934 to 1936 and as first secretary of the provincial Party organization from 1937 to 1939. See L.P. Gordeeva, "L.M. Kaganovich i V.M. Molotov – rukovoditeli Nizhegorodskoi gubernii (1918–1920)," in Pelevina and Soina, *Rossiia i Nizhegorodskii krai*, 241–4; V.I. Belous, ed., *Politicheskaia elita Nizhegorodskoi oblasti, 1917–1995* (Nizhnii Novgorod: FISNIMO NNGU, 1995), 39–40.
11 TsANO, R-6205, op. 1, d. 2, l. 2ob.

12 Tarkhanov and Kavtaradze, *Architecture of the Stalin Era*, 13; Hudson, *Blueprints in Blood*, 172.

13 "S plenuma gorkoma VKP (b)," *Gor'kovskii rabochii* 7 (4 March 1934): 1; "Arkhitektory – k s'ezdu sovetov," *Gor'kovskii rabochii* 199 (25 Oct. 1934): 4; "Gorod v budushchem," *Gor'kovskii rabochii* 210 (7 Nov. 1934): 3. This was done as preparation for the upcoming Conference of the Union of Soviet Architects. For more, see Hudson, *Blueprints in Blood*, 146, 172–9.

14 "Bread and circus" alludes to Stephen Kotkin's characterization of the Soviet moral economy as a combination of official goods ("bread") and illegal trade ("circus"). The denunciation of those engaged in illegal trade was a circus, or absurd show, because dysfunction in the Soviet economy made the black market a necessity (Kotkin, *Magnetic Mountain*, 238–79).

15 On the role of rituals in making the state identifiable, see Kertzer, *Rituals, Politics, and Power*, 28.

16 On public and hidden transcripts, see James Scott, *Dominations and the Arts of Resistance: Hidden Transcripts* (New Haven: Yale University Press, 1992), 17–44, 56–7.

17 TsANO, R-6205, op. 1, d. 4, ll. 52, 116–25; V.F. Boronin, "Proekt i stroitel'naia praktika," *Gor'kovskii rabochii* 32 (9 Feb.1936): 2.

18 TsANO, R-6205, op. 1, d. 2, l. 2ob; d. 4, ll. 121ob–122 and 125.

19 Ibid., d. 3, ll. 145–6. Anatolii Fedorovich Zhukov was reportedly a "Moscow" architect; Bubnov and Orel'skaia, *Arkhitektura goroda Gor'kogo*, 42.

20 Brooks, *Thank You, Comrade Stalin!*, 127. Note that Robert Tucker has also referred to those awarded honours and privileges as the new "service nobility." *Stalin in Power: The Revolution from Above, 1928–1941* (New York: Norton, 1990), 323.

21 For more on this pact with power, see Catriona Kelly, "New Boundaries for the Common Good," 245; Sheila Fitzpatrick, "Professors and Soviet Power," in *The Cultural Front: Power and Culture in Revolutionary Russia* (Ithaca: Cornell University Press, 1992), 55–64.

22 TsANO, R-6205, op. 1, d. 4, ll. 115–115ob.

23 On the role of the 1936 Constitution in establishing a new *soslovie* (caste) system, one in which architects would join the "intellectual stratum," see Fitzpatrick, "Ascribing Class," 745–70.

24 Under Catherine II and her successors, all provincial chief architects earned noble status. See Filatov, *Nizhegorodskoe zodchestvo*, 71, 78–9. On the way in which provincial nobles exported the capital's aesthetic and social practices to the provinces, serving as emissaries of the capital's culture, see P.R. Roosevelt, *Life on the Russian Country Estate: A Social and Cultural History* (New Haven: Yale University Press, 1995).

25 On the role of private space in fostering the self-reflection essential to liberal subjectivity, see Otter, *Victorian Eye*, 46–54.

26 The role of the collective in shaping individual selfhood is explored in Oleg Kharkhordin, *The Collective and the Individual in Russia: A Study of Practices* (Berkeley: University of California Press, 1999). Kharkhordin contrasts the privacy of the Western confessional to the Orthodox tradition of "doing penance in the public gaze," a practice appropriated – in reinvented form – by the Bolsheviks.

27 In 1932, on Ivanitskii's behalf, the Industrial Commission set up a 2½ month exhibit of its city zoning plan in the local Historical-Revolutionary Museum. See GARF, A-314, op. 1, d. 7496, l. 8.

28 GARF, A-314, op. 1, d. 7496, l. 8. Afanas'ev, "Biuro planirovki rabotaet bez uchastiia mass," *Gor'kovskii rabochii* 5 (3 June 1932): 2.

29 TsANO, R-6205, op. 1, d. 2, l. 9; d. 4, ll. 101 and 173ob–174.

30 I.E. Geimanson, "Ploshchad' v Gor'kom," *Arkhitekturnaia gazeta* 8 (8 Feb. 1936): 3.

31 Nikolai Ushakov, "Kreml' i Sovetskaia ploshchad'," *Gor'kovskii rabochii* 21 (Feb. 1936): 2; A.F. Zhukov, "Kak rekonstruirovat' Sovetskuiu ploshchad'," *Gor'kovskii rabochii* 48 (28 Feb. 1936): 2.

32 "Planirovka g. Gor'kogo: sostavlena skhema proekta," *Gor'kovskii rabochii* 25 (1 Feb. 1936): 2; V. Gradskii, "Budushchee nashego goroda," 26 (2 Feb. 1936): 2; TsANO, R-6205, op. 1, d. 2, l. 2ob.

33 "Kak obsuzhdaetsia plan rekonstruktsii goroda," *Gor'kovskii rabochii* 50 (2 March 1936): 2.

34 On the centrality of the press to the creation of such a public culture, see Brooks, *Thank You, Comrade Stalin!*, 3–18, 69.

35 "Planirovka goroda Gor'kogo: sostavlena skhema proekta," *Gor'kovskii rabochii* 25 (1 Feb. 1936): 2; N.A. Solofnenko, "Arkhitekturnyi obraz goroda," *Gor'kovskii krai* 1 (1936): 98–103.

36 For a sample of this debate, see A.F. Zhukov, "Kak rekonstruirovat' Sovetskuiu ploshchad'," *Gor'kovskii rabochii* 48 (28 Feb. 1936): 2; A.A. Iakovlev, Jr., "Sleduet li snosit' kremlevskuiu stenu?" *Gor'kovskii rabochii* 48 (28 Feb. 1936): 2; A.I. Velikorechin, "Kreml' nado sokhranit'," *Gor'kovskii rabochii* 48 (28 Feb. 1936): 2. For "closed" debates among elites, see TsANO, R-2697, op. 1, d. 36, ll. 24–5; GARF, A-314, op. 1, d. 7504, ll. 162–3; TsANO, R-2697, op. 1, d. 49, ll. 17–18.

37 A.M. Shirkov, "Gde postroit' pamiatnik A.M. Gor'komu," *Gor'kovskii rabochii* 183 (10 Aug. 1936): 3; N.A. Solofnenko, "Pamiatnik Alekseiu Maksimovichu Gor'komu," *Gor'kovskii rabochii* 193 (22 Aug. 1936): 3; V. Mikhailovskii, "O pamiatnike k Mininu," *Gor'kovskii rabochii* 32 (9 Feb.1939): 3.

38 See, e.g.,V.A. Orel'skii, "Ispol'zovat' tsvetnuiu shtukaturku," *Gor'kovskii rabochii* 176 (22 July 1936): 2; "Kakim dolzhen byt' zhiloi dom?" *Gor'kovskii rabochii* 125 (2 June 1936): 2; V.N. Rymarenko, "Nuzhny komnaty dlia khraneniia velosipedov," *Gor'kovskii rabochii* 176 (22 July 1936): 2; D.P. Sil'vanov, "Pri kazhdoi kvartire – balkon," *Gor'kovskii rabochii* 176 (22 July 1936): 2.

39 "Segodnia v Gor'kom," *Gor'kovskii rabochii* 165 (20 July 1936): 1.

40 N. Burlakov, "Osushenie zarech'ia," *Gor'kovskii rabochii* 51 (3 March 1936): 2; V.S. Sovetov, "Voprosy vodnogo khoziaistva i gidrotekhniki," *Gor'kovskii rabochii* 52 (4 March 1936): 2.

41 A.M. Khomutov, "K chemu parkovyi most?" *Gor'kovskii rabochii* 48 (28 Feb. 1936): 2.

42 F. Lbov, "Radio – v plan rekonstruktsii," *Gor'kovskii rabochii* 48 (28 Feb. 1936): 2.

43 Iu.M. Kossoi, *Vash drug tramvai* (Nizhnii Novgorod: Elen'; Iabloko, 1996), 33, 55–6; "Pokhvalinskii elevator ne sleduet zakryvat'," *Nizhegorodskaia kommuna* 300 (29 Dec. 1928): 3; "Nuzhen li Pokhvalinskii elevator?," *Nizhegorodskaia kommuna* 293 (18 Dec. 1928): 3.

44 Tregubov, "Vosstanovit' elevatory," *Gor'kovskii rabochii* 222 (23 Sept. 1936): 2; "Vmesto elevatorov – eskalatory," *Gor'kovskii rabochii* 168 (23 July 1936): 2.

45 I.F. Neiman, "Vzgliad v budushchee goroda Gor'kogo," *Gor'kovskii rabochii* 259 (10 Nov. 1937): 3.

46 Western analysts erroneously date the start of such Soviet consultation to the 1970s. See R.A. French and F.E. Ian Hamilton, "Is There a Socialist City?," in *The Socialist City: Spatial Structure and Urban Policy*, ed. R.A. French and F.E. Ian Hamilton (Indianapolis: Wiley, 1979), 7. To learn more about such consultation in the Brezhnev period, see V. Glazychev, "'The City of the People' and Problems of Its Formation," in *Cities of Europe: The Public's Role in Shaping the Urban Environment*, ed. Tjeerd Deelstra and Oleg Ianitskii (Moscow: Mezhdunarodnye otnoshenia, 1991), 111.

47 V. Iakovlev and N. Ushakov, "Vystavka proektnykh rabot po rekonstruktsii Gor'kogo," *Gor'kovskii rabochii* 154 (8 July 1937): 3; A. Dzhorogov, "Vtoroi etap," *Gor'kovskii rabochii* 77 (4 April 1938): 2.

48 N.A. Solofnenko, "Gor'kovskii dom pionerov," *Gor'kovskii rabochii* 202 (2 Sept. 1936): 2; B.Sh., "Popravki k proektu. Kakim dolzhen byt' Dvorets pionerov," *Gor'kovskii rabochii* 220 (23 Sept. 1936): 3; S.V. Skipetrova, "Dvorets schastlivykh rebiat," *Gor'kovskaia oblast'* 7 (July 1937): 46–52.

49 Matthew Lenoe, *Closer to the Masses: Agitation, Propaganda, and the "Stalinization" of the Soviet Press, 1922–1930* (Pittsburgh: University of Pittsburgh Press, 1998).

50 Marshall McLuhan, *Understanding Media: The Extensions of Man* (New York: McGraw-Hill, 1964), 23.

51 In a sense, this campaign combined the agitational and propaganda functions of Soviet media, which Frank Ellis identifies with "spoken" and "written" media, respectively. Contrary to what Ellis suggests, however, the campaign left space for mass participation in theoretical debate. See Frank Ellis, "Media as Social Engineer," in Kelly and Shepherd, *Russian Cultural Studies*, 198–200.

52 On how architects seek to "forge" a receptive audience, see Groys, *The Total Art of Stalinism*.

53 Author's interview of S.L. Agafonov in the City of Nizhnii Novgorod in summer 2005.

54 N.A. Solofnenko and V.E. Iakovlev, "Dadim g. Gor'komu vysokokachestvennyi proekt," *Gor'kovskii rabochii* 165 (20 July 1936): 1. "Rekonstruktsiia goroda – delo vsei gorodskoi partorganizatsii," *Gor'kovskii rabochii* 165 (20 July 1936): 1.

55 Hoffman, *Stalinist Values*, 158–9. Some of the popular responses to the draft of the 1936 Constitution were published in Lewis Siegelbaum et al., eds., *Stalinism as a Way of Life: A Narrative in Documents* (New Haven: Yale University Press, 2004).

56 In this, the "popular voice" represented by Lengiprogor's campaign resembled that of Soviet elections, which were not democratic by Western standards, but which nonetheless effected genuine participation in the political system. See Theodore H. Friedgut, *Political Participation in the USSR* (Princeton: Princeton University Press, 1979).

57 On the "economy of the gift," see Brooks, *Thank You, Comrade Stalin!*, 58, 83–105, 127.

58 See TsANO, R-2697, op. 1, d. 18, ll. 3ob, 16. Markeev and Glazov, "Nedobrokachestvennaia produktsiia gorproekta: o proekte zhilogo doma zavoda 'Novoe Sormovo,'" *Gor'kovskii rabochii* 175 (2 Aug. 1937): 2. N.V. Dem'ianov, "Reshitel'no usilit' tempy gorodskogo stroitel'stva," *Gor'kovskii rabochii* 123 (1 July 1938): 2. TsANO, R-2697, op. 1, d. 18, l. 24.

59 TsANO, R-6205, op. 1, d. 1, l. 1.

60 Wendy Goldman traces the origins of the vast "snowball" of terror to the campaign for democracy in the factories. For more, see *Terror and Democracy in the Age of Stalin: The Social Dynamics of Repression* (Cambridge: Cambridge University Press, 2007).

61 See "Rezul'tat narusheniia vnutripartiinoi demokratii," *Gor'kovskii rabochii* 56 (10 March 1937): 2; GOPANO, f. 772, op. 6, d. 43, ll. 89–90. For two recent books that offer a powerful reinterpretation of the purges in the Soviet Union, see Paul Hagenloh, *Stalin's Police: Public Order and Mass Repression in*

the USSR, 1926–1941 (Washington, DC: Woodrow Wilson Center Press, and Baltimore: Johns Hopkins University Press, 2009). Also see David Shearer, *Policing Stalin's Socialism: Repression and Social Order in the Soviet Union, 1924–1953* (Stanford: Hoover Institution Press, and New Haven: Yale University Press, 2009).

62 "Sobranie sovetskogo aktiva," *Gor'kovskii rabochi* 87 (16 April 1937): 2. Soviet authorities promised rehabilitation to another group of once vilified "class aliens," also on condition that they serve the state "honourably." For more on the rehabilitation of these "special settlers," see Viola, *The Unknown Gulag*, 95.

63 For more on this bottom-up resentment, as unleashed through the purges, see Sheila Fitzpatrick, "How the Mice Buried the Cat: Scenes from the Great Purges of 1937 in the Russian Provinces," *Slavic Review* 52 (July 1993): 299–320.

64 For Kashnikov's quote, see TsANO, R-6205, op. 1, d. 13, l. 3.

65 Compare their behaviour to the ritualized scientific disputation discussed in Kojevnikov, "Games of Stalinist Democracy," 140–70. On the mock show trials, which were scripted but whose outcomes were not perfectly controlled, see Elizabeth Wood, *Performing Justice: Agitation Trials in Early Soviet Russia* (Ithaca: Cornell University Press, 2005), 151.

66 TsANO, R-2697, Op. 1, d. 57, ll. 8–28.

67 For the bid for such a House of Architects, see TsANO, R-6205, op. 1, d. 10, ll. 1–1ob. They received the building in 1973. See "Dom arkhitektora," *Gor'kovskii rabochii* 154 (4 July 1973): 1.

68 TsANO, R-6205, op. 1, d. 1, ll. 37–37ob and 26–26ob; d. 3, ll. 110–11; d. 4, ll. 9–9ob, 27.

69 Blumenfeld, *Life Begins at 65*, 130.

70 Hudson, *Blueprints in Blood*, 147–63, 179, 186.

71 Vera Dunham, *In Stalin's Time: Middle-Class Values in Soviet Fiction* (Durham: Duke University Press, 1990).

72 On the improved image of the engineer in Soviet literature from 1938 to 1939, see Katerina Clark, "The Changing Image of Science and Technology in Soviet Literature," in Graham, *Science and the Soviet Social Order*, 274, 279.

73 On such postwar demands, see Jeffrey W. Jones, *Everyday Life and the "Reconstruction" of Soviet Russia during and after the Great Patriotic War, 1943–1948* (Bloomington: Slavica, 2008), 77. Also see Zubkova, *Russia after the War*.

74 Ia. Kokushkin, "Realen li proekt planirovki Sormova, razrabotannyi Giprogorom?" *Krasnyi Sormovich* 278 (4 Dec. 1936): 2.

75 N.A. Solofnenko, "Arkhitekturnyi obraz goroda," *Gor'kovskii krai* 1 (1936): 98. TsANO, R-2697, op. 1, d. 36, l. 60.

76 TsANO, R-2697, op. 1, d. 36, l. 46ob; GARF, A-314, op. 1, d. 7501, l. 121. For Lengiprogor's response, see GARF, A-314, op. 1, d. 7501, l. 108.

77 GARF, A-314, op. 1, d. 7509, ll. 97–8 and 28.

78 Ia. Kokushkin, "Realen li proekt planirovki Sormova, razrabotannyi Giprogorom?" *Krasnyi Sormovich* 278 (4 Dec. 1936): 2; Ia. Kokushkin, "Rykovskii poselok podlezhit snosu," *Krasnyi Sormovich* 209 (10 Sept. 1936): 3.

79 GARF, A-314, op. 1, d. 7508, ll. 12ob–13ob.

80 N.A. Solofnenko, "Realen li proekt planirovki Sormova? Otvet tov. A. Kokushkinu," *Gor'kovskii rabochii* 295 (23 Dec. 1936): 2.

81 For the petition that followed, see GARF, A-314, op. 1, d. 7508, ll. 12ob–13ob.

82 For reviews prompted by the Kokushkin affair, see GARF, A-314, op. 1, d. 7501, ll. 105–7; d. 7506, ll. 1–8ob; d. 7508, ll. 2–2ob.

83 Ibid., d. 7509, l. 125.

84 F.V. Popov, "Zakliuchenie ekspertizy," *Gor'kovskii rabochii* 66 (21 March 1936): 2.

85 RGAE, f. 293, op. 3, d. 319, l. 108. Also see "Postanovlenie Gor'kovskogo kraiispolkoma i kraikoma VKP (b) ot 17 iiulia 1936 g., "Ob osnovnykh polozheniiakh po sostavleniiu general'nogo plana rekonstruktsii goroda Gor'kogo," *Gor'kovskii rabochii* 164 (19 July 1936): 1.

86 "Ekspertnyi soviet o proekte rekonstruktsii goroda," *Gor'kovskii rabochii* 185 (14 Aug. 1937): 2. The Russian Commissariat of the Municipal Economy (NKKKh RSFSR) and the Supreme Council of the Municipal Economy (VSKKh pri TsIK SSSR) approved plans for the ensemble along the Oka River in Jan. 1937. GARF, A-314, op. 1, d. 7509, l. 37.

87 GARF, A-314, op. 1, d. 7505, l. 141 and 32; d. 7510, ll. 7–8.

88 GARF, A-314, op. 1, d. 7508, ll. 35–7. Belous, *Politicheskaia elita*, 39–40. On purges in the Gorky region, see also S.M. Shimovolos and M.Iu. Gusev, eds., *Kniga pamiati zhertv politicheskikh repressii v Nizhegorodskoi oblasti*, vol. 1 (Nizhnii Novgorod: Nizhegorodskii pechatnik, 1997); A.N. Golubinova et al., eds., *Kniga pamiati zhertv politicheskikh repressii v Nizhegorodskoi oblasti*, vol. 2 (Nizhnii Novgorod: Nizhegorodskii pechatnik, 2001); L.P. Gordeeva et al., eds., *Zabveniiu ne podlezhit*, vol. 1, *O repressiiakh 30-kh – nachala 50-kh godov v Nizhegorodskoi oblasti* (Nizhnii Novgorod: Volgo-Viatskoe, 1993).

89 TsANO, R-2697, op. 1, d. 57, ll. 14ob–15.

90 GARF, A-314, op. 1, d. 7501, l. 123. Accusations of stonewalling continued to plague the Council in 1938. See TsANO, R-6205, op. 1, d. 13, ll. 2–3.

91 TsANO, R-2697, op. 1, d. 57, ll. 5–6 and 13–13ob.

92 GARF, A-314, op. 1, d. 7508, ll. 35–7; d. 7502, ll. 28 and 38. TsANO, R-2697, op. 1, d. 57, ll. 7–20.

93 GARF, A-314, op. 1, d. 7510, ll. 26–8; d. 7501, ll. 3–8.
94 See both the previous chapter and TsANO, R-2697, op. 1, d. 8, ll. 42–3; d. 57, ll. 20ob, 22–4; GARF, A-314, op. 1, d. 7509, l. 2.
95 The council demanded these from Ivanitskii (TsANO, R-2697, op. 1, d. 20, ll. 1–1ob) and from Lengiprogor (ibid., d. 57, ll. 20ob and 22).
96 GARF, A-314, op. 1, d. 7502, l. 10.
97 Scott, *Domination and the Arts of Resistance*, 196, 156–82.
98 J. Arch Getty attributes the Great Purges to Moscow's (somewhat futile) struggle for power over regional parties, which were notorious for poor record keeping and "cliques." The city council's behaviour in many ways resembles the local Party behaviour that Getty describes in his book. See *Origins of the Great Purges: The Soviet Communist Party Reconsidered, 1933–1938* (Cambridge: Cambridge University Press, 1985).
99 TsANO, R-2697, op. 1, d. 57, l. 9ob.
100 On other contexts in which Soviet officials used two competing languages – in this case, one for public propaganda and another for administrative discussion, see Donald J. Raleigh, "Languages of Power: How Saratov Bolsheviks Imagined Their Enemies," *Slavic Review* 57/2 (1998): 320–49.

6 A City That Builds Itself: The Limits of Technocracy

1 Vladimir Mayakovsky, "Prikaz po armii iskusstva," *Iskusstvo kommuny* 1/7 (Dec. 1918): 1.
2 TsANO, R-6205, op. 1, d. 1, ll. 35–6.
3 TsANO, R-2697, op. 1, d. 20, ll. 7–7ob and 87–8; d. 57, l. 14; d. 8, ll. 42–3.
4 GARF, A-314, op. 1, d. 7499, ll. 46–7; d. 7508, ll. 4–6. TsANO, R-6205, op. 1, d. 1, ll. 15ob–16. GARF, A-314, op. 1, d. 7497, ll. 19–20, 31ob.
5 The phrase "high-quality plan" alludes both to Boris Groys' analysis of Stalinist architecture ("The Art of Totality, 96–124) and to Solofnenko's own words, as printed in N.A. Solofnenko and V.E. Iakovlev, "Dadim g. Gor'komu vysokokachestvennyi proekt," *Gor'kovskii rabochii* 165 (20 July 1936): 1.
6 Homes built by ordinary citizens became an essential component of the state's housing program in the Stalin period (Smith, *Property of Communists*, 26). Also see Stephen Emmett Harris, "Moving to the Separate Apartment: Building, Distributing, Furnishing, and Living in Urban Housing in Soviet Russia, 1950s–1960s" (doctoral dissertation, University of Chicago, 2003).
7 On the highly informal and personalized nature of Soviet administration, see Graeme Gill, "The Communist Party and the Weakness of Bureaucratic Norms," in *Russian Bureaucracy and the State: Officialdom from Alexander III to*

Vladimir Putin, ed. Don K. Rowney and Eugene Huskey (London: Palgrave Macmillan, 2009), 118–34.

8   On illicit postwar construction, see Qualls, *From Ruins to Reconstruction*, 76–7. On later conflicts with industry, see Gregory D. Andrusz, *Housing and Urban Development in the USSR* (London: Macmillan, 1984), 47–51, 80.

9   On "backwardness," defined in terms of missing institutions and specialists, see N.V. Baranov, *Glavnyi arkhitektor goroda: Tvorcheskaia i organizatsionnaia deiatel'nost'* (Moscow: Stroiizdat, 1979). Baranov attributed many of the failures of planning in the 1930s to the lack of a chief city architect (p. 6). For further commentary on "missing" institutions, see Parkins, *City Planning in Soviet Russia*, 50, and Andrew Day, "The Rise and Fall of Stalinist Architecture," in Cracraft and Rowland, *Architectures of Russian Identity*, 176–7.

10   Charles Hachten offers a succinct analysis of the state's embrace of local autonomy, even as it advanced the myth of centralized control, in "Separate yet Governed: The Representation of Soviet Property Relations in Civil Law and Public Discourse," in Siegelbaum, *Borders of Socialism*, 65–82.

11   On the formation of the APU, see TsANO, R-2697, op. 1, d. 20, ll. 69–70.

12   GARF, A-314, op. 1, d. 7494, ll. 48–9; d. 7499, ll. 104–21, 144.

13   In 1933, the Central Executive Committee (TsIK) and the Soviet Council of People's Commissars (Sovnarkom SSSR) decreed that no institution could build in a municipality without respecting the construction laws and technical norms of the city council. GARF, R-7544, op. 1, d. 92, ll. 5–7.

14   TsANO, R-2697, op. 1, d. 42, ll. 18–18ob; d. 45, l. 2.

15   Ibid., d. 20, l. 87.

16   GARF, A-314, op. 1, d. 7508, ll. 3–6.

17   TsANO, R-6205, op. 1, d. 4, ll. 40ob and 57; TsANO R-2697, op. 1, d. 20, l. 7ob; GARF, A-314, op. 1, d. 7508, l. 5.

18   TsANO, R-6205, op. 1, d. 4, ll. 24–6.

19   GARF, A-314, op. 1, d. 7510, l. 8. TsANO, R-2697, op. 1, d. 20, l. 5.

20   TsANO, R-2697, op. 1, d. 12, ll. 3–6. Orel'skaia, "Arkhitektura gorodov," 110.

21   "Polozhenie ob ekspertnom-arkhitekturnom sovete pri prezidiume Gor'kovskogo gorsoveta," in TsANO, R-2698, op. 2, d. 4, ll. 7–8ob. TsANO, R-2697, op. 1, d. 38, ll. 7–8.

22   TsANO, R-2697, op. 1, d. 57, ll. 10–10ob.

23   For a report of the Supreme Council of the Economy on this matter, see RGAE, d.4372, op. 33, d. 950, l. 101. In response to this problem, authorities proposed aerial surveys (RGAE, d.4372, op. 33, d. 950, ll. 97–97ob). Note that these problems inhibited attempts to properly inventory the housing stock.

24   TsANO, R-2697, op. 1, d. 20, ll. 7–7ob; GARF, A-314, op. 1, d. 7497, ll. 43–5;

GOPANO, f. 30, op. 1, d.867, l. 3. In the Russian language, lots are "designated" or "set apart," but not "severed." The Russian phrase is *udeliat' uchastok* (to set apart a lot), not *otdeliat'* (to sever).

25 TsANO, R-6205, op. 1, d. 4, ll. 18–18ob; TsANO, R-2697, op. 1, d. 36, l. 46ob.

26 See "Novye proekty blagoustroistva," *Gor'kovskii rabochii* 83 (11 April 1937): 2. GARF, A-314, op. 1, d. 7502, l. 44; d. 7501, ll. 108–108ob.

27 GARF, A-314, op. 1, d. 7494, l. 49.

28 Ibid., d. 7497, l. 45. TsANO, R-2697, op. 1, d. 20, l. 1.

29 TsANO, R-6205, op. 1, d. 13, ll. 2–3. GARF, A-314, op. 1, d. 7497, l. 32ob.

30 Near the Stankozavod and Red Etna factories in 1938, some buildings had been erected on swampy soil lying outside the boundaries of the designated lot. TsANO, R-2697, op. 1, d. 57, l. 11ob.

31 On the qualifications of local specialists, see Bubnov and Orel'skaia, *Arkhitektura goroda Gor'kogo*, 38–9. On Stalin's support for technical rather than broadly theoretical education, see Bailes, *Technology and Society*, 163–70, as well as Harley Balzer, "Engineers: The Rise and Decline of a Social Myth," in Graham, *Science and the Soviet Social Order*, 153–6. Also see Gail Lapidus, "Educational Strategies and Cultural Revolution," in Fitzpatrick, *Cultural Revolution in Russia*, 84–5, and Cooke, *Russian Avant-Garde*, 9, 168–9.

32 TsANO, R-6205, op. 1, d. 1, ll. 3–4 and 39.

33 Ibid., ll. 6ob–8, 17–51, and 77; d. 4, ll. 31, 54–5; d. 7, ll. 36–36ob; d. 14, l. 4.

34 Ibid., d. 3, l. 72. In some cases, crowded living conditions proved as problematic as crowded work conditions (ibid., d. 1, ll. 26–26ob). Such problems were reportedly typical. See the *Harvard Project on the Soviet Social System*, schedule A, vol. 22, case 446 (interviewer J.O., type A4): male, 35, Russian architectural engineer (Kiev design bureau), Widener Library, Harvard University, pp. 8–10, sequence 8–10.

35 TsANO, R-6205, op. 1, d. 4, ll. 24–6 and 48; d. 1, ll. 13–36.

36 Ibid., d. 1, ll. 5, 10–11, 23, 28–28ob, and 32–43; d. 3, l. 56. For a report of similar troubles in Soiuztransproekt in Ukraine, see the *Harvard Project on the Soviet Social System*, schedule A, vol. 27, case 526 (interviewer A.P., type A4): male, 39, Ukrainian engineer (Soiuztransproekt), Widener Library, Harvard University, p. 8, sequence 8. Also see Bukhalov, "Proekty i smety 'na glazok' udorozhaiut stroitel'stvo," *Gor'kovskii rabochii* 36 (10 April 1934): 2.

37 On poor pay, see Hudson, *Blueprints in Blood*, 142.

38 TsANO, R-2697, op. 1, d. 42, ll. 18–18ob; d. 45, l. 2.

39 It occasionally reviewed projects submitted by state ministries, but only when (1) construction was to take place in the city and (2) provincial authorities permitted this. This likely required the permission of the ministry involved. See TsANO, R-2697, op. 1, d. 38, ll. 7–8; "Polozhenie

ob ekspertnykh sovetakh oblasti," in TsANO, R-2698, op. 2, d. 4, ll. 11ob–12.

40 "Polozhenie ob ekspertnom-arkhitekturnom sovete pri prezidiume Gor'kovskogo gorsoveta," TsANO, R-2698, op. 2, d. 4, ll. 8–8ob.

41 GOPANO, f. 30, op. 1, d.867, ll. 1 and 3. TsANO, R-6205, op. 1, d. 1, ll. 22–3, 30, and 32–4.

42 TsANO, R-6205, op. 1, d. 1, ll. 13–50; TsANO, R-2697, op. 1, d. 20, ll. 1ob and 70; TsANO, R-6205, op. 1, d. 1, l. 20, and d. 3, l. 107; TsANO, R-2698, op. 2, d. 4, ll. 7–8ob.

43 Day, "The Rise and Fall of Stalinist Architecture," 181.

44 TsANO, R-6205, op. 1, d. 1, l. 16ob. In many ways, Zhukov was advocating the revival of nineteenth-century architectural controls. On these controls, see A.I. Vlasiuk, "Evoliutsiia stroitel'nogo zakonodatel'stva Rossii v 1830e–1910e gody," in *Pamiatniki russkoi arkhitektury i monumental'nogo iskusstva*, ed. V.P. Vygolov (Moscow: Nauka, 1985), 232.

45 TsANO, R-6205, op. 1, d. 4, ll. 112ob–113, and 128; d. 1, l. 3–5. For Vesnin's words, see Hudson, *Blueprints in Blood*, 175. (Note that my own interpretation differs from that of Hudson.)

46 TsANO, R-6205, op. 1, d. 4, ll. 31 and 100.

47 Ibid., ll. 48, 57, and 113–14.

48 Shul'pin, "Pretenzii k arkhitektoru," *Gor'kovskii rabochii* 29 (5 Feb. 1936): 2.

49 GOPANO, f. 30, op. 1, d. 121, ll. 5–8. Gunov, "Otstroennye doma v 'karantine,'" *Gor'kovskii rabochii* 42 (20 Feb. 1933): 3. Gur'ianova, "Mertvyi shtil'," *Gor'kovskii rabochii* 29 (22 April 1935): 3.

50 Ivanov, "Nalitso vsego 8% rabochikh," *Gor'kovskaia kommuna* 90 (18 April 1933): 2.

51 In the postwar period, the city council's office of municipal services (*gorkomkhoz*) would have had a vested interest in delaying such construction, since such departments had the right to fine homebuilders who failed to complete construction on their allotment within a pre-stipulated time. See Hachten, "Property Relations and the Economic Organization of Soviet Russia," 318.

52 GOPANO, f. 30, op. 1, d. 1119, l. 28ob.

53 The same held true in Moscow, where about 30 per cent of construction proceeded without state approval or inspection, even along the main traffic arteries of the city – at least, during the First Five-Year Plan. See Hudson, *Blueprints in Blood*, 142.

54 "Chertezhi, materialy – stroikam," *Gor'kovskii rabochii* 29 (22 April 1935): 3.

55 Zimin, "Stroikam – tochnye tekhnicheskie dokumenty," *Gor'kovskii rabochii* 42 (20 Feb. 1933): 3; V. Tsaregradskii, "Na stroike tsentral'noi gostinitsy," *Gor'kovskii rabochii* 80 (7 April 1936): 2.

56 GOPANO, f. 30, op. 1, d. 121, ll. 3–5; d. 1119, l. 29. Also see O. Litinskii,
    "Stroitel'stvu ne vidno kontsa," *Gor'kovskii rabochii* 250 (29 Oct.
    1935): 2; Viktor Gorbynov, "Ispraviv, vnov' prislat'," *Gor'kovskii rabochii* 46 (24 Feb.
    1933): 3; "Tikho v kabinetakh Gordorstroia," *Gor'kovskii rabochii* 7 (4 March 1934): 2.

57 Bukhalov, "Proekty i smety 'na glazok' udorozhaiut," 2; Zimin, "Stroikam –
    tochnye tekhnicheskie dokumenty," 3.

58 Gunov, "Otstroennye doma v 'karantine,'" 3; Tsaregradskii, "Pochemu defit-
    sitny mestnye stroimaterialy," *Gor'kovskii rabochii* 63 (17 March 1935): 2; N.V.
    Dem'iakov, "254 novykh zdanii," *Gor'kovskii rabochii* 196 (27 Aug. 1938): 2.

59 GOPANO, f. 30, op. 1, d. 867, l. 4; F. Kitsis, "Pochemu vysoka stoimost'
    stroitel'stva? (Otklik na stat'iu tt. Molchanova i Agafonova)," *Gor'kovskii
    rabochii* 181 (9 Aug. 1937): 2.

60 GARF, A-314, op. 1, d. 7494, l. 48.

61 The provincial party organization called for the local production of
    construction materials. *Rezoliutsii aprel'skogo plenuma Nizhkraikoma VKP(b)*
    (Nizhnii Novgorod: Kraiizdat, 1932), 7. But key factories such as the asphalt
    factory were never built. "Tikho v kabinetakh Gordorstroia," *Gor'kovskii
    rabochii* 7 (4 March 1934): 2. Also see GOPANO, f. 30, op. 1, d. 121, ll. 5–6;
    TsANO, R-6205, op. 1, d. 4, ll. 39–40.

62 Discussions of this problem were extensive, both in the press and at state,
    Party, and professional meetings. See TsANO, R-2697, op. 1, d. 42, l. 30ob;
    d. 36, l. 57ob; d. 57, l. 15. GARF, R-7544, op. 1, d. 77, ll. 2ob–3. V. Tsaregrad-
    skii, "Stroikam goroda – krepkuiu bazu stroimaterialov," *Gor'kovskii rabochii*
    86 (14 April 1936): 2; I. Sidorov, "Promyshlennost' stroimaterialov v tret'em
    piatiletki," *Gor'kovskaia oblast'* 1 (1937): 75–9; M.I. Dekabrun and S.I. Kop'ev,
    "Voprosy organizatsii stroitel'stva po g. Gor'komu," *Gor'kovskaia oblast'* 7
    (1937): 37–45.

63 On the black market's role in the overall Soviet economy, see Elena
    Osokina, *Za fasadom "Stalinskogo izobiliia": Raspredelenie i rynok v snabzhenii
    naseleniia v gody industrializatsii, 1927–1941* (Moscow: Rosspen, 1998).

64 For more, see Paul Gregory, *The Political Economy of Stalinism: Evidence from
    the Soviet Secret Archives* (New York: Cambridge University Press, 2003).

65 GOPANO, f. 30, op. 1, d. 121, ll. 4–6. "Zhulikov iz gor'komstroia i raikom-
    stroia k otvetu," *Gor'kovskii rabochii* 46 (24 Feb. 1933): 3.

66 F. Kitsis, "Pochemu vysoka stoimost' stroitel'stva?" 2; "Zhulikov iz
    gor'komstroia i raikomstroia k otvetu," 3; Molchanov and Agafonov, "Snizit'
    sebestoimost' stroitel'stva," *Gor'kovskii rabochii* 169 (26 July 1937): 2.

67 TsANO, R-6205, op. 1, d. 4, l. 8ob, 11, 13, and 31; d. 3, ll. 128–9.

68 *Harvard Project on the Soviet Social System*, schedule B, vol. 5, case no. 615
    (Interviewer A.P., type B2), Widener Library, Harvard University, p. 1,
    sequence 1.

69 Molchanov and Agafonov, "Snizit' sebestoimost' stroitel'stva," *Gor'kovskii rabochii* 169 (26 July 1937): 2; Bukhalov, "Proekty i smety 'na glazok' udorozhaiut stroitel'stvo," *Gor'kovskii rabochii* 36 (10 April 1934): 2; B.V. Zhadin, "Kak ne nado stroit': brakodely iz tresta 'Sevstroiput,'" *Gor'kovskii rabochii* 227 (March 1937): 2.

70 GOPANO, f. 30, op. 1, d. 1119, l. 29ob; "Ni planov, ni materialov," *Gor'kovskii rabochii* 56 (9 March 1935): 3; M.V., "Istoriia povtoriaetsia: o stroitel'stve tsentral'noi i sormovskoi gostinits," *Gor'kovskii rabochii* 186 (15 Aug. 1937): 2.

71 TsANO, R-6205, op. 1, d. 3, l. 123. N. Tret'iakov, "Chto delaet gosstroikontrol'?" *Gor'kovskii rabochii* 148 (1 July 1938): 1. GARF, R-7544, op. 1, d. 77, l. 2ob.

72 GOPANO, f. 30, op. 1, d. 1119, l. 28ob.

73 For such local complaints, see B.V. Zhadin, "Kak ne nado stroit': Brakodely iz tresta Sevstroiput'," *Gor'kovskii rabochii* 227 (March 1937): 2; TsANO, R-6205, op. 1, d. 3, ll. 47, and 67; d. 4, ll. 24–6. Balzer, "Engineers," in Graham, *Science and the Soviet Social Order*, 143. On the attempt to better train foremen and builders in the 1940s, see Smith, *Property of Communists*, 54–5, 113.

74 TsANO, R-6205, op. 1, d. 4, ll. 14ob–15; RGAE, f. 4372, op. 36, d. 1661, ll. 55–6; TsANO, R-6205, op. 1, d. 1, l. 39ob. Charles Hachten also discusses the power of high-priority enterprises over local government; see "Property Relations," 99–101, 114–15, 118.

75 R.S. Semenov, "Vtoroi god raboty sovetov goroda," *Gor'kovskii rabochii* 67 (22 March 1936): 2. Also see TsANO, R-2697, op. 1, d. 18, l. 27; d. 57, l. 14. These documents date to 1938, but squatting was clearly a problem as early as 1930 or 1931, if not before.

76 Sakhan, "Chertezhi, materialy," 3. TsANO, R-2697, op. 1, d. 57, l. 11ob.

77 Decrees in October 1937 and April 1939 permitted individual citizens to claim credits for housing construction, making it possible for individual initiative to drive the Soviet housing program. For more, see Smith, *Property of Communists*, 26, 154, 180.

78 Soviet law in the 1920s guaranteed to citizens freedom from eviction for three years after having made renovations or repairs to the building in which they lived. Hachten, "Property Relations," 95.

79 Viktor Gorbynov, "Ispraviv, vnov' prislat'," *Gor'kovskii rabochii* 46 (24 Feb. 1933): 3.

80 Eremin et al., "Dobit'sia polnoi pobedy,' *Nizhegorodskaia kommuna* 38 (8 Feb. 1931): 3; TsANO, R-6205, op. 1, d. 4, ll. 16–16ob.

81 For more on these property relations, see Hachten, "Property Relations," and Smith, *Property of Communists*.

82 N. Tret'iakov, "Chto delaet gosstroikontrol'?" *Gor'kovskii rabochii* 148 (1 July 1938): 1; Gunov, "Otstroennye doma v 'karantine,'" 3.

83 For more on this issue, see Harris, "Resisting the Plan in the Urals," 202.

84 N.S. Sboev, "Na lesakh arkhitektora ne vidno," *Gor'kovskii rabochii* 29 (5 Feb. 1936): 2; D. Sil'vanov, "Eshche raz ob arkhitektorskom nadzore," *Gor'kovskii rabochii* 83 (11 April 1937): 2; Zimin, "Na stroike doma zhelezno-dorozhnikov net bol'shevistskogo rukovodstva," *Gor'kovskii rabochii* 36 (13 Feb. 1933): 3.

85 TsANO, R-6205, op. 1, d. 3, ll. 145–6. Zhukov's words indirectly testify to the paucity of women in governance and in planning. For more on architectural education for women in Russia and the Soviet Union, see Cooke, *Russian Avant-Garde*, 12–13.

86 Hudson, *Blueprints in Blood*, 195–6.

87 TsANO, R-6205, op. 1, d. 1, ll. 40ob–51; d. 3, ll. 61 and 110–11.

88 *Harvard Project on the Soviet Social System*, schedule A., vol. 4, case 34 (interview by E.H., type A2): male 39, Russian watch repairer and mason, Widener Library, Harvard University, p. 26, sequence 26.

89 TsANO, R-6205, op. 1, d. 1, ll. 16 and 36. GOPANO, f. 30, op. 1, d. 1119, l. 29ob; d. 867, ll. 1–2.

90 TsANO, R-6205, op. 1, d. 3, ll. 61 and 66.

91 This information comes from the author's spring 2001 discussion with Olga Vladimirovna Orel'skaia, an architect in present-day Nizhnii Novgorod. While the story may have been altered through telling and retelling, debates over paint colour did, in fact, pit architects against builders. Consider, for instance, Zhukov's controversial demand for white paint. TsANO, R-6205, op. 1, d. 3, ll. 126–7 and 145–6.

92 TsANO, R-6205, op. 1, d. 3, l. 98.

93 Ibid., d. 4, ll. 24–8; d. 1, ll. 16–16ob.

94 On demands for a high-quality plan, see Groys, "The Art of Totality," 96–124.

95 TsANO, R-6205, op. 1, d. 1, l. 16ob.

7 Performing Socialism: Connecting Space to Self

1 Thomas More, *Utopia & A Dialogue of Comfort (1516)* (London: J.M. Dent and Sons, 1946), 461.

2 The Soviet state had long conflated public dress and behaviour with moral and social health. See Eric Naiman, *Sex in Public: The Incarnation of Early Soviet Ideology* (Princeton: Princeton University Press, 1999); Anne Gorsuch, *Youth in Revolutionary Russia: Enthusiasts, Bohemians, Delinquents* (Bloomington: Indiana University Press, 2000).

3 As Priestland would emphasize, planners and the Party had competing visions of popular mobilization; for a study of four distinct Soviet
approaches to such mobilization, see *Stalinism and the Politics of Mobilization*,
1–57.
4 V.F. Grechukho, "Za gorod–krasavets," *Gor'kovskii rabochii* 225 (27 Nov.
1934): 4.
5 GOPANO, f. 30, op. 1, d. 1110, l. 33; *Materialy k otchetu o rabote gorsoveta*
(Gorky: Gorsovet, 1935), 48; F. Smirnov, "Kul'turnoe blagoustroistvo ordenonosnomu kraiu," *Vlast' sovetov* 13 (1934): 45–6. On financial shortfalls,
see "Na kraevom s'ezde sovetov," *Gor'kovskii rabochii* 1 (1 Jan. 1935): 1. The
mobilization of the population for such matters as home repair continued
into the postwar period (Hachten, "Property Relations," 180–1).
6 F. Smirnov, "Kul'turnoe blagoustroistvo ordenonosnomu kraiu," *Vlast' sovetov* 13 (1934): 45–6; TsANO, f. R-78, op. 2, d. 68, l. 43ob.
7 GOPANO, f. 30. op. 1, d. 1110, ll. 27 and 56.
8 GARF, R-7544, op. 1, d. 174, ll. 27–8; S. Tseitlin, "100 tysiach trudodnei
na bor'bu za chistotu i kul'turu," *Gor'kovskii rabochii* 61 (12 May 1934): 3;
Eidman, "Kak my organizovali i proveli konkurs na luchshuiu deputatskuiu
gruppu i sektsiiu po gorodu Gorky," *Rabota sovetov* 11–12 (1932); Avtozavod
District Council, *Usloviia konkursa na luchshuiu uchastkovuiu, deputatskuiu
gruppu* ... (Avtozavod: Gorsovet, 1935); *Plan meropriiatii po blagoustroistvu* ...
na 1935 g. (Avtozavod: Raisovet, 1935); *Materialy k otchetu*, 170–2. Also see
GOPANO, f. 1065, op. 1, d. 10, ll. 73–6.
9 On these earlier *massovki*, see Lenoe, *Closer to the Masses* (2004), 38.
10 *Materialy k otchetu*, 52; "U nikh uchit'sia obraztsovomu ukhodu za svoim
zhilishchem," *Gor'kovskii rabochii* 127 (31 July 1934): 3.
11 TsANO, f. R-78, op. 2, d. 265a, ll. 37–37ob; R.S. Semenov, "Vtoroi god raboty
sovetov goroda," *Gor'kovskii rabochii* 67 (22 March 1936): 2.
12 On the Soviet press as an agent of social organization, see Thomas C.
Wolfe, *Governing Soviet Journalism: The Press and the Socialist Person after Stalin*
(Bloomington: Indiana University Press, 2005), 7, 18–19, 70; Lenoe, *Closer to
the Masses* (2004), 235–7.
13 For an analysis of how Soviet morality was forged through public/collective
performance, see Kharkhordin, *The Collective and the Individual in Russia*.
14 R.S. Semenov, "Vtoroi god raboty sovetov goroda," 2. GOPANO, f. 30, op. 1,
d.1110, ll. 37, and 43–8.
15 GOPANO, f. 30, op. 1, d. 1262, ll. 105–6, 127; "Litso novykh raionov
goroda," *Gor'kovskii rabochii* 43 (21 Feb. 1935): 3; "Gorod budet tsvesti,"
Leninskaia smena 222 (27 Sept. 1934): 4; "Osennee ozelenenie," *Gor'kovskii
rabochii* 219 (22 Sept. 1936): 4; "Po-boevomu vziat'sia za blagoustroistvo

goroda," *Gor'kovskii rabochii* 56 (9 March 1935): 3; TsANO, f. R-78, op. 2, d. 265a, ll. 1–122. GOPANO, f. 30, op. 1, d. 1110, ll. 25–9.

16 For an excellent, in-depth study of how spatial organization was identified with both individual and collective morality, see Christine Varga-Harris's unpublished book manuscript, "Constructing the Soviet Hearth: Home, Citizenship and Socialism During the Khrushchev Era."

17 Sheila Fitzpatrick, *The Cultural Front: Power and Culture in Revolutionary Russia* (Ithaca: Cornell University Press, 1992), 215–17, 227; Boym, *Common Places*, 105; Catriona Kelly and Vadim Volkov, "Directed Desires: *Kul'turnost'* and Consumption," in Kelly and Shepherd, *Constructing Russian Culture*, 293–313.

18 Vadim Volkov, "The Concept of *Kultur'nost*': Notes on the Stalinist Civilizing Process," in Fitzpatrick, *Stalinism: New Directions*, 209–30.

19 Sheila Fitzpatrick, *Everyday Stalinism: Ordinary Life in Extraordinary Times – Soviet Russia in the 1930s* (New York: Oxford University Press, 1999), 83.

20 Susan Reid, "Cold War in the Kitchen: Gender and the Destalinization of Taste in the Soviet Union under Khrushchev," *Slavic Review* 61/2 (2002): 211–52. In Soviet thought, outward discipline was viewed as central to the development of will, efficiency, and smartness (Hoffman, *Stalinist Values*, 42, 134–45).

21 "Kul'turnye zhelenye dorozhnye vagony," *Gor'kovskii rabochii* 56 (10 March 1937): 2; "Sobranie sovetskogo aktiva," *Gor'kovskii rabochii* 87 (16 April 1937): 2; "'Melochi,'" *Gor'kovskii rabochii* 171 (28 July 1937): 2; Amy E. Randall, "'Revolutionary Bolshevik Work': Stakhanovism in Retail Trade," *Russian Review* 59/3 (2000): 425–41.

22 On the power of ritual to establish and sustain hierarchy, see Kertzer, *Ritual, Politics, and Power*, 10, 25.

23 Consider the improved image of the engineer in Soviet literature from 1938 to 1939, as discussed in Clark, "The Changing Image of Science and Technology in Soviet Literature," 274, 279.

24 Julie Hessler, "Cultured Trade: The Stalinist Turn towards Consumerism," in Fitzpatrick, *Stalinism: New Directions*, 182–209; Katherine Verdery, *What Is Socialism? And What Comes Next* (Princeton: Princeton University Press, 1996), chapter 1.

25 "O resheniiakh zabyli," *Gor'kovskii rabochii* 200 (26 Oct. 1934): 2; "Tsvety k stankam," *Gor'kovskii rabochii* 33 (6 April 1934): 2.

26 On the city beautiful as an agent of distraction, see Peter Hall, *Cities of Tomorrow: An Intellectual History of Urban Planning and Design in the Twentieth Century*, 3rd ed. (Oxford: Blackwell, 2002). On "spectacular" distraction from social discontents, see Vanessa Schwartz, *Spectacular Realities: Early Mass Culture in Fin-de-Siècle France* (Berkeley: University of California Press, 1999).

27 Hoffman, *Stalinist Values*, 73–4, 107.

28 "Proletarskomu Kanavinu – sotsialisticheskoe blagoustroistvo!" *Gor'kovskii rabochii* 30 (3 April 1934): 1.

29 See M.F., "Chistka ozdorovila partorganizatsiiu," *Gor'kovskii rabochii* 220 (21 Nov. 1934): 2; "Proletarskomu Kanavinu – sotsialisticheskoe blagoustroistvo!" *Gor'kovskii rabochii* 30 (3 April 1934): 1; "Eshche raz ob ochistke goroda," *Gor'kovskii rabochii* 172 (30 July 1938): 4.

30 On biological metaphors, also see Richard Pipes, *The Russian Revolution* (New York: Random House, 1990), 790–1.

31 On Russia as a gardening state, see Peter Holquist, "To Count, to Extract, and to Exterminate: Population Statistics and Population Politics in Late Imperial and Soviet Russia," in *A State of Nations: Empire and Nation-Making in the Age of Lenin and Stalin*, ed. R.G. Suny and T. Martin (New York: Oxford University Press, 2001), 111–44. Also see Amir Weiner, ed., *Landscaping the Human Garden: Twentieth-Century Population Management in Comparative Framework* (Stanford: Stanford University Press, 2003).

32 Joyce, *Rule of Freedom*, 62–97, 175, 248.

33 For statistics on access to sewer, running water, garbage, and the like in 1947, see Filtzer, *The Hazards of Urban Life*, 28–38, 76–7. Although Filtzer's data derive from a later period, the picture that he depicts applies to the 1930s city, too.

34 "Legkie goroda," *Gor'kovskii rabochii* 190 (14 Oct. 1934): 3.

35 V.E. Iakovlev, "Zachem nam nuzhen proekt planirovki goroda?" *Gor'kovskii rabochii* 40 (19 Feb. 1936): 2.

36 P. Vysotskii, Mikh. Polonskii, and K. Smirnov, "Gorky – promyshlennyi tsentr, krupneishii gorod strany," *Gor'kovskaia kommuna* 245 (24 Oct. 1939): 2; V. Gradskii, "Budushchee nashego goroda," 26 (2 Feb. 1936): 2. V.E. Iakovlev, "Zachem nam nuzhen proekt planirovki goroda?" *Gor'kovskii rabochii* 40 (19 Feb. 1936): 2.

37 See Mumford, *The Culture of Cities*, 41–4. For more on the impact of greenhouses on planning ideas, see Mumford, *The City in History*, 474–6.

38 "Mama – nalivai!" *Gor'kovskii rabochii* (1935).

39 Hoffman, *Stalinist Values*, 23–5; Rebecca Balmas Neary, "Domestic Life and the Activist Wife in the 1930s Soviet Union," in Siegelbaum, *Borders of Socialism*, 107–22; Fitzpatrick, *The Cultural Front*, 232.

40 V. Tsaregradskii, "Ne znakomaia ulitsa," *Gor'kovskii rabochii* 94 (23 April 1935): 3; "Pesok ostupaet," *Gor'kovskii rabochii* 49 (26 April 1934): 3; "Segodnia v Gor'kom," *Gor'kovskii rabochii* 149 (702) (1 July 1936): 1.

41 D.K. Zutte, "Domokhoziaiki – bol'shaia sila," *Gor'kovskii rabochii* 127 (31 July 1934): 3.

42 On women's role in sustaining male productivity, see Neary, "Domestic Life," 110–11. On *poshlost'*, see Boym, *Common Places*, 47–60.

43 "Domokhoziaiki – bol'shaia sila," *Gor'kovskii rabochii* 127 (31 July 1934): 3. On the liminal nature of public-private "boundaries," see Boym, *Common Places*, 2–3; Lewis Siegelbaum, Introduction, in Siegelbaum, *Borders of Socialism*, 1–7.

44 GOPANO, f. 30, op. 1, d. 1110, ll. 20–50.

45 On gender constructs and the travails of working women, see Choi Chatterjee, *Celebrating Women: Gender, Festival Culture, and Bolshevik Ideology, 1910–1939* (Pittsburgh: University of Pittsburgh Press, 2002); Wendy Goldman, *Women at the Gates: Gender and Industry in Stalin's Russia* (New York: Cambridge University Press, 2002).

46 "Kommandiry chistoty," *Gor'kovskaia kommuna* 73 (28 March 1941): 3; RGASPI, f. 77 (A.A. Zhdanov), op. 1. d. 191, l. 7; TsANO, f. R-78, op. 2, d. 265a, ll. 12 and 38–38ob.

47 "Proletarskomu Kanavinu – sotsialisticheskoe blagoustroistvo!" *Gor'kovskii rabochii* 30 (3 April 1934): 1; "K 1 maia okonchatel'no ochistit' gorod!," *Gor'kovskii rabochii* 50 (27 April 1934): 1.

48 "Za zelenyi, blagoustroennyi gorod," *Gor'kovskii rabochii* 64 (16 May 1934): 1; "Ne skryt' bol'she griazi i musora," *Gor'kovskii rabochii* 39 (14 April 1934): 3; V. Gradskii, "Naberezhnuiu Oki sdelat' obratsovnei," *Gor'kovskii rabochii* 63 (17 March 1935): 2.

49 Nik., "Khlebozavod no. 1 posle chistki," *Gor'kovskii rabochii* 101 (29 June 1934): 2.

50 "Tsvety k stankam," *Gor'kovskii rabochii* 33 (6 April 1934): 2.

51 "Sdelaem nashi goroda i poselki chistymi i blagoustroennymi," *Gor'kovskaia kommuna* 60 (13 March 1941): 1; "Za zelenyi, blagoustroennyi gorod," *Gor'kovskii rabochii* 64 (16 May 1934): 1.

52 "Tsvety k stankam," *Gor'kovskii rabochii* 33 (6 April 1934): 2.

53 TsANO, f. R-78, op. 2, d. 265a, l. 12.

54 Consider postwar letters to newspapers, in which citizens demanded improved living conditions. For an example of such letters, see Stephen Bittner, *The Many Lives of Khrushchev's Thaw: Experience and Memory in Moscow's Arbat* (Ithaca: Cornell University Press, 2008), chapter 5.

55 Hachten, "Property Relations," 196–7, 329. Note that all such hegemonic transcripts co-opt, responding in some way to popular demand (Scott, *Domination and the Arts of Resistance*, 18).

56 T. Pachina, "Remont zhilfonda zakonchim v srok," *Gor'kovskii rabochii* 221 (26 Sept. 1938): 4.

57 GOPANO, f. 30. op. 1, d. 1110, ll. 27ob–28.

58 On free action within prescribed boundaries as the quintessential Soviet dilemma, see Alexei Yurchak, *Everything Was Forever, until It Was No More*, 10–13.

59 See Lars Lih on Lenin's attitude to "spontaneity," in "How a Founding Document Was Found, or One Hundred Years of Lenin's *What Is To Be Done?*," *Kritika: Explorations in Russian and Eurasian History* 4/1 (2003): 5–49. Also see Anna Krylova, "Beyond the Spontaneity-Consciousness Paradigm: 'Class Instinct' as a Promising Category of Political Analysis," *Slavic Review* 62/1 (Spring 2003): 1–23, in which the notion of "class instinct" is proposed as an analytical category that bridges the false dichotomy between "spontaneity" and "consciousness," as presented in Western scholarship on this issue.

60 As Scott notes, this dilemma faced all social engineers; see *Seeing Like a State*, 114.

61 D.V. Rudakov, "Ne stikhiino, a organizovanno provodit' ozelenenie ulits," *Gor'kovskii rabochii* 100 (28 June 1934): 3.

62 V. Tsaregradskii, "Ne znakomaia ulitsa," *Gor'kovskii rabochii* 94 (23 April 1935): 3.

63 GOPANO, f. 30, op. 1, d. 1110, l. 34; TsANO, f. R-78, op. 2, d. 265a, l. 25.

64 GOPANO, f. 30, op. 1, d. 1110, ll. 43–4 and 58.

65 Ibid., l. 33.

66 D.V. Rudakov, "Ne stikhiino, a organizovanno provodit' ozelenenie ulits," *Gor'kovskii rabochii* 100 (28 June 1934): 3.

67 "K 1 maia okonchatel'no ochistit' gorod!," *Gor'kovskii rabochii* 50 (27 April 1934): 1. On nationwide garbage-collection problems, see Filtzer, *The Hazards of Urban Life*, 47–8, 63–5.

68 "Za zelenyi, blagoustroennyi gorod," *Gor'kovskii rabochii* 64 (16 May 1934): 1; S.S. Stankov, "Neotlozhnye zadachi zelenego stroitel'stva," *Gor'kovskii rabochii* 59 (10 May 1934): 4.

69 G.V. Greiber, "Litso ulitsy," *Gor'kovskii rabochii* 90 (20 April 1937): 2; TsDNINO, f. 30, op. 1, d. 1110, l. 19.

70 Fitzpatrick, *Everyday Stalinism*, 34–5.

71 D.V. Rudakov, "Ne stikhiino, a organizovanno provodit' ozelenenie ulits," *Gor'kovskii rabochii* 100 (28 June 1934): 3.

72 R.S. Semenov, "Vtoroi god raboty sovetov goroda," *Gor'kovskii rabochii* 67 (22 March 1936): 2.

73 Stephen Frank, "Confronting the Domestic Other: Rural Popular Culture and Its Enemies in Fin-de-Siècle Russia," in *Cultures in Flux: Lower-Class Values, Practices, and Resistance in Late Imperial Russia*, ed. S. Frank and M. Steinberg (Princeton: Princeton University Press, 1994), 100.

74 On the constative and performative elements of Soviet discourse, see Yurchak, *Everything Was Forever*, 11–22.

75 Kertzer, *Ritual, Politics, and Power*, 69–78. (The quote comes from p. 78.)
76 On the decimation of these committees, see "Ozhivit' rabotu ulichnykh komitetov," *Gor'kovskii rabochii* 73 (31 March 1938): 2.
77 On "architecture of awe," see Tarkhanov and Kavtaradze, *Architecture of the Stalin Era*, 182.
78 For more on the battle for cultured homes and streets during the Khrushchev era, see Susan E. Reid, "The Meaning of Home: 'The Only Bit of the World You Can Have to Yourself,'" in Siegelbaum, *Borders of Socialism*, 145–70.

Conclusion: Living Socialism in the Shadow of the Political

1 TsANO, R-2697, op. 1, d. 57, l. 9ob.
2 The general city plan was never submitted to the SNK RSFSR (RGAE, f. 9432, op. 1, d. 205, l. 34ob).
3 Trube, *Naselenie goroda Gor'kogo*, 23.
4 RGAE, f. 4372, op. 36, d. 1661, ll. 55–9; Poliakov, *Spravochnik arkhitektora*, 20; Parkins, *City Planning in Soviet Russia*, 18–19.
5 A. Mostakov, "Skhematizm v planirovke gorodov," *Arkhitektura SSSR* 6 (1936) 30, as referred to in Parkins, *City Planning in Soviet Russia*, 19.
6 On these various tropes, see Katerina Clark, *The Soviet Novel: History as Ritual* (Chicago: University of Chicago Press, 1981).
7 On the stylistic evolution of the Socialist Realist genre, see Tarkhanov and Kavtaradze, *Architecture of the Stalin Era*, 182. On the openness inherent to Socialist Realism as an aesthetic practice, see Lahusen, "Socialist Realism in Search of Its Shores," 661–86.
8 The concept of a "cultural ecosystem" comes from Clark, *Petersburg*, ix–x.
9 For Stephen Kotkin, the concept of living space testified to the Soviet state's enduring commitment to social engineering. As noted in this chapter, however, "living space" could mean much more. For Kotkin's discussion of living space, see his *Magnetic Mountain*, 160–97.
10 "Scenario of power" is a direct allusion to Richard Wortman, *Scenarios of Power: Myth and Ceremony in Russian Monarchy from Peter the Great to the Abdication of Nicholas II* (Princeton: Princeton University Press, 2006).
11 Kertzer, *Ritual, Politics, and Power*, 153, 174. Stalin acknowledged his inability to control motives. See Brooks, *Thank You, Comrade Stalin!*, 67–8.
12 On off-stage scripts, or "hidden transcripts," see Scott, *Domination and the Arts of Resistance*, 50.
13 My comments here are inspired by Mikhail Bakhtin, *Problems of Dostoevsky's Poetics*, edited and translated by Caryl Emerson (Minneapolis: University of Minnesota Press, 1984).

14 Yurchak, *Everything Was Forever*, 12–16. Party leaders, too, might speak of a situation using two competing conceptual frameworks, only one of which was meant for public consumption. See Donald J. Raleigh, "Languages of Power: How Saratov Bolsheviks Imagined Their Enemies," *Slavic Review* 57/2 (1998): 320–49.

15 On the role of the architectural metaphor in Derrida's thought, see Max Wigley, *The Architecture of Deconstruction*.

16 Kertzer, *Ritual, Politics, and Power*, 4.

17 Tarkhanov and Kavtaradze, *Architecture of the Stalin Era*, 182.

18 Day, "The Rise and Fall of Stalinist Architecture," 172–93. Also see Martine Mespoulet, "Survival Strategies in the Soviet Bureaucracy: The Case of the Statistics Administration," in Rowney and Huskey, *Russian Bureaucracy and the State*.

Glossary

absolute space – the totality of space, including all that cannot be represented in a textual, visual, or verbal frame

"across the river" settlement plan – see *zarechnoe rasselenie*

All-Union Council for the Municipal Economy (VSKKh pri TsIK SSSR) – responsible for municipal development in the Soviet Union

APU – Architecture and Planning Administration

ARU – Association of Architects-Urbanists, an urban planning organization belonging to the rationalist school, founded by Nikolai A. Ladovskii in 1928

Avtostroi – state agency responsible for building the automobile factory in Avtozavod during the First Five-Year Plan

Avtozavod – southwestern district of present-day Nizhnii Novgorod; site of a Ford factory and its socialist city

blagoustroistvo – urban improvement (i.e., landscaping, architecture, and infrastructure)

Central Committee of the Communist Party (TsK VKP[b], TsK KPSS) – governing apparatus of the Communist Party, selected the secretariat (responsible for all appointments to Party and state posts) and the Politburo (the most powerful policy-making apparatus in the Soviet Union)

chistka – purge or "cleanup," may refer to political purge or to such mundane activities as snow and waste removal

Communist Youth League (Komsomol) – political organization for the education and mobilization of Soviet youth

compact plan – the zoning plan approved for the City of Gorky in 1935; an updated version of *zarechnoe rasselenie*, or "across the river" settlement

constructivism – school of architecture in which the aesthetic of a building is defined by its function and by the materials out of which it is crafted

detal'nye plany – detailed plans; projects for specific buildings and infrastructure, drafted in the fourth and final stage of city planning

Expert Architectural Council (EAS) – also called the "Expert Council," responsible for the approval of all architectural projects for the City of Gorky

fourth wall – in theatre, the imaginary wall separating the actors from the audience

GAZ – Gorky Automobile Factory, located in Avtozavod

general'nyi plan – general city plan, drafted in the third stage of the city planning process; a project for the placement of roads, bridges, and other fundamental infrastructure

Giprogor – see Mosgiprogor and Lengiprogor

GlavAPU – Main Architecture and Planning Administration of the Russian Federation, an agency subordinate to the Russian Commissariat of the Municipal Economy

gorod-krasavits – city beautiful

Gorproekt – a municipal project agency, responsible for designs for civic buildings

Gosplan – State Planning Committee, existed at both Russian (Gosplan RSFSR) and Soviet (Gosplan SSSR) levels of governance

Gorstroiproekt – a project agency, produced a new city plan for Avtozavod in 1935

Industrial Commission (PK NMMI) – worked on the Nizhnii Novgorod city plan from 1928 to 1931, affiliated with NMMI

izbushki – small huts

Kanavino – a district of Nizhnii Novgorod, located on the left bank of the Oka River

Kraiproekt – provincial design bureau, specialized in the production of industry-related architectural projects

kremlin – a fortress or walled city; in this study, kremlin refers almost exclusively to Nizhnii Novgorod's sixteenth-century fortress

kul'turnost' – culturedness

Lengiprogor – Leningrad State Institute of City Planning, worked on the Gorky city plan after 1935

MAO – Moscow Architectural Society

meridian construction – construction in which a building is situated with its length following a north-south axis, maximizing interior exposure to sunlight through windows facing west and east

Mosgiprogor – Moscow State Institute of City Planning, responsible for city planning in Nizhnii Novgorod/Gorky from 1931 to 1935

MVTU – Moscow Higher Technical Institute, its students authored the initial design for the socialist city of Avtozavod in 1930

nagornoe rasselenie – hilltop settlement, one of the proposed zoning plans for the City of Nizhnii Novgorod in 1931

Nizhgubkommunotdel – Province of Nizhnii Novgorod Department of the Municipal Economy

NKVD RSFSR – Russian Commissariat of Internal Affairs

NMMI – Nizhnii Novgorod Mechanics and Machine-Building Institute

obshchestvennitsy – society women

OGPU – United State Political Administration (1923–1934), state political police

OSA – Union of Contemporary Architects, a constructivist architectural organization founded by the Vesnin brothers and Moisei Ginzburg in 1925

planirovanie – economic and social planning

planirovka – zoning or spatial planning; second stage of city planning (after *planirovanie*)

promezhutochnoe rasselenie – interspersed settlement, see also *rassredotochennyi gorod*

rassredotochennyi gorod – dispersed city, marked by scattered pockets of settlement

rationalism – in architecture, a school of aesthetics that displayed strong concern for how colour and form would impact the human psyche

Russian Commissariat of the Municipal Economy (NKKKh RSFSR) – responsible for Russian municipal affairs, including the production and approval of city plans

Russian Council of People's Commissars (SNK RSFSR, Sovnarkom RSFSR) – supreme executive and administrative body of the Russian Soviet Federated Socialist Republic, consisting of the heads of Russian commissariats

Scientific-Technical Council (NTS NKKKKh RSFSR) – organ of the Russian Commissariat of the Municipal Economy, an expert panel that ruled on matters related to city planning and public health

Sormovo – a district of Nizhnii Novgorod, located on the northwestern outskirts of the city; known for heavy industry

Soviet Council of People's Commissars (SNK SSSR, Sovnarkom SSSR) – until 1946, the highest executive and administrative body of the Union of Soviet Socialist Republics

Stakhanovite – an individual known for extraordinary feats of productivity, as inspired by the achievements of the coal miner Alexei Stakhanov in 1935

Stalinskaia zabota – Stalinist care

star-city plan – the fourth of the Industrial Commission's proposed zoning plans of 1931

strelka – an arrow-shaped promontory formed by the confluence of the Volga and Oka rivers

Supreme Council of the Economy (VSNKh SSSR) – also called "Vesenkha," responsible for the supervision of nationalized industries to 1932

trudovoi zaem – labour tax; state exploitation of unpaid, supposedly volunteer labour

Union of Soviet Architects – formed in 1932 to unite architects in the Soviet Union behind a shared, state-controlled social and aesthetic program

Vkhutein – Higher State Art and Technical Institute, dissolved in 1930; successor to Vkhutemas

Vkhutemas – Higher State Art and Technical Studios, founded in 1920 to train future Soviet designers and builders, became a site of avant-garde experimentation in design; reorganized to form Vkhutein in 1926

Vodokhoziaistvennyi Otdel – see Water Management Section

VOPRA – All-Union Association of Proletarian Architects, formed in 1929 with the aim of creating truly "proletarian" architecture, dissolved in 1932

Water Management Section – part of the Leningrad Scientific Research Institute of the Municipal Economy (LNIKKh), responsible for drafting plans for the melioration of the left bank region of the City of Gorky in 1935 to 1936

zarechnoe rasselenie – across the river settlement, one of the four zoning plans proposed by the Industrial Commission in 1931; in it, both residential and industrial development were planned for the left bank of the Oka River; after 1935, identified as the "compact plan"

References

Primary Sources

Archives

MUSEUM OF THE HISTORY OF THE GORKY AUTOMOBILE FACTORY
Liubimov, S.M. "Vospominaniia i razdum'ia." Nizhnii Novgorod: Muzei istorii
    OAO GAZa, n.d.
Sur'ianinov, G.M. "Ne srazu sotsgorod stroilsia ... ," from "Vospominaniia
    byvshego glavnogo inzhenera UKSa GAZa Sur'ianinova." Nizhnii Novgorod:
    Muzei istorii OAO GAZa, n.d.
Sur'ianinov, G.M. "Kak eto bylo: letopis' organizatsii stroitel'stva, proektirova-
    niia, vypolneniia stroitel'stva, rasshireniia, vosstanovleniia i rekonstruktsii
    Gor'kovskogo avtomobil'nogo zavoda. Nizhnii Novgorod: Muzei istorii OAO
    GAZa, 1980.

CENTRAL STATE ARCHIVE OF THE PROVINCE OF NIZHNII NOVGOROD (TsANO)
Fond 2431   Office for the Construction of the Nizhnii Novgorod Automobile
            Factory
Fond 2561   District Provisional Executive Committee of Avtozavod
Fond R-78[1]   Design trust "Gorproekt"
Fond R-2697 City of Gorky Bureau for Architecture and Construction
Fond R-2698 Expert Architectural Council (EAS)
Fond R-2711 City of Gorky Office of Municipal Services (Gorkomkhoz)

---

1 The designations R- and A- were required by archivists when I conducted my original
  research. Although such designations have fallen out of use, I retain these here. – HD.

Fond R-2717   City of Nizhnii Novgorod/Gorky Planning Commission
Fond R-5317   Province of Nizhnii Novgorod Department of the Municipal
              Economy
Fond R-6205   Union of Soviet Architects, branch of the Province of Gorky

RUSSIAN STATE ARCHIVE OF LITERATURE AND ART (RGALI)
Fond 2991, op. 1 A.P. Ivanitskii

RUSSIAN STATE ECONOMIC ARCHIVE (RGAE)
Fond 293   Soviet Academy of Architecture and Construction
Fond 4372   Gosplan SSSR
Fond 9432   Committee of Architectural Affairs (under the Council of
              Ministers)

STATE ARCHIVE OF THE RUSSIAN FEDERATION (GARF)
Fond A-314   Commissariat of the Municipal Economy (NKKKh RSFSR)
Fond A-262   Gosplan RSFSR
Fond R-7544   All-Union Council of the Municipal Economy (VSKKh TsIK
              SSSR)

STATE SOCIAL-POLITICAL ARCHIVE OF THE PROVINCE OF NIZHNII NOVGOROD (GOPANO)
Fond 30   City of Gorky Party Committee (Gorkom)
Fond 772   Komsomol of the City of Gorky
Fond 1065   Party Committee of the Sverdlovsk District of the City of Gorky

Nizhnii Novgorod Periodicals

Biulleten' arkhitektury
Gor'kovskii rabochii
Izvestiia Vremennogo biuro TSK VKP(b)
Krasnyi Sormovich
Leninskaia smena
Nizhegorodskaia/Gor'kovskaia kommuna
Nizhegorodskii krai/Gor'kovskaia oblast'
*Nizhegorodskii ezhegodnik: administrativno-khoziaistvennyi spravochnik po Nizhnemu-
    Novgorodu i gubernii*
Nizhegorodskoe khoziaistvo
Rabota sovetov
Zapiski kraevedov: ocherki, vospominaniia, stat'i, dokumenty, khronika

Architecture Periodicals

Arkhitektura SSSR
Arkhitekturnaia gazeta
Arkhitekturnoe nasledstvo
Proekt Rossiia/Project Russia
Sovetskaia arkhitektura

Secondary Sources

Adrianov, Iurii, and Valerii Shamshurin. *Staryi Nizhnii: istoriko-literaturnye ocherki.* Nizhnii Novgorod: SMM, 1994.

Afanas'ev, K.N., and V.E. Khazanova, eds. *Iz istorii sovetskoi arkhitektury, 1917–1925: dokumenty i materialy.* Moscow: Akademiia Nauk SSSR, 1963.

Agafonov, Sviatoslav L. *Gorod Gorky.* Arkhitektura gorodov SSSR. Moscow: Akademiia arkhitektury SSSR, 1949.

– *Kamennaia letopis' goroda.* Gorky: Volgo-Viatskoe, 1971.

– *Nizhegorodskii kreml': Arkhitektura, istoriia, restavratsiia.* Gorky: Volgo-Viatskoe, 1976.

Andrusz, Gregory D. *Housing and Urban Development in the USSR.* London: Macmillan, 1984.

"Architectural Guide to Nizhnii Novgorod." *Proekt Rossii: arkhitektura, dizain, tekhnologiia* 4 (1997): 49–64.

Arkhangel'skii, Sergei Ivanovich, ed. *Nizhnii Novgorod v XVII veke: sbornik dokumentov: Iz materialov k istorii Nizhnego Novgoroda i ego okrugi.* Gorky: Gor'kovskoe knizhnoe izdatel'stvo, 1961.

Arzhanova, V.F., and I.M. Gur'ev, eds. *Ocherki istorii Gor'kovskoi organizatsii KPSS, 1918–1941.* Gorky: Volga-Viatskoe, 1966.

Ashavskii, I.M. *Sotsgorod Nizhegorodskogo avtozavoda.* Nizhnii Novgorod: Nizhegorodskoe izdatel'stvo, 1932.

Attwood, Lynne, and Catriona Kelly. "Programmes for Identity: The 'New Man' and the 'New Woman.'" In *Constructing Russian Culture in the Age of Revolution: 1881–1940*, ed. Catriona Kelly and David Shepherd, 256–90. Oxford: Oxford University Press, 1998.

Austin, Richard Cartwight. *Building Utopia: Erecting Russia's First Modern City, 1930.* Kent: Kent State University Press, 2004.

Badcock, Sarah. *Politics and the People in Revolutionary Russia: A Provincial History.* Cambridge: Cambridge University Press, 2007.

Bailes, Kendall E. "Alexei Gastev and the Soviet Controversy over Taylorism, 1918–1924." *Soviet Studies* 29/3 (1977): 373–394.

– *Technology and Society under Lenin and Stalin: Origins of the Soviet Technical Intelligentsia, 1917–1941.* Princeton: Princeton University Press, 1978.
– "The American Connection: Ideology and the Transfer of American Technology to the Soviet Union, 1917–1941." *Comparative Studies in Society and History* 23/3 (1981): 421–48.
Bakhtin, Mikhail. *Problems of Dostoevsky's Poetics.* Transl. Caryl Emerson. Minneapolis: University of Minnesota Press, 1984.
Balzer, Harley D. "Engineers: The Rise and Decline of a Social Myth." In *Science and the Soviet Social Order*, ed. Loren R. Graham, 141–67. Cambridge: Harvard University Press, 1990.
– "The Engineering Profession in Tsarist Russia." In *Russia's Missing Middle Class: The Professions in Russian History*, ed. Harley D. Balzer, 55–88. Armonk: M.E. Sharpe, 1996.
Baranov, Nikolai V. *Glavnyi arkhitektor goroda: Tvorcheskaia i organizatsionnaia deiatel'nost'.* Moscow: Stroiizdat, 1979.
Barkhin, Mikhail G. *Metod raboty zodchego: Iz opyta raboty sovetskoi arkhitektury, 1917–1957 gg.* Moscow: Stroiizdat, 1981.
Bassin, Mark, Christopher Ely, and Melissa Stockdale, eds. *Space, Place, and Power in Modern Russia: Essays in the New Spatial History.* Dekalb: Northern Illinois University Press, 2010.
Bater, James H. *The Soviet City: Ideal and Reality.* Beverly Hills: Sage, 1980.
Baulina, Valentina V. *Gde otdykhaiut gor'kovchan'e.* Gorky: Volga-Viatskoe, 1971.
Beaujour, Elizabeth Klosty. "Architectural Discourse and Early Soviet Literature." *Journal of the History of Ideas* 44/3 (1983): 477–95.
Beissinger, Mark R. *Scientific Management, Socialist Discipline, and Soviet Power.* Cambridge: Harvard University Press, 1988.
Belenko, Iurii G., and G.I. Pylaeva, eds. *Gor'kovskii dizel'nyi: Ocherki istorii zavoda "Dvigatel' Revoliutsii."* Moscow: Mysl', 1985.
Belous, V.I., ed. *Politicheskaia elita Nizhegorodskoi oblasti 1917–1995: Nauchno-spravochnoe izdanie.* Nizhnii Novgorod: FISNIMO NNGU, 1995.
Benjamin, Walter. "The Task of the Translator." In *Illuminations.* Intro. Hannah Arendt. Transl. Harry Zohn, 69–82. New York: Schocken, 1986.
Bernatskii, L.N., F.E. Vol'sov, and E.V. Milanovskii. *Opolzni srednego i nizhnego Povolzh'ia i mery bor'by s nimi.* Moscow: Glavnaia redaktsiia stroitel'noi literatury, 1935.
Bittner, Stephen. *The Many Lives of Khrushchev's Thaw: Experience and Memory in Moscow's Arbat.* Ithaca: Cornell University Press, 2008.
Bliznakov, Milka. "Soviet Housing during the Experimental Years, 1918–1933." In *Russian Housing in the Modern Age: Design and Social History*, ed. William Craft Brumfield and Blair A. Ruble, 85–148. Washington, DC: Woodrow Wilson Center Press, and Cambridge: Cambridge University Press, 1993.

Bodenschatz, Harald, and Christiane Post, eds. *Städtebau im Schatten Stalins: Die internationale Suche nach der sozialistischen Stadt in der Sowjetunion, 1929–1935*. Berlin: Verlagshaus Braun, 2003.

Bogoroditskaia, N.A. "Stranichki istorii Nizhegorodskoi iarmarki." *Voprosy Istorii (SSSR)* 10 (1979): 179–83.

Bogoroditskaia, N.A., and N.F. Filatov, eds. *XVI Vserossiiskaia promyshlennaia i khudozhestvennaia vystavka 1896 goda v Nizhnem Novgorode: Ocherki istorii*. Nizhnii Novgorod: FISNIMO NNGU, 1996.

Bondarenko, I.A., ed. *Stolichnyi gorod*. Moscow: URSS, 1998.

Boym, Svetlana. *Common Places: Mythologies of Everyday Life in Russia*. Cambridge: Harvard University Press, 1994.

Brandenberger, David. *National Bolshevism: Stalinist Mass Culture and the Formation of Modern Russian National Identity, 1931–1956*. Cambridge: Harvard University Press, 2002.

Brooks, Jeffrey. *Thank You, Comrade Stalin! Soviet Public Culture from Revolution to Cold War*. Princeton: Princeton University Press, 2000.

Brower, Daniel R. *The Russian City between Tradition and Modernity, 1850–1900*. Berkeley: University of California Press, 1990.

– "Urban Revolution in Late Imperial Russia." In *The City in Late Imperial Russia*, ed. Michael F. Hamm, 319–54. Bloomington: Indiana University Press, 1986.

Brown, Kate. *A Biography of No Place: From Ethnic Borderland to Soviet Heartland*. Cambridge: Harvard University Press, 2005.

Brumfield, William Craft. *A History of Russian Architecture*. Cambridge: Cambridge University Press, 1993.

Brumfield, William Craft, ed. *Reshaping Russian Architecture: Western Technology, Utopian Dreams*. Washington, DC: Woodrow Wilson International Center for Scholars, and Cambridge: Cambridge University Press, 1990.

Brumfield, William Craft, and Blair A. Ruble, eds. *Russian Housing in the Modern Age: Design and Social History*. Washington, DC: Woodrow Wilson Center Press, and Cambridge: Cambridge University Press, 1993.

Bubnov, Iurii Nikolaevich. *Arkhitektura Nizhnego Novgoroda serediny XIX – nachala XX veka*. Nizhnii Novgorod: Volgo-Viatskoe, 1990.

– *Vserossiiskaia promyshlennaia i khudozhestvennaia vystavka 1896 goda v Nizhnem Novgorode: K 100-letiiu so dnia otkrytiia*. Nizhnii Novgorod: Dekom, 1996.

Bubnov, Iurii N., and Olga V. Orel'skaia. *Arkhitektura goroda Gor'kogo: Ocherki istorii, 1917–1985*. Gorky: Volgo-Viatskoe, 1986.

Buchli, Viktor. *An Archaeology of Socialism*. Oxford: Berg, 1999.

Castillo, Greg. "Stalinist Modern: Constructivism and the Soviet Company Town." In *Architectures of Russian Identity: 1500 to the Present*, ed. James Cracraft and Daniel B. Rowland, 135–49. Ithaca: Cornell University Press, 2003.

Certeau, Michel de. *The Practice of Everyday Life*. Berkeley: University of California Press, 1984.

Chatterjee, Choi. *Celebrating Women: Gender, Festival Culture, and Bolshevik Ideology, 1910–1939*. Pittsburgh: University of Pittsburgh Press, 2002.

Clark, Katerina. "Changing Historical Paradigms in Soviet Culture." In *Late Soviet Culture from Perestroika to Novostroika*, ed. Thomas Lahusen and Gene Kuperman. Durham: Duke University Press, 1993.

– "The Changing Image of Science and Technology in Soviet Literature." In *Science and the Soviet Social Order*, ed. Loren R. Graham, 266–79. Cambridge: Harvard University Press, 1990.

– *Petersburg: Crucible of Cultural Revolution*. Cambridge: Harvard University Press, 1995.

– "Socialist Realism and the Sacralizing of Space." In *The Landscape of Stalinism: The Art and Ideology of Soviet Space*, ed. E.A. Dobrenko and Eric Naiman, 3–18. Seattle: University of Washington Press, 2003.

– *The Soviet Novel: History as Ritual*. Chicago: University of Chicago Press, 1981.

Clements, Barbara Evans. *Bolshevik Women*. Cambridge: Cambridge University Press, 1997.

Colton, Timothy J. *Moscow: Governing the Socialist Metropolis*. Cambridge: Harvard University Press, 1995.

Cooke, Catherine. *Russian Avant-Garde: Theories of Art, Architecture, and the City*. London: Academy Editions, 1995.

Cooke, Catherine, V.P. Tolstoi, and I.M. Bibikova, eds. *Street Art of the Revolution: Festivals and Celebrations in Russia, 1918–1933*. London: Vendome, 1990.

Cracraft, James. *The Petrine Revolution in Russian Architecture*. Chicago: University of Chicago Press, 1988.

Cracraft, James, and Daniel B. Rowland, eds. *Architectures of Russian Identity: 1500 to the Present*. Ithaca: Cornell University Press, 2003.

Crowley, David, and Susan Emily Reid, eds. *Socialist Spaces: Sites of Everyday Life in the Eastern Bloc*. Oxford and New York: Berg, 2002.

Czaplicka, John, Blair A. Ruble, and Lauren Crabtree, eds. *Composing Urban History and the Constitution of Civic Identities*. Washington, DC: Woodrow Wilson Center Press, and Baltimore: Johns Hopkins University Press, 2003.

Czaplicka, John, Nida Gelazis, and Blair A. Ruble, eds. *Cities after the Fall of Communism: Reshaping Cultural Landscapes and European Identity*. Washington, DC: Woodrow Wilson Center Press, and Baltimore: Johns Hopkins University Press, 2009.

David-Fox, Michael. *Revolution of the Mind: Higher Learning among the Bolsheviks, 1918–1929*. Ithaca: Cornell University Press, 1997.

Davidovich, Vladimir G., and Tat'iana A. Chizhikova. *Aleksandr Ivanitskii*. Moscow: Stroiizdat, 1973.

Day, Andrew. "Building Socialism: The Politics of the Soviet Cityscape in the Stalin Era." Doctoral dissertation, Columbia University, 1998.

– "The Rise and Fall of Stalinist Architecture." In *Architectures of Russian Identity*, ed. James Cracraft and Daniel B. Rowland, 172–93. Ithaca: Cornell University Press, 2003.

Deelstra, Tjeerd, and Oleg Ianitskii, eds. *Cities of Europe: The Public's Role in Shaping the Urban Environment*. Moscow: Mezhdunarodnye otnoshenia, 1991.

Dobrenko, E.A. "Socialism as Will and Representation, or What Legacy Are We Rejecting?" Transl. Jesse Savage and Gust Olsen. *Kritika: Explorations in Russian and Eurasian History* 5/4 (2004): 675–708.

– *The Political Economy of Socialist Realism*. Transl. Jesse Savage. New Haven: Yale University Press, 2007.

Dobrenko, E.A., and Eric Naiman. *The Landscape of Stalinism: The Art and Ideology of Soviet Space*. Seattle: University of Washington Press, 2003.

Dunham, Vera. *In Stalin's Time: Middle-Class Values in Soviet Fiction*. Cambridge: Cambridge University Press, 1976.

Easter, Gerald. *Reconstructing the State: Personal Networks and Elite Identity in Soviet Russia*. Cambridge: Cambridge University Press, 2000.

Ellis, Frank. "Media as Social Engineer." In *Russian Cultural Studies: An Introduction*, ed. Catriona Kelly and David Shepherd, 192–222. Oxford: Oxford University Press, 1998.

Ely, Christopher D. "The Origins of Russian Scenery: Volga River Tourism and Russian Landscape Aesthetics." *Slavic Review* 62/4 (2003): 666–82.

– *This Meager Nature: Landscape and National Identity in Imperial Russia*. DeKalb: Northern Illinois University Press, 2002.

– "Street Space and Political Culture in St. Petersburg under Alexander II." In *Space, Place, and Power in Modern Russia*, ed. Mark Bassin, Christopher Ely, and Melissa Stockdale, 167–94. Dekalb: Northern Illinois University Press, 2010.

Evgrafov, F.G. "Kommunisty oblasti v bor'be za industrializatsiiu narodnogo khoziaistva." *Istoriia partiinoi organizatsii. Podborka broshiur*. Gorky: Znanie, 1967.

Fadeev, V.P., Z.K. Zvezdin, and N.I. Kuprianova, eds. *Istoriia industrializatsii Nizhegorodskogo/Gor'kovskogo kraia (1926–1941)*. Gorky: Volga-Viatskoe, 1968.

Fedorov, G. *Sotsialisticheskii gorod Gorky*. Gorky: OGIZ, 1939.

Fedorov, Valerii D. *Liudi novykh zavodov: rabochie Nizhegorodskogo kraia v pervoi piatiletke*. Gorky: Volgo-Viatskoe, 1981.

Fedorov, Valerii D. et al., eds. *Rossiia i Nizhegorodskii krai: aktual'nye problemy istorii: Materialy chtenii pamiati N.M. Dobrotvora 24–25 aprelia 1997 g.* Nizhnii Novgorod: NGPU, 1998.

Fedoseev, P.N., K.U. Chernenko, and A.G. Egorov, eds. *KPSS SSSR v resoliutsiiakh i resheniiakh s'ezdov, konferentsii, i plenumov TsK, 1898–1970*. 8th rev. ed., vol. 4 (1927–1931). Moscow: Politicheskaia literatura, 1931.

Filatov, Nikolai F. *Nizhegorodskoe zodchestvo XVII – nachala XX veka.* Gorky: Volgo-Viatskoe, 1980.
– *Nizhnii Novgorod: Arkhitektura XIV – nachala XX veka: entsiklopediia Nizhegorod-skogo kraia.* Nizhnii Novgorod: "Nizhegorodskie novosti," 1994.
– "Staryi gorodok XII veka v ust'e Oki – predshestvennik Nizhnego Novgoroda." In *Nizhegorodskie issledovaniia po kraevedeniiu i arkheologii: Ezhegod-nik,* 104–8. Nizhnii Novgorod: Nizhegorodskii gumanitarnyi tsentr, 1999.
Filtzer, Donald. *Soviet Workers and Stalinist Industrialization: The Formation of Modern Soviet Production Relations, 1928–1941.* Armonk: M.E. Sharpe, 1986.
– *The Hazards of Urban Life in Late Stalinist Russia: Health, Hygiene, and Living Standards, 1943–1953.* New York: Cambridge University Press, 2010.
Fitzpatrick, Anne Lincoln. *The Great Russian Fair: Nizhnii Novgorod, 1840–90.* London: Macmillan, 1990.
Fitzpatrick, Sheila. "Ascribing Class: The Construction of Identity in Soviet Russia." *Journal of Modern History* 65/4 (1993): 745–70.
– *The Cultural Front: Power and Culture in Revolutionary Russia.* Ithaca: Cornell University Press, 1992.
– *Education and Social Mobility in the Soviet Union, 1921–1934.* Cambridge: Cambridge University Press, 1979.
– *Everyday Stalinism: Ordinary Life in Extraordinary Times – Soviet Russia in the 1930s.* New York: Oxford University Press, 1999.
– "How the Mice Buried the Cat: Scenes from the Great Purges of 1937 in the Russian Provinces." *Russian Review* 52/3 (1993): 299–320.
– "Ordzhonikidze's Takeover of Vesenkha: A Case Study in Soviet Bureaucratic Politics." *Soviet Studies* 37/2 (1985): 153–72.
Fitzpatrick, Sheila, ed. *Cultural Revolution in Russia, 1928–1931.* Bloomington: Indiana University Press, 1978.
– *Stalinism: New Directions.* London: Routledge, 2000.
Frank, Stephen, and Mark Steinberg, eds. *Cultures in Flux: Lower-Class Values, Practices, and Resistance in Late Imperial Russia.* Princeton: Princeton University Press, 1994.
French, Richard Antony. *Plans, Pragmatism, and People: The Legacy of Soviet Planning for Today's Cities.* Pittsburgh: University of Pittsburgh Press, 1995.
French, Richard Antony, and F.E. Ian Hamilton, eds. *The Socialist City: Spatial Structure and Urban Policy.* New York: Wiley, 1979.
Friedgut, Theodore H. *Political Participation in the USSR.* Princeton: Princeton University Press, 1979.
Galai, Iu.G., N.A. Kuznetsova, and V.A. Shamshurin, eds. *Gorod slavy i vernosti Rossii: Materialy istoriko-kraevedcheskoi konferentsii, posviashchennoi 775–letiiu Nizhnego Novgoroda.* Nizhnii Novgorod: Gorodskoe upravlenie kul'tury, 1996.

Garanina, L.F. *Gorod Gorky: Putevoditel'*. Gorky: Volga-Viatskoe, 1964.

Gastev, Alexei. *Poeziia rabochego udara*. Petrograd: Proletkul't, 1918.

Gatsiskii, Alexander S., ed. *Nizhegorodskii letopisets*. Nizhegorodskie byli. Nizhnii Novgorod: Nizhegorodskaia iarmarka, 2001.

Geldern, James von. *Bolshevik Festivals, 1917–1920*. Berkeley: University of California Press, 1993.

Gerasimova, Katerina. "The Soviet Communal Apartment." In *Beyond the Limits: The Concept of Space in Russian History and Culture*, ed. Jeremy Smith, 107–31. Helsinki: SHS, 1999.

Getty, J. Arch. *Origins of the Great Purges: The Soviet Communist Party Reconsidered, 1933–1938*. Cambridge: Cambridge University Press, 1985.

Gill, Graeme. "The Communist Party and the Weakness of Bureaucratic Norms." In *Russian Bureaucracy and the State: Officialdom from Alexander III to Vladimir Putin*, ed. Don K. Rowney and Eugene Huskey, 118–34. Basingstoke: Palgrave Macmillan, 2009.

Ginzburg, Moisei Ia. *Zhilishche: Opyt piatiletnei raboty nad problemoi zhilishcha*. Moscow: Gosstroiizdat, 1934.

Glazychev, V. "'The City of the People' and Problems of Its Formation." In *Cities of Europe: The Public's Role in Shaping the Urban Environment*, ed. Tjeerd Deelstra and Oleg Ianitskii. Moscow: Mezhdunarodnye otnoshenia, 1991.

Goldman, Wendy. *Terror and Democracy in the Age of Stalin: The Social Dynamics of Repression*. Cambridge: Cambridge University Press, 2007.

– *Women at the Gates: Gender and Industry in Stalin's Russia*. Cambridge: Cambridge University Press, 2002.

– *Women, the State, and Revolution: Soviet Family Policy and Social Life, 1917–1936*. Cambridge: Cambridge University Press, 1993.

Golubinova, A.N., N.Iu. Gusev, V.I. Zhil'tsov, V.V. Smirnov, and V.A. Kharlamov, eds. *Kniga pamiati zhertv politicheskikh repressii v Nizhegorodskoi oblasti*. 2 vols. Nizhnii Novgorod: OAO "Nizhegorodskii pechatnik," 2001.

Gordeeva, L.P. "L.M. Kaganovich i V.M. Molotov – rukovoditeli Nizhegorodskoi gubernii (1918–1920)." In *Rossiia i Nizhegorodskii krai: Aktual'nye problemy istorii. (Materialy v pamiati N.M. Dobrotvora 24–25 aprelia 1997 g.)*, 241–4. Nizhnii Novgorod: Nizhegorodskii gumanitarnyi tsentr, 1998.

Gordeeva, L.P., V.A. Kazakov, V.P. Kiselev, V.V. Smirnov, eds. *Zabveniiu ne podlezhit*, vol. 1, *O repressiiakh 30-kh – nachala 50-kh godov v Nizhegorodskoi oblasti*. Nizhnii Novgorod: Volgo-Viatskoe, 1993.

Gorsuch, Anne. *Youth in Revolutionary Russia: Enthusiasts, Bohemians, Delinquents*. Bloomington: Indiana University Press, 2000.

Graham, Loren R. *The Ghost of the Executed Engineer: Technology and the Fall of the Soviet Union*. Cambridge: Harvard University Press, 1993.

Graham, Loren R., ed. *Science and the Soviet Social Order.* Cambridge: Harvard University Press, 1990.

Gregory, Paul. *The Political Economy of Stalinism: Evidence from the Soviet Secret Archives.* Cambridge: Cambridge University Press, 2003.

Groys, Boris. "The Art of Totality." In *The Landscape of Stalinism: The Art and Ideology of Soviet Space,* ed. E.A. Dobrenko and Eric Naiman, 96–124. Seattle: University of Washington Press, 2003.

– *The Total Art of Stalinism: Avant-Garde, Aesthetic Dictatorship, and Beyond.* Transl. Charles Rougle. Princeton: Princeton University Press, 1992.

Guillén, Mauro F. "Scientific Management's Lost Aesthetic: Architecture, Organization, and the Taylorized Beauty of the Mechanical." *Administrative Science Quarterly* 42/2 (1997): 682–715.

Gulianitskii, N.F., ed. *Moskva i slozhivshiesia russkie goroda XVIII – pervoi poloviny XIX vekov.* Moscow: Stroiizdat, 1998.

Hachten, Charles. "Property Relations and the Economic Organization of Soviet Russia, 1941–1948." Doctoral dissertation, University of Chicago, 2005.

– "Separate yet Governed: The Representation of Soviet Property Relations in Civil Law and Public Discourse." In *Borders of Socialism: Private Spheres of Soviet Russia,* ed. Lewis Siegelbaum, 65–82. New York: Palgrave Macmillan, 2006.

Hagenloh, Paul. *Stalin's Police: Public Order and Mass Repression in the USSR, 1926–1941.* Washington, DC: Woodrow Wilson Center Press, and Baltimore: Johns Hopkins University Press, 2009.

Hall, Peter Geoffrey. *Cities of Tomorrow: An Intellectual History of Urban Planning and Design in the Twentieth Century.* 3rd ed. Oxford: Blackwell, 2002.

Hamm, Michael F., ed. *The City in Late Imperial Russia.* Bloomington: Indiana University Press, 1986.

– *The City in Russian History.* Lexington: University Press of Kentucky, 1976.

Harris, James. *The Great Urals: Regionalism and the Evolution of the Soviet System.* Ithaca: Cornell University Press, 1999.

– "Resisting the Plan in the Urals, 1928–1956, or Why Regional Officials Needed 'Wreckers' and 'Saboteurs.'" In *Contending with Stalinism: Soviet Power and Popular Resistance in the 1930s,* ed. Lynne Viola, 201–28. Ithaca and London: Cornell University Press, 2002.

Harris, Stephen Emmett. "Moving to the Separate Apartment: Building, Distributing, Furnishing, and Living in Urban Housing in Soviet Russia, 1950s–1960s." Doctoral dissertation, University of Chicago, 2003.

Herlihy, Patricia. *Odessa: A History, 1794–1914.* Cambridge: Harvard University Press, 1987.

Hessler, Julie. "Cultured Trade: The Stalinist Turn towards Consumerism." In *Stalinism: New Directions,* ed. Sheila Fitzpatrick, 182–209. London and New York: Routledge, 2000.

Hirsch, Francine. *Empire of Nations: Ethnographic Knowledge and the Making of the Soviet Union*. Ithaca: Cornell University Press, 2005.

Hoffman, David. *Peasant Metropolis: Social Identities in Moscow, 1929–1941*. Ithaca: Cornell University Press, 1994.

– *Stalinist Values: The Cultural Norms of Modernity, 1917–1941*. Ithaca: Cornell University Press, 2003.

Hogan, Heather. *Forging Revolution: Metalworkers, Managers, and the State in St. Petersburg, 1890–1914*. Bloomington: Indiana University Press, 1993.

Hoisington, Sona Stephan. "'Ever Higher': The Evolution of the Project for the Palace of Soviets." *Slavic Review* 62/1 (2003): 41–68.

Holquist, Peter. "To Count, to Extract, and to Exterminate: Population Statistics and Population Politics in Late Imperial and Soviet Russia." In *A State of Nations: Empire and Nation-Making in the Age of Lenin and Stalin*, ed. Ronald Grigor Suny and Terry Martin, 111–44. New York: Oxford University Press, 2001.

Hough, Jerry. *The Soviet Union and Social Science Theory*. Cambridge: Harvard University Press, 1979.

Howard, Ebenezer. *Garden Cities of Tomorrow*. London: S. Sonnenschein, 1902.

Hrytsak, Yaroslav, and Victor Susak. "Constructing a National City: The Case of L'viv." In *Composing Urban History and the Constitution of Civic Identities*, ed. John J. Czaplicka, Blair A. Ruble, and Lauren Crabtree. Washington, DC: Woodrow Wilson Center Press, and Baltimore: Johns Hopkins University Press, 2003.

Hudson, Hugh D. *Blueprints and Blood: The Stalinization of Soviet Architecture, 1917–1937*. Princeton: Princeton University Press, 1994.

Hughes, Thomas. *American Genesis: A Century of Invention and Technological Enthusiasm, 1870–1970*. New York: Viking, 1989.

Hutchinson, John F. *Politics and Public Health in Revolutionary Russia*. Baltimore: Johns Hopkins University Press, 1990.

Iurin, B.D., and E.V. Shvorak, eds., *Gor'kovskii avtomobil'nyi: Ocherki istorii zavoda*. Moscow: VTsSPS Profizdat, 1964.

Jones, Jeffrey W. *Everyday Life and the "Reconstruction" of Soviet Russia during and after the Great Patriotic War, 1943–1948*. Bloomington: Slavica, 2008.

Joyce, Patrick. *The Rule of Freedom: Liberalism and the Modern City*. New York: Verso, 2003.

Kelly, Catriona. "New Boundaries for the Common Good." In *Constructing Russian Culture in the Age of Revolution, 1881–1940*, ed. Catriona Kelly and David Shepherd, 238–55. Oxford: Oxford University Press, 1998.

Kelly, Catriona, and David Shepherd, eds. *Constructing Russian Culture in the Age of Revolution: 1881–1940*. Oxford: Oxford University Press, 1998.

Kertzer, David I. *Ritual, Politics, and Power*. New Haven: Yale University Press, 1988.

Khan-Magomedov, Selim O. *Pioneers of Soviet Architecture: The Search for New Solutions in the 1920s and 1930s.* Transl. Alexander Lieven. London: Thames and Hudson, 1987 [1983].

Kharkhordin, Oleg. *The Collective and the Individual in Russia: A Study of Practices.* Berkeley: University of California Press, 1999.

Khazanova, Vigdariia E. *Sovetskaia arkhitektura pervoi piatiletki: Problemy goroda budushchego.* Moscow: Nauka, 1980.

Khmel'nitskii, Dmitrii. *Arkhitektura Stalina: Psikhologiia i stil'.* Moscow: Progress-Traditsiia, 2007.

Khokhlov, A.F. *Universitet, rozhdennyi trizhdy: Istoriia sozdaniia i stanovleniia Nizhegorodskogo universiteta.* Nizhnii Novgorod: Nizhegorodskii universitet, 1998.

Khorev, B.S. *Gor'kovskaia oblast': Ekonomiko-geograficheskie ocherki.* 2nd ed. Gorky: Volgo-Viatskoe, 1967.

Khramtsovskii, Nikolai I. *Kratkii ocherk istoriia i opisanie Nizhnego Novgoroda.* Nizhnii Novgorod: Nizhegorodskaia iarmarka, 1998.

Kir'ianov, I.A. *K voprosu o vremeni osnovaniia goroda Gor'kogo.* Gorky: Gosudarstvennoe knizhnoe izdatel'stvo, 1956.

Kirichenko, Evgeniia I., and Elena G. Shcheboleva. *Russkaia provintsiia.* Kul'turnoe nasledie Rossii. Moscow: Nash dom; L'Age d'Homme, 1997.

Kirschenbaum, Lisa. "Place, Memory, and the Politics of Identity: Historical Buildings and Street Names in Leningrad–St. Petersburg." In *Space, Place, and Power in Modern Russia: Essays in the New Spatial History,* ed. Mark Bassin, Christopher Ely, and Melissa Stockdale, 243–60. Dekalb: Northern Illinois University Press, 2010.

Kiselev, I.I., V.Ia. Dobrokhotov, et al., eds. *Gor'kovskii avtomobil'nyi.* Moscow: Mysl', 1981.

Kivelson, Valerie A., and Robert H. Green, eds. *Orthodox Russia: Belief and Practice under the Tsars.* University Park: Pennsylvania State University Press, 2003.

Kojevnikov, Alexei. "Games of Stalinist Democracy: Ideological Discussions in Soviet Sciences, 1947–1952." In *Stalinism: New Directions,* ed. Sheila Fitzpatrick, 140–70. New York: Routledge, 2000.

Kopp, Anatole. "Foreign Architects in the Soviet Union during the First Five-Year Plans." In *Reshaping Russian Architecture: Western Technology, Utopian Dreams,* ed. William C. Brumfield and Blair A. Ruble, 176–214. Washington, DC: Woodrow Wilson International Center for Scholars; Cambridge and New York: Cambridge University Press, 1990.

– *Town and Revolution: Soviet Architecture and City Planning, 1917–1935.* Transl. Thomas E. Burton. New York: Braziller, 1970.

Kossoi, Iu.M. *Vash drug tramvai, 1896–1996: Vek Nizhegorodskogo tramvaia.* Nizhnii Novgorod: Elen' Iabloko, 1996.

Kotkin, Stephen. *Magnetic Mountain: Stalinism as a Civilization*. Berkeley: University of California Press, 1995.

– "Shelter and Subjectivity in the Stalin Period: A Case Study of Magnitogorsk." In *Russian Housing in the Modern Age: Design and Social History*, ed. William Craft Brumfield and Blair A. Ruble, 171–210. Washington, DC: Woodrow Wilson Center Press; Cambridge and New York: Cambridge University Press, 1993.

Kozonim, A.V. *Istoriia "Krasnogo Sormovo."* Moscow: Mysl', 1969.

Krylova, Anna. "Beyond the Spontaneity-Consciousness Paradigm: "Class Instinct" as a Promising Category of Political Analysis." *Slavic Review* 62/1 (2003): 1–23.

Küntzel, Kristina. *Von Nižnij zu Gor'kij: Metamorphosen einer russischen Provinzstadt*. Stuttgart: Franz Steiner Verlag, 2001.

Lahusen, Thomas. "Socialist Realism in Search of Its Shores: Some Historical Remarks on the 'Historically Open Aesthetic System of the Truthful Representation of Life.'" In *Socialist Realism without Shores*, ed. Thomas Lahusen and E.A. Dobrenko. Durham: Duke University Press, 1995.

Lavrov, Vitaly A. "Avtostroi – sotsialisticheskii gorod." *Stroitel'stvo Moskvy* 4 (1930): 20–4.

Lefebvre, Henri. *The Production of Space*. Transl. Donald Nicholson-Smith. Oxford: Blackwell, 1991.

– *The Urban Revolution*. Transl. Robert Bononno. Minneapolis: University of Minnesota Press, 2003.

Lenoe, Matthew. *Closer to the Masses: Agitation, Propaganda, and the "Stalinization" of the Soviet Press, 1922–1930*. Pittsburgh: University of Pittsburgh Press, 1998.

– *Closer to the Masses: Stalinist Culture, Social Revolution, and Soviet Newspapers*. Cambridge: Harvard University Press, 2004.

Lewin, Moshe. "Who Was the Soviet Kulak?" *Soviet Studies* 18/2 (1966): 189–212.

Lih, Lars. "How a Founding Document Was Found, or One Hundred Years of Lenin's *What Is to Be Done?*" *Kritika: Explorations in Russian and Eurasian History* 4/1 (2003): 5–49.

Lincoln, W. Bruce. *In the Vanguard of Reform: Russia's Enlightened Bureaucrats, 1825–1861*. Dekalb: Northern Illinois University Press, 1982.

Lubrano, Linda L., and Susan Solomon, eds. *The Social Context of Soviet Science*. Boulder: Westview Press, 1980.

Maddox, Stephen. "Healing the Wounds: Commemorations, Myths, and the Restoration of Leningrad's Imperial Heritage, 1941–1950." Doctoral dissertation, University of Toronto, 2008.

Maier, Charles. S. "Between Taylorism and Technocracy: European Ideologies and the Vision of Industrial Productivity in the 1920s." *Journal of Contemporary History* 5/2 (1970): 27–61.

– *In Search of Stability: Explorations in Historical Political Economy.* Cambridge: Cambridge University Press, 1987.

Martin, Terry. *The Affirmative Action Empire: Nations and Nationalism in the Soviet Union, 1932–1939.* Ithaca: Cornell University Press, 2001.

Mashkovtsev, V.P., and T.P. Vinogradova. *Tsarstvenno postavlennyi gorod: Nizhnii Novgorod v staroi otkrytke.* Vladimir: Posad, 2000.

Materialy k otchetu o rabote gorsoveta. Gorky: Gorsovet, 1935.

McLeod, Mary. "'Architecture or Revolution': Taylorism, Technocracy, and Social Change." *Art Journal* 43/2 (1983): 132–47.

McLuhan, Marshall. *Understanding Media: The Extensions of Man.* New York: McGraw-Hill, 1964.

Mel'nikov, A.P. *Ocherki bytovoi istorii Nizhegorodskoi iarmarki.* 2nd ed. Nizhnii Novgorod: Nizhegorodskii komp'iuternyi tsentr, 1993 [1917].

Mespoulet, Martine. "Survival Strategies in the Soviet Bureaucracy: The Case of the Statistics Administration." In *Russian Bureaucracy and the State: Russian Officialdom from Alexander III to Vladimir Putin,* ed. Don K. Rowney and Eugene Huskey. Basingstoke: Palgrave Macmillan, 2009.

Michels, Georg Bernhard. *At War with the Church: Religious Dissent in Seventeenth-Century Russia.* Stanford: Stanford University Press, 1999.

Miliutin, Nikolai Aleksandrovich. "Osnovnye voprosy zhilishchno-bytovogo stroitel'stva SSSR." *Sovetskaia arkhitektura* 1 (1931): 2–4.

– *Sotsgorod: The Problem of Building Socialist Cities.* Transl. Anatole Senkevich. Cambridge: MIT Press, 1974.

Miller, Martin A. *Freud and the Bolsheviks: Psychoanalysis in Imperial Russia and the Soviet Union.* New Haven: Yale University Press, 1998.

Moss, Anne Eakin. "Stalin's Harem: The Spectator's Dilemma in Late 1930s Soviet Film." *Studies in Russian and Soviet Cinema* 3/2 (2009): 157–72.

Mumford, Lewis. *The City in History: Its Origins, Its Transformation, and Its Prospects.* New York: Harcourt, Brace, and World, 1961.

– *The Culture of Cities.* New York: Harcourt, Brace, 1938.

Muravlev, A.N. "Sotsgorod avtozavoda im. Molotova (k 10-ti letiiu so dnia osnovaniia)." *Biulleten' arkhitektury,* 24–5. Gorky, 1940.

Murray, John. *Politics and Place Names: Changing Names in the Late Soviet Period.* Birmingham: University of Birmingham Press, 2000.

Naiman, Eric. *Sex in Public: The Incarnation of Early Soviet Ideology.* Princeton: Princeton University Press, 1999.

Neary, Rebecca Balmas. "Domestic Life and the Activist Wife in the 1930s Soviet Union." In *Borders of Socialism: Private Spheres of Soviet Russia,* ed. Lewis Siegelbaum, 107–22. London: Palgrave Macmillan, 2006.

Nikanorov, I. "Avtostroi." *Revoliutsiia i kul'tura* 1 (15 Jan. 1930): 76–7.

Nikulina. E.G. "General'nyi plan 1935 i istoricheskaia gorodskaia tkan'." In *Stolichnyi gorod*, ed. I.A. Bondarenko, 277–84. Moscow: URSS, 1998.

Northrop, Douglas. *Veiled Empire: Gender and Power in Stalinist Central Asia*. Ithaca: Cornell University Press, 2003.

Obertreis, Julia. "The Changing Image of the 'Individual' Apartment in the 1920s and 1930s: Individualism versus the Collective in Soviet Discourse on Housing." Paper presented at the 34th National Convention of the AAASS, Pittsburg, Pennsylvania, 21 Nov. 2002.

Olwig, Kenneth. *Landscape, Nature, and the Body Politic from Britain's Renaissance to America's New World*. Madison: University of Wisconsin Press, 2002.

Opolovnikov, Alexander V, and Elena A. Opolovnikova. *The Wooden Architecture of Russia: Houses, Fortifications, Churches*, ed. David Buxton. New York: Harry N. Abrams, 1989.

Orel'skaia, Olga V. *Arkhitektura epokhi sovetskogo avangarda v Nizhnem Novgoroda*. Nizhnii Novgorod: Promgrafika, 2005.

– "Arkhitektura gorodov Gor'kovskoi aglomeratsii 1920kh–1930kh godov: Gorky, Balakhna, Dzerzhinsk." Unpublished dissertation, Moscow Institute of Architecture, 1982.

– "Eksperiment prodolzhaetsia: iz istorii sovetskoi arkhitektury." *Zapiski kraevedov:ocherki, vospominaniia, stat'i, dokumenty, khronika*, ed. N.I. Kuprianova and I.V. Sidorov, 39–48. Gorky: Volga-Viatskoe, 1981.

Osokina, Elena A. "Economic Disobedience under Stalin." In *Contending with Stalinism: Soviet Power and Popular Resistance in the 1930s*, ed. Lynne Viola, 178–200. Ithaca: Cornell University Press, 2002.

– *Za fasadom "Stalinskogo izobiliia": Raspredelenie i rynok v snabzhenii naseleniia v gody industrializatsii, 1927–1941*. Moscow: Rosspen, 1998.

Otter, Chris. *The Victorian Eye: A Political History of Light and Vision in Britain, 1800–1910*. Chicago: University of Chicago Press, 2008.

Paperny, Vladimir. *Kul'tura dva*. Moscow: Novoe literaturnoe obozrenie, 1996.

Parkins, Maurice Frank. *City Planning in Soviet Russia, with an Interpretative Bibliography*. Chicago: University of Chicago Press, 1953.

Pelevina, T.I., A.I. Eliseev, and I.A. Kir'ianov, eds. *Ulitsy goroda Gor'kogo: Spravochnik*. Gorky: Volgo-Viatskoe, 1972.

Poliakov, N.Kh., ed. *Spravochnik arkhitektora*, vol. 2, *Gradostroitel'stvo*. Moscow: Akademiia arkhitektura SSSR, 1946.

Priestland, David. *The Politics of Mobilization: Ideas, Power, and Terror in Interwar Russia*. New York: Oxford University Press, 2007.

Puzis, G. *Kommunal'noe i zhilishchnoe khoziaistvo SSSR za 15 let*. Moscow: Gosudarstvennoe sotsial'no-ekonomicheskoe izdatel'stvo, 1932.

Qualls, Karl D. "Accommodation and Agitation in Sevastopol: Redefining

Socialist Space in the Postwar 'City of Glory.'" In *Socialist Spaces: Sites of Everyday Life in the Eastern Bloc*, ed. David Crowley and Susan Reid, 23–45. Oxford: Berg, 2002.

– *From Ruins to Reconstruction: Urban Identity in Soviet Sevastopol after World War Two*. Ithaca: Cornell University Press, 2009.

Rabinbach, Anson. *The Human Motor: Energy, Fatigue, and the Origins of Modernity*. New York: Basic Books, 1990.

Rae, John B. *The American Automobile Industry*. Boston: Twayne Publishers, 1984.

Raleigh, Donald J. "Languages of Power: How Saratov Bolsheviks Imagined Their Enemies." *Slavic Review* 57/2 (1998): 320–49.

Randall, Amy E. "'Revolutionary Bolshevik Work': Stakhanovism in Retail Trade." *Russian Review* 59/3 (2000): 425–41.

Rees, E.A. *Decision-Making in the Stalinist Command Economy, 1932–37*. London: Macmillan; New York: St. Martin's Press, 1997.

Reid, Susan E. "Cold War in the Kitchen: Gender and the Destalinization of Taste in the Soviet Union under Khrushchev." *Slavic Review* 61/2 (2002): 211–52.

– "The Meaning of Home: 'The Only Bit of the World You Can Have to Yourself.'" In *Borders of Socialism: Private Spheres of Soviet Russia*, ed. Lewis Siegelbaum, 145–70. New York: Palgrave Macmillan, 2006.

Rieber, Alfred J. "The Rise of Engineers in Russia." *Cahiers du monde russe et soviétique* 31/4 (1990): 539–68.

Roosevelt, Priscilla R. *Life on the Russian Country Estate: A Social and Cultural History*. New Haven: Yale University Press, 1995.

Rosenberg, William. "Russian Labour and Bolshevik Power after October." *Slavic Review* 44/2 (1985): 213–38.

Rowney, Don K. *Transition to Technocracy: The Structural Origins of the Soviet Administrative State*. Ithaca: Cornell University Press, 1989.

Rowney, Don K., and Eugene Huskey, eds. *Russian Bureaucracy and the State: Officialdom from Alexander III to Vladimir Putin*. Basingstoke: Palgrave Macmillan, 2009.

Ruble, Blair A. "From Palace Square to Moscow Square: St. Petersburg's Century-Long Retreat from Public Space." In *Reshaping Russian Architecture: Western Technology, Utopian Dreams*, ed. William C. Brumfield and Blair A. Ruble. Washington, DC: Woodrow Wilson International Center for Scholars, and Cambridge: Cambridge University Press, 1990.

– *Leningrad: Shaping a Soviet City*. Berkeley: University of California Press, 1990.

– "Moscow's Revolutionary Architecture and Its Aftermath: A Critical Guide." In *Reshaping Russian Architecture: Western Technology, Utopian Dreams*, ed. William C. Brumfield and Blair A. Ruble. Washington, DC: Woodrow Wilson

International Center for Scholars, and Cambridge: Cambridge University Press, 1990.

Rydell, Robert W. *The World of Fairs: The Century-of-Progress Expositions.* Chicago: University of Chicago Press, 1993.

Sabsovich, Leonid M. *Goroda budushchego i organizatsiia sotsialisticheskogo byta.* Moscow: Tekhnicheskoe izdatel'stvo, 1929.

Schönle, Andreas. "Garden of the Empire: Catherine's Appropriation of the Crimea." *Slavic Review* 60/1 (2001): 1–23.

Schultz, Kurt S. "Building the 'Soviet Detroit: The Construction of the Nizhnii Novgorod Automobile Factory, 1927–1932.'" *Slavic Review* 49/2 (1990): 200–12.

– "The American Factor in Soviet Industrialization: Fordism and the First Five-Year Plan, 1928–1932." Doctoral dissertation, Ohio State University, 1993.

Schwartz, Vanessa. *Spectacular Realities: Early Mass Culture in Fin-de-Siècle France.* Berkeley: University of California Press, 1999.

Scott, James C. *Domination and the Arts of Resistance: Hidden Transcripts.* New Haven: Yale University Press, 1990.

– *Seeing Like a State: How Certain Schemes to Improve the Human Condition Have Failed.* New Haven: Yale University Press, 1998.

Semenov, A.A., and M.M. Khorev, eds. *Andrei Osipovich Karelin: Tvorcheskoe nasledie.* Nizhnii Novgorod: Arnika, 1994.

Sezneva, Olga. "Dual History: The Politics of the Past in Kaliningrad, Former Königsberg." In *Composing Urban History and the Constitution of Civic Identities,* ed. John J. Czaplicka, Blair A. Ruble, and Lauren Crabtree, 58–85. Washington, DC: Woodrow Wilson Center Press; Baltimore: Johns Hopkins University Press, 2003.

– "Tenacious Place, Contingent Homeland: Making History and Community in the Repopulated City of Kaliningrad." Doctoral dissertation, New York University, 2005.

Shearer, David. "The Language and Politics of Socialist Rationalization." *Cahiers du Monde russe et soviétique* 32/4 (1991): 581–608.

– *Policing Stalin's Socialism: Repression and Social Order in the Soviet Union, 1924–1953.* Stanford: Hoover Institution Press, and New Haven: Yale University Press, 2009.

Shimovolos, S.M., and M.Iu. Gusev, eds., *Kniga pamiati zhertv politicheskikh repressii v Nizhegorodskoi oblasti,* vol. 1, Nizhnii Novgorod: Nizhegorodskii pechatnik, 1997.

Shomysov, N.M. *Geologicheskie ekskursii po Gor'kovskoi oblasti.* Gorky: Gor'kovskoe knizhnoe izdatel'stvo, 1954.

Shumilkin, Sergei Mikhailovich. "Arkhitektura kupecheskikh postroek Nizhnego Novgoroda i iarmarki XIX–nachala XX vv." In *Arkhitektura v istorii rus-skoi kul'tury*, ed. I.A. Bondarenko, 158–67. Moscow: Kollektiv avtorov, 1996.

– "Nizhegorodskaia iarmarka." *Arkhitekturnoe nasledstvo USSR* 29 (1981): 80–9.

Shvidkovsky, Dimitri. "Catherine the Great's Field of Dreams: Architecture and Landscape in the Russian Enlightenment." In *Architectures of Russian Identity: 1500 to the Present*, ed. James Cracraft and Donald Rowland, 51–65. Ithaca: Cornell University Press, 2003.

Siegelbaum, Lewis. *Cars for Comrades: The Life of the Soviet Automobile*. Ithaca: Cornell University Press, 2008.

– *Stakhanovism and the Politics of Productivity in the USSR, 1935–1941*. Cambridge: Cambridge University Press, 1990.

Siegelbaum, Lewis, ed. *Borders of Socialism: Private Spheres of Soviet Russia*. New York: Palgrave Macmillan, 2006.

Siegelbaum, Lewis, and Andrei Sokolov, eds. *Stalinism as a Way of Life: A Narrative in Documents*. New Haven: Yale University Press, 2004.

Slezkine, Yuri. "Naturalists Versus Nations: Eighteenth-Century Russian Scholars Confront Ethnic Diversity." In *Russia's Orient: Imperial Borderlands and Peoples, 1700–1917*, ed. Daniel R. Brower and Edward J. Lazzerini, 27–57. Bloomington: Indiana University Press, 1997.

Smirnova, Liudmila M. *Nizhnii Novgorod do i posle: Istoriko-literaturnye ocherki*. Nizhnii Novgorod: Begemot, 1996.

Smirnova, Liudmila M., and T.P. Zvantseva. *Tserkvi Nizhnego Novgoroda, unich-tozhennye i utselevshie: Kratkii putevoditel' po staromu gorodu*. Nizhnii Novgorod: Nizhegorodskoe knizhnoe izdatel'stvo, 1991.

Smith, Mark B. *Property of Communists: The Urban Housing Program from Stalin to Khrushchev*. Dekalb: Northern Illinois University Press, 2010.

Solomon, Susan Gross. "Reflections on Western Studies of Soviet Science." In *The Social Context of Soviet Science*, ed. Linda L. Lubrano and Susan Gross Solomon, 1–30. Boulder: Westview, 1980.

Solomon, Susan Gross, ed. *Doing Medicine Together: Germany and Russia between the Wars*. Toronto and Buffalo: University of Toronto Press, 2006.

Starr, S. Frederick. "Visionary Town Planning during the Cultural Revolution." In *Cultural Revolution in Russia, 1928–1931*, ed. Sheila Fitzpatrick, 207–38. Bloomington: Indiana University Press, 1978.

Steinberg, Mark. "Workers on the Cross: Religious Imagination in the Lives of Russian Workers." *Russian Review* 53/2 (1994): 213–39.

Stites, Richard. "Iconoclastic Currents in the Russian Revolution: Destroying and Preserving the Past." In *Bolshevik Culture: Experiment and Order in the Russian Revolution*, ed. Abbott Gleason, Peter Kenez, and Richard Stites, 1–24. Bloomington: Indiana University Press, 1985.

– *Revolutionary Dreams: Utopian Vision and Experimental Life in the Russian Revolution*. New York: Oxford University Press, 1989.
– *The Women's Liberation Movement in Russia*. Princeton: Princeton University Press, 1978.
– "World Outlook and Inner Fears in Soviet Science Fiction." In *Science and the Soviet Social Order*, ed. Loren R. Graham. Cambridge: Harvard University Press, 1990.
Tarkhanov, Alexei, and Sergei Kavtaradze. *Architecture of the Stalin Era*. New York: Rizzoli, 1992.
Taubman, William. *Governing Soviet Cities: Bureaucratic Politics and Urban Development in the USSR*. New York: Praeger, 1973.
Thurston, Robert W. *Liberal City, Conservative State: Moscow and Russia's Urban Crisis, 1906–1914*. New York: Oxford University Press, 1987.
Trube, Lev L. *Naselenie goroda Gor'kogo*. Gorky: Volga-Viatskoe, 1982.
Trube, Lev L., and Anatolii F. Shubin. *Gor'kovskaia oblast': Priroda i naselenie*. Gorky: Volgo-Viatskoe, 1968.
Tucker, Robert. *Stalin in Power: The Revolution from Above, 1928–1941*. New York: Norton, 1990.
Tumarkin, Nina. *Lenin Lives: The Lenin Cult in Soviet Russia*. Cambridge: Harvard University Press, 1997.
Verdery, Katherine. *What Is Socialism? And What Comes Next*. Princeton: Princeton University Press, 1996.
Viola, Lynne. *The Best Sons of the Fatherland: Workers in the Vanguard of Soviet Collectivization*. Oxford and New York: Oxford University Press, 1989.
– *Peasant Rebels under Stalin: Collectivization and the Culture of Peasant Resistance*. New York: Oxford University Press, 1996.
– *The Unknown Gulag: The Lost World of Stalin's Special Settlements*. New York: Oxford University Press, 2007.
Viola, Lynne, ed. *Contending with Stalinism: Soviet Power and Popular Resistance in the 1930s*. Ithaca: Cornell University Press, 2002.
Vlasiuk, A.I. "Evoliutsiia stroitel'nogo zakonodatel'stva Rossii v 1830e–1910e gody." In *Pamiatniki russkoi arkhitektury i monumental'nogo iskusstva*, ed. V.P. Vygolov. Moscow: Nauka, 1985.
Volkov, Vadim. "The Concept of Kultur'nost': Notes on the Stalinist Civilizing Process." In *Stalinism: New Directions*, ed. Sheila Fitzpatrick, 209–30. London: Routledge, 2000.
Volkov, Vadim, and Catriona Kelly. "Directed Desires: *Kul'turnost'* and Consumption." In *Constructing Russian Culture in the Age of Revolution: 1881–1940*, ed. Catriona Kelly and David Shepherd, 291–313. Oxford: Oxford University Press, 1998.

Wagner, William G. "Paradoxes of Piety: The Nizhegorod Convent of the Exaltation of the Cross, 1807–1935." In *Orthodox Russia: Belief and Practice under the Tsars*, ed. Valerie A. Kivelson and Robert H. Greene, 211–38. University Park: Pennsylvania State University Press, 2003.

Weiner, Amir, ed. *Landscaping the Human Garden: Twentieth-Century Population Management in Comparative Framework*. Stanford: Stanford University Press, 2003.

Welter, Volker M. "From *locus genii* to Heart of the City: Embracing the Spirit of the City." In *Modernism and the Spirit of the City*, ed. Iain Boyd Whyte, 35–56. London: Routledge, 2003.

Whyte, Iain Boyd, ed. *Modernism and the Spirit of the City*. London: Routledge, 2003.

Wigley, Mark. *The Architecture of Deconstruction: Derrida's Haunt*. Cambridge: MIT Press, 1996.

Wilkins, Mira, and Frank E. Hill. *American Business Abroad: Ford on Six Continents*. Detroit: Wayne State University Press, 1964.

Wolfe, Thomas C. *Governing Soviet Journalism: The Press and the Socialist Person after Stalin*. Bloomington: Indiana University Press, 2005.

Wood, Elizabeth. *Performing Justice: Agitation Trials in Early Soviet Russia*. Ithaca: Cornell University Press, 2005.

Wortman, Richard. *Scenarios of Power: Myth and Ceremony in Russian Monarchy from Peter the Great to the Abdication of Nicholas II*. Princeton: Princeton University Press, 2006.

Yurchak, Alexei. *Everything Was Forever, until It Was No More: The Last Soviet Generation*. Princeton: Princeton University Press, 2005.

Zhdanov, A.A. *O gorodskom khoziaistve Nizhnego Novgoroda*. Gorky: OGIZ, 1932.

– *Otchet o rabote kraikoma*. Gorky: OGIZ, 1932.

Zitser, Ernest. *The Transfigured Kingdom: Sacred Parody and Charismatic Authority at the Court of Peter the Great*. Ithaca: Cornell University Press, 2004.

Zubkova, Elena. *Russia after the War: Hopes, Illusions, Disappointments, 1945–1957*. Transl. and ed. Hugh Ragsdale. Armonk: M.E. Sharpe, 1998.

Index

absolute space, 13–14, 65
agency of the material, 55, 59, 191n91
All-Russian Industrial and Art Exhibition (1896), 32–3
All-Union Association of Proletarian Architects (VOPRA), 7, 46, 51
All-Union Tractor and Automobile Association (VATO), 50, 189n75
architects: ennoblement under Catherine II, 203n24; generations of, 6–9, 11, 14, 52, 90, 99, 120, 151, 168, 173nn17, 26; intellectual stratum, as part of, 114, 203n23; provincial conference of (1936), 112–15; Soviet nobility, 113–14, 120, 203n20; training, 69, 90, 98, 133–5; victimhood, question of, 10–11; working conditions, 134–5
Architecture and Planning Administration (APU), 97–8, 102, 106, 117–18, 122, 124, 127, 128–33, 137–8, 142, 148–9, 152, 162, 164, 210n11
Arkhangel'sk, 69
Art Institute of Kiev, 99
Association for Urban-Municipal Construction, 75

Association of Architects-Urbanists (ARU), 46, 48–9
Austin Company, 53–7
Avant-garde, 6–7, 10–11, 15, 18, 32–3, 40–3, 46, 51, 56, 60–4, 91, 136
Avtostroi, 43, 45–51, 54, 56–8
Avtozavod: blagoustroistvo in, 75, 158; building socialist city of, 55–63, 191n94; competition for socialist city of, 42–55, 63; in fourth zoning plan for Greater Nizhnii Novgorod, 79; in iconographic plan, 104, 108; left-bank settlement of, 82–3, 84–6, 90–3; visionary planning in, 15, 46–51, 60–1

Baku, 69
baroque city planning, 28
Benjamin, Walter, 12–13
Béthencourt y Molina, Augustin de, 30
blagoustroistvo: campaigns for, 148–53, 157–60; relationship to culturedness (kul'turnost'), 147, 151–2, 160–1; relationship to purge (chistka), 153–7
Bogorad, Daniil Il'ich, 195n45